WOMEN ARTISTS
IN HISTORY

Third Edition

• • • • • • • • • • • •

Women Artists in History

From antiquity

to the present

Wendy Slatkin

University of Redlands
Redlands, California

PRENTICE HALL

Upper Saddle River, New Jersey 07458

Library of Congress Cataloging-in-Publication Data

SLATKIN, WENDY
  Women Artists in History : from antiquity to the present / Wendy
Slatkin. — 3rd ed.
    p.   cm.
  Includes bibliographical references.
  ISBN 0–13–432873–6
  1. Women artists—Biography   I. Title
N43.S57   1997
704′.042—dc20
                                                95–41184
                                                CIP

Acquisitions editor: Bud Therien
Assistant editor: Marion Gottlieb
Editorial production/supervision
  and interior design: F. Hubert
Manufacturing buyer: Bob Anderson

© 1997, 1990, 1985 by Prentice-Hall, Inc.
Simon & Schuster / A Viacom Company
Upper Saddle River, New Jersey 07458

Printed in the United States of America

10   9   8   7   6   5   4   3

ISBN 0-13-432873-6

PRENTICE-HALL INTERNATIONAL (UK) LIMITED, *London*
PRENTICE-HALL OF AUSTRALIA PTY. LIMITED, *Sydney*
PRENTICE-HALL CANADA INC., *Toronto*
PRENTICE-HALL HISPANOAMERICANA, S.A., *Mexico*
PRENTICE HALL OF INDIA PRIVATE LIMITED, *New Delhi*
PRENTICE-HALL OF JAPAN, INC., *Tokyo*
SIMON & SCHUSTER PTE. LTD., *Singapore*
EDITORA PRENTICE-HALL DO BRASIL, LTDA., *Rio de Janeiro*

for my parents,
Helen and Robert Slatkin,
and to the memory of my grandmother,
Bertha Gleischman

CONTENTS

PART II. EUROPE: 1450–1800

8. Italy: 1450–1650 • 63

9. Northern Europe: 1600–1700 • 81

PART IV. THE TWENTIETH CENTURY

Preface

> *We can blow up the canon . . . History is*
> *what groups write as they come to power.*
> AMY RICHLIN[1]

> *The person who does the looking is the person*
> *with the power. No doubt about it: looking is power,*
> *but so, too, is the ability to make someone look.*
> MICHAEL ANN HOLLY[2]

During the course of my reading, in preparation for this revision of *Women Artists in History,* these two statements seemed to stand out as markers of my intentions for this project. This book asks students to do two things: to look at some "canonical" works of art in new ways and to look in new directions, i.e., to redirect the looking process, in order to ask questions relevant to the women who lived and worked in that historical context.

In the process of this revision, the title of the book, *Women Artists in History,* became an inaccurate description of its contents. I have gone well beyond a discussion of the role of women creators in the production of "high art," i.e., painting, sculpture, and architecture, to include images of women and women as patrons. However, in order to maintain continuity with the earlier editions, I have retained the name, despite its limitations.

This third edition of *Women Artists in History* takes as full advantage as possible of the wealth of recent feminist research in the history of art. The broadest definitions of "feminist interventions" into the discipline have been used to provide a conduit for this research into the classroom. The text has been substantially revised and the issues follow, to a great extent, the course of the findings of a generation of brilliant, dedicated scholars. If the preceding edition appeared to some simply to add women to a preexisting art historical canonical structure, this edition should not be vulnerable to such criticism.

The most extensive revisions have occurred in those portions addressing the history of art prior to 1600. It is in these fields that the new research has most significantly expanded and altered our understanding of women's contributions to visual culture.

However, the contributions of women creators must continue to remain in the foreground of discussion, since this has been the area where mainstream texts seem to overwhelm, if not ignore, the presence of women.

Since post-structuralist theoretical perspectives have thrown many of the categories of art history into semiotic "skepticism," the emphasis within the chapters has been on specific issues or works of art in which a feminist reading has impacted interpretation.

The topics, then, follow the course of the current state of research. It is, to a great extent, the feminist scholarly gaze that has determined the structure of this text.

ACKNOWLEDGMENTS

I wish to thank first my editor at Prentice Hall, Bud Therien, for his support of this rewriting of *Women Artists in History*. Assistant editor, Marion Gottlieb, has been wonderful—patient, helpful, and sustaining throughout this process. It has been a joy to work with Frank Hubert as production editor. He has been efficient, responsive, and supportive. The constructive criticism of scholars, including JoAnn Wein, George Gorse, and Martin Rosenberg, was extremely valuable. Conversations with JoAnn Wein and John Brownfield were most helpful at an extremely crucial stage in the creative process of this revision. Comments by the following individuals who reviewed the manuscript were extremely helpful: Shirley W. Byrd, San Jose State University; George L. Gorse, Pomona College; Rita Parham McCaslin, James Madison University; Ann Roberts, Lake Forest College; Martin Rosenberg, University of Nebraska at Omaha; Jean Owens Schaefer, University of Wyoming; Jo Ann Wein, State University College, Oneonta, New York. Finally, my students at the University of Redlands have been my first sounding board for many of the new ideas incorporated here. They have been the living, breathing receptors of this book, and they have tolerated my preliminary conceptualizations with great good humor and given me significant feedback. Thanks also to Sandy Richey of the Armacost Library, University of Redlands, and Terre Hodgson for her assistance in securing photo permissions.

WENDY SLATKIN

WOMEN ARTISTS
IN HISTORY

Introduction

FEMINIST SCHOLARLY REAPPRAISALS

The opportunity to rewrite this book occurs nearly eight years after the second edition was composed. During this time, an enormous outpouring of convincing and compelling scholarship has been published. Every time period, nearly every creator, and absolutely every underlying principle on which the first two editions were based has been thoughtfully and frequently brilliantly argued by an international community of feminist scholars.

Therefore, it is on a much broader and more solid foundation of scholarship that this third edition can be constructed. Griselda Pollock's excellent term "feminist interventions"[1] describes well these reappraisals in the discipline of art history. We now can take a much more varied approach to the range of available evidence in different periods than was possible when this book was first conceived. The structure and the format of the text have been revised to incorporate this body of scholarly work.

These "interventions" may be identified in the following ways:

1. The reconstitution of individual creator's careers. Scholars have worked on issues of attribution and iconographical analysis. There now exists a fuller understanding of the historical context for interpreting both the works of art themselves and the conditions in which specific women artists functioned as professionals.

2. An examination of the gender biases of the discourses that defined the category "Art," biases which often eliminated women's creative activity from inclusion in the texts in which the "History of Art" was codified. In their important theoretical text, *Old Mistresses*, Pollock and Parker first articulated the ideological underpinnings of the exclusion of women and their works from the canonical art historical texts.[2] Since the publication of their book in 1981, over a decade of effort by scholars has disrupted, destabilized, and illuminated the masculinist underpinnings of this exclusion of women from full participation in the cultural productions that form the "History of Art."

3. The role of women as patrons. In certain epochs, women could participate in cultural production not through direct creation of works of art, but rather through the commissioning of works of art and through influence exerted on male artists. The issues of patronage or "matronage" (Deborah Cherry's term[3]) can also be expanded to include the ways in which women's lives were affected by the physical structure of domestic architecture, such as Roman villas and Renaissance palaces.

4. Analysis of the institutional structures of the art world and their impact on the ability of women to become practicing professional artists. Scholars have examined the roles of guilds and art academies, for example, to learn the ways in which the highly specialized skills necessary to become an artist were taught in order to better understand the discriminatory conditions in which women operated.

5. The construction of gender in visual images. Women have appeared as images in representations since the oldest existing paleolithic sculptures. There has hardly ever been an epoch in which images of women did not exist. To interpret the appearance of the sign "Woman" in representations has motivated scholars to employ a range of art historical strategies. Scholarship into the imagery of women has led to discussions of pornography and efforts to situate such representations within the discourses of sexuality.

All such strategies have persuasive validity, and it is my position, writing in 1995, to accept all such interventions into the discourses of art history as valuable. Feminist scholars have actively and convincingly engaged in a reexamination of the fundamental premises of their areas and periods of specialization, and to limit or define those efforts that deal with women creators is totally contradictory to the spirit of feminist scholarship. It is neither possible nor desirable to force "feminist art history" into a unified "school" or methodology. The works are too diverse, the ways in which they were created and defined in various periods too different to permit a single unified methodological approach. This book is an attempt to present to the introductory-level college student some insight into the processes of feminist art historical interpretation. The examples in this text demonstrate a variety of ways in which a work can be effectively interpreted to illuminate the concerns of one half of the population of any given culture.

SEMIOTICS, DECONSTRUCTION, AND ART HISTORY

Semiotics, or the study of "signs," has a complex history beginning in the writings of Saussure and Pierce in the early twentieth century. Mieke Bal and Norman Bryson have outlined a semiotic system appropriate for the history of art.[4] These authors refer to the "theoretical skepticism of semiotics" and develop their interpretive model on the foundation not only of semioticians, but also on the philosophical concepts articulated in the writings of Jacques Derrida, known as "deconstruction." As defined by Jonathan Culler, the term "deconstruction" "demonstrates the difficulties of any theory that would define meaning in a univocal way."[5] Derrida claims that since "deconstruction is never concerned only with signified content but especially with the conditions and assumptions of discourse, with frameworks of enquiry, [deconstruction] engages the institutional structures governing our practices, competencies, performances."[6]

Thus each basic category utilized in this book can be opened up to a scrutiny that essentially breaks down and "deconstructs" any confidence in "truth," intellectual certainty, or the precise definition of "meaning" or interpretation in a work of art.

According to Bal and Bryson, the following basic concepts are all subject to destabilization or "problematization."

Women
Artist
Art history
Historical context
Meaning and the "truth" of interpretation
Audience and reception theory

Clearly the title of this book, *Women Artists in History*, is resting on cultural categorizations that are complex and open to debate. The issues raised in each of these categories may be briefly summarized as follows:

Women. As Denise Riley notes, the term "women" is "a volatile collectivity in which female persons can be very differently positioned, so that the apparent continuity of the subject of 'women' isn't to be relied on . . . being a woman is also inconstant, and can't provide an ontological foundation."[7]

Artist. Foucault and Barthes in a series of influential theoretical works have forced the category of the "author" into its own problematic. As Bal and Bryson note, "authorship is an elaborate work of framing, something we elaborately produce rather than something we simply find."[8] Reliance on the monograph, the book-length essay which focuses on the individual creator, is theoretically suspect in this intellectual system. As Pollock notes, "archaic individualism [is] at the heart of art historical discourse."[9]

Art history. Pollock has defined the academic discipline of art history as "a masculinist discourse, party to the social construction of sexual difference."[10] Obviously, this book and other studies which dissect art historical discourse for gender bias must treat "Art History" as a fluid field of inquiry rather than a closed body of knowledge.

Historical context. "Context can always be extended; it is subject to the same process of mobility that is at work in the semiosis of the text or artwork that 'context' is supposed to delimit and control . . . it cannot be taken for granted that the evidence that makes up 'context' is going to be any simpler or more legible than the visual text upon which such evidence is to operate."[11]

Meaning and the "truth" of interpretation. In semiotic terms, "polysemy" is the word that defines the fluidity of meaning in works of art. "There can be no such thing as a fixed, pre-determined, or unified meaning." Most pertinent to deconstruction is Derrida's concept of "dissemination" which is, as Bal notes, "the most radical endorsement of the view that no interpretation can be privileged over any other . . . the affirmation of a single meaning is profoundly motivated by socially relevant power positions."[12]

Audience and reception theory. Who are the receivers of works of art? How is information decoded from the image? "Semiotic analysis draws attention to the plurality and unpredictability at work in contexts of reception, in the forms of looking that have produced the discursive configurations evident in the archive."[13] Gender plays a key role here. It matters whether men or women, as gendered subjects, are doing the looking. But how one may identify what it means to be a "woman looking" is also difficult to define with intellectual certainty.

What does remain for art history as concrete evidence are the works of art themselves, the "visual texts" or the "objects." Therefore, various headings in each chapter of this book link the creator of the work with the title of the specific object which is the focus of discussion. The information provided is selected for its relevance to the interpretation of that specific work of art.

However it is not possible, or even desirable as some feminists have argued, to ignore or eliminate issues of "quality" in the selection process. To do so would negate the struggles and efforts of so many of these creators. To become a "painter," a "sculptor," or (in the case of Julia Morgan) an "architect" involved for women in the periods since 1550 an acceptance of the "rules of the game." To enter the arena of painting was to challenge many of the fundamental assumptions on which the discourses of patriarchy were grounded. Since the Renaissance, art was a profession, and women who entered this professional arena produced works that could only be judged by the criteria of excellence of its institutional matrix, whether it was the French Royal Academy of the eighteenth century or the New York art world of the 1940s and '50s. There were no alternative systems of evaluation.

Quite obviously, these institutions and their critical discourses were dominated by men. Most artists were men, most patrons were men, most writers of critical texts were men. The criteria of excellence were invented and perpetuated by men. When women chose to become artists, as defined by their specific culture, they accepted those standards, since there were no other options. The campaigns to gain admission into the Royal Academy in London, or to the *Ecole des Beaux-Arts* in Paris, were efforts to improve women's training so they could compete with their male contemporaries since critics and other members of their audience employed a unified system of critical criteria. The difficulties inherent in this undertaking were great and frequently insurmountable.

Despite this, the evidence of the surviving body of works of art attributed to women creators documents the historical reality that women artists accepted the inequities and struggled to meet the criteria established by the male-dominated art world. If these creators could recognize and accept the reality of male-defined standards for excellence, contemporary art historians must as well. Perhaps we should not wonder why so few women managed to meet those criteria, but rather how any women at all surmounted the immense difficulties of patriarchal society to create works that met such stringent critical standards. These criteria may be summarized in the following four categories:

1. *Stylistic or technical innovation.* A number of artists have developed methods of painting and sculpture that are different from any previous style. These artists usually are members of an avant-garde group. This category applies most frequently to artists living in the late nineteenth and the twentieth centuries, when stylistic innovation has been most valued. However, Rosalba Carriera, for example, was a technical innovator in the lower-status categories of miniature painting and pastel portraiture during the eighteenth century.

2. *Compositional or iconographic originality.* Some artists have been singled out because they invented a new format, compositional arrangement, or structure for painting or sculpture. For example, the originality of Clara Peeters lies more in her compositions and the selected viewpoint of her still lifes than in her method of paint application. A number of artists have invented new subjects, sometimes based specifically on their experiences as women. Other artists have developed new variations or layers of meaning for subjects regularly depicted by their male colleagues. Artemisia Gentileschi, Judith Leyster, Harriet Hosmer, and Käthe Kollwitz are examples of artists who have created new iconographies based on their personal identities as women.

3. *Influence on other artists.* One standard regularly applied by art historians to evaluate the contribution of an artist to the history of art is the extent to which that artist's imagery or technique influenced the works of other artists. Certain artists, such as Angelica Kauffman, exerted a decisive and widespread influence on the art of their contemporaries.

4. *Recognition within the culture.* Many of the artists to be discussed were widely appreciated during their lifetimes. They received official and critical recognition and occupied positions of prominence in the contemporary culture. Rachel Ruysch, Elisabeth Vigée-Lebrun, and Rosa Bonheur are examples of artists whose careers belong in this category.

For the purposes of this book, an additional criterion has been used. I am most interested in those works which question, challenge, and/or redefine the social and cultural construction of the category "woman"—the "signs" of gender, in semiotic terms, that provide insight into the ways in which representations both reflected, modified, and/or resisted the dominant discourses of "woman." Such gender signs are crucial to the identities of the creators who are the focus of our attention. Whenever possible, priority has been given to images created by women in which their interpretation can illuminate some aspect of the construction of gender issues for the culture.

This book has an audience clearly in mind. The text is targeted at undergraduate students in introductory level art history courses. It is intended to be used in conjunction with another, longer, widely available text. Within the physical confines of what can be included here, i.e., the number of pages and quantity of illustrations as established by my publisher, I have selected the issues and concepts on those "objects" customarily discussed in introductory level survey courses. Then, I have written the text in a way to communicate these ideas as clearly as possible to the student beginning his or her study of art history.

CHAPTER 1

• • • • • • • • •

Prehistory

THE NATURE OF THE EVIDENCE

The historical era is defined by the survival of the earliest written records in the third millennium B.C. The past 5,000 years are a relatively recent epoch in human history. Written documents emerge from civilizations in which both patriarchal institutions and a class structure with a ruling elite and slaves exist. Therefore, the archeological evidence from the thousands of years of social organizations that preceded the third millennium B.C. have provided a source of great attention for feminist scholars. Is there evidence of social groups in which men and women occupy similar positions of status in the community? Is there any evidence in prehistory of societies organized as "matriarchies," i.e., societies in which women were more important than men? The fascination with prehistory for today's feminists reflects the need for alternative models for gender relationships in contemporary society.

ART OF THE UPPER PALEOLITHIC ERA

The surviving art works of this epoch fall into three categories: (a) cave paintings in France and Spain, (b) stone objects, decorated with designs, which most often have animal motifs, and (c) female statuettes.

Female Statuettes

For contemporary feminists, the most interesting groups of objects are the sculptured female figurines. Over sixty figures have been found over a wide area of Europe, from southwestern France to eastern Russia. The oldest examples have been dated to the Upper Paleolithic era, and most appear to have been created within a relatively short time span of 2,000 years, i.e., between 25,000 B.C. and 23,000 B.C. Most of these examples have been carved in stone or mammoth ivory, although a few are modeled from baked clay. As a group, they are quite small in scale, the largest being 22 cm. tall.

- ## Upper Paleolithic Hunting and Gathering Societies, *"Venus" of Willendorf*

This figure, excavated at Willendorf, in Austria, is commonly known as the *"Venus" of Willendorf*, using the name of the Roman goddess of love and fertility. Obviously, naming such an image "Venus" is an anachronism. Roman civilization would only develop nearly 25,000 years later than the creation of this work, and the beliefs attached to "Venus" as a Roman deity were surely vastly different from concepts of female divinity in these societies.

The sculpture is characteristic of this group of Paleolithic figures in its treatment of female anatomy. The image is a nude human identifiable as a woman by the enlarged breasts, stomach, buttocks, and thighs. Like the other sculptures in this group, the figure is faceless, armless, and lacking feet.

In formulating an interpretation of the meaning of these objects, it is important to pay attention to the evidence of archeological excavations. Most such figurines have been found in houses or homesites. They are usually excavated as single objects, along with flint tools and other debris. Margaret Ehrenberg summarizes the interpretation of these statuettes into two categories. Some scholars have argued that these images are the representation of a "Mother Goddess" or fertility goddess. However, despite the appeal

Fig. 1–1. *Venus of Willendorf.*
c. 30,000–25,000 B.C. Limestone.
Height 4³⁄₈ in.   *(Naturhistorisches
Museum, Vienna)*

of such a concept, Ehrenberg argues against the assumption that these figures provide evidence of a universal religion based on a unified concept of a female goddess.[1]

The societies in which these statuettes were created were composed of small-scale populations which survived by gathering or foraging plant foods, whenever possible, and hunting animals. These men and women lived in very cold climates, on the edges of glacial ice sheets where foraging would have been difficult and meat would have been the mainstay of the diet. Religions based on personified deities are very unusual in such societies, which have been studied in recent times.

Ehrenberg argues convincingly for the second interpretation. These images served as aids in sympathetic magic to promote fertility in women of the community. She cites examples among North American Indian tribes such as the Zuñi or west African tribes in which a model of the hoped-for child is carried until the woman gives birth. After the pregnancy or successful birth of the child was achieved the figure could be discarded, or retained and used as a doll.

However, it is not necessary to commit to a single unifying explanation or interpretation for all the figures.

- **Neolothic Agricultural Societies, Statuette from the Cyclades**

Most of the surviving sculptures of the Neolithic period may be dated in a much more recent historical epoch, stretching from 5500 to 3000 B.C. Small-scale sculptures depicting women have been located throughout Europe and in southwest Asia. They are especially numerous in the Mediterranean islands from the Cyclades, in the east, to Majorca.

The figures from the Cyclades have been found mainly in graves, rather than in settlements like the Upper Paleolithic figures. Both male and female figures have been excavated. Like the older examples, such as the *"Venus" of Willendorf* (Fig. 1–1), a range of interpretations have been proposed to explain their significance. Compared with these older statuettes, the differences are quite distinct. These figures have all their body parts, from head to feet. They are relatively flat, and arms are incised across the stomach. The enlargement of breasts, stomach, and buttocks visible in the Willendorf figure is no longer apparent. Instead, a highly simplified conceptual treatment of anatomy is used, one which provided inspiration to early-twentieth-century modernist sculptors such as Brancusi.

One especially significant difference is in the nature of the societies in which these images were made. By the time these works were created, agriculture was well established throughout the Mediterranean world. Our knowledge of contemporary communities in which agriculture is practiced reveals a number of consistent factors. When the plough is employed and animals are domesticated, the agricultural work is done mainly by men. In horticultural societies in which other tools such as hoes or digging sticks are used, women are mainly responsible for agricultural production.

Ehrenberg believes that women can be credited with the discovery of agriculture. Since women were most probably responsible for gathering plant foods, they would have developed specialized knowledge about the growth of plants. Eventually,

Fig. 1–2. Cycladic Figure from Amorgos. c. 3000 B.C. Marble.
Height 2 ft. 6$\frac{1}{4}$ in.   *(Ashmolean Museum, University of Oxford)*

the conscious planting and cultivation of grains would have led to two important consequences: a change from a nomadic to a sedentary living situation and an increase in population due to the improved and more dependable food sources. If women were cultivating the crops, it is possible that they would likely have been responsible for inventing the necessary tools. Heavier, more solid containers, probably made from pottery, would have been desirable to store the increased food supply. The oldest examples of pottery have been found at sites in the same regions in which farming first appears in southwestern Asia. With this sedentary lifestyle and food supplies such as cereals appropriate to young children to supplement breast milk, women could have given birth to more children, leading to population increases.[2]

In contemporary times, there is a significant correlation between non-plough agriculture, matrilineal and matrilocal systems, and an enhanced status for women. By the time records were kept, the shift had been made in Egypt and the ancient Near East to plough agriculture, patrilocal residence, patrilineal descent and land ownership, and the domestication of animals. Ehrenberg concludes that when men took over most of the agricultural work, the social status of women declined.

Another theory traces the origins of male dominance to the development of patrilocality.[3] When women moved into their husband's kin group, their labor could be effectively exploited for the creation of commodities for exchange. Female subordination then established the necessary labor force for the emergence of private property and the state.[4]

In the absence of concrete evidence, it is very difficult to determine the extent of women's participation in craft activity. We simply do not know whether women were responsible for the creation of fertility figurines, clay pots, or woven baskets. However, we can assume that women were responsible for the creation of cloth. Elizabeth Barber has accumulated a vast body of evidence documenting the production of textiles in the Neolithic and Bronze Ages. Based on her analysis of the data, she concludes that nearly all textile workers during these epochs were women.[5] Barber builds her case by associating the production of woven cloth for household use as a task consistent with child rearing, and thus appropriate to women.[6]

It is important to remember that the existence of these small sculptures does not necessarily tell us about the organization of society, the division of labor between the sexes, or the relative status of women and men in communities of the prehistoric past.

The survival of these statuettes, as well as mythological references, have elicited many speculations about the existence in prehistoric culture of societies organized as matriarchies. There is no consensus among scholars that this was the case. On the contrary, "motherhood has often placed abstract *woman* on a pedestal, but it has at the same time left concrete *women* in the home and powerless. Reverence . . . does not necessarily result from, or lead to, the high status or power of the revered object that is symbolically presented."[7] Contemporary anthropologists generally discount any arguments for the widespread existence of matriarchies in prehistory.

That there are biological differences between men and women is clear and undeniable. But biology alone does not determine the roles, activities, and status differences between men and women in any given culture. "The chief importance of biological sex in determining social roles is in providing a universal and obvious division around which other distinctions can be organized."[8] Although every society has some sort of division of tasks by sex, the assignment of any particular task to one sex or the other varies enormously from culture to culture. Biologically determinist theories are an inadequate explanation for the success of male dominance in early civilizations.

Suggestions for Further Reading

BARBER, ELIZABETH, *Prehistoric Textiles: The Development of Cloth in the Neolithic and Bronze Ages* (Princeton, NJ: Princeton University Press, 1991).

BARBER, ELIZABETH, *Women's Work: The First 20,000 Years; Women, Cloth and Society in Early Times* (New York: Norton, 1994).

CONKEY, MARGARET W., and JOAN M. GERO (eds.), *Engendering Archaeology: Women and Prehistory* (Cambridge, MA: Basil Blackwell, 1991).

COONTZ, STEPHANIE, and PETA HENDERSON (eds.), *Women's Work, Men's Property: The Origins of Gender and Class* (London: Verso, 1986).

EHRENBERG, MARGARET, *Women in Prehistory* (Norman: University of Oklahoma Press, 1989).

GADON, ELINOR, *The Once and Future Goddess: A Symbol for Our Time* (San Francisco: Harper and Row, 1989).

GIMBUTAS, MARIJA, *The Language of the Goddess* (San Francisco: Harper and Row, 1989).

JOHNSON, BUFFIE, *Lady of the Beasts: Ancient Images of the Goddess and Her Sacred Animals* (San Francisco: Harper and Row, 1988).

REITER, RAYNA R. (ed.), *Toward an Anthropology of Women* (New York: Monthly Review Press, 1975).

Chapter 2

• • • • • • • • • •

The Ancient Near East

THE NATURE OF THE EVIDENCE

Archeological Evidence

By the third millennium B.C. the subordination of women in a patriarchal social structure was well under way. A leading scholar of this period, Julia Asher Grève notes the existence of a small population of upper class women in the ruling families, some of whom served as high priestesses. There existed an equally small middle class of women with married status whose spouses were priests, or temple or palace administrators. The largest group was composed of women employed by temple and palace, the working women.[1]

Examinations of skeletons show an average life expectancy of 25 to 35 years, with death due to childbearing accounting for the shortened life spans of women.

Written Records

In the culture of the "fertile crescent" in the ancient Near East, political power became centralized in the hands of male military leaders, and hierarchical class stratification of the society began. Women were excluded from decision making and became another form of private property. This process is documented by the marriage laws that controlled women's lives to a great extent. Marriages were arranged by parents. The groom paid a "bride's price" to the parents of the bride. Daughters from poor families were sold into marriage or slavery to improve the family's financial situation. After marriage the husband became undisputed head of the family. He could divorce his wife quite easily or sell or pawn her and his children to pay off his debts. While husbands could maintain concubines, a wife's adultery became a crime punishable by death. Children, like wives, were considered property of economic value.[2]

There is no evidence for female infanticide in Mesopotamia because the more children a man possessed, the greater his economic worth became. Abortion was considered a serious crime, and the society encouraged numerous births. A woman who was a mother had higher status and better legal rights than a woman who was not.

Because the main occupation of most women was the bearing and raising of children, the education of daughters focused on instruction in household tasks, which included weaving, needlework, and music making. However, women were not totally excluded from the economy.

Women do seem to have had equal rights in some legal and financial transactions.[3] Wives had the right to use their own dowry after their husband's death. Therefore, some upper-class women were active in business affairs. Such women were literate and signed documents and contracts in their own names. They could buy and sell slaves and other forms of property. Women could act as witnesses in court. A few women were priestesses living in convents and conducting a wide variety of business affairs independently of men.

Lower-class women and female slaves were active in many types of jobs and contributed to the economic development of their societies in the ancient Near East. Women were scribes, midwives, singers, tavern-keepers, and even chemists (thirteenth century B.C.). Records from as early as the third millennium B.C. show that women were brewers, cooks, and agricultural workers, occupations associated with women into the eighteenth century A.D.

One significant occupation of women in Mesopotamia continued to be their predominance in the making of textiles, a laborious and time-consuming activity which, as noted in Chapter 1, could be done in the home and was therefore well suited to women. The fibers of flax, cotton, or wool first had to be cleaned and prepared and spun into thread. Then the thread was woven into cloth. Clothing was often decorated with embroidery. All these tasks were the exclusive concern of women. Female slaves who were skilled weavers were highly valued and in great demand in the ancient Near East. The upper classes purchased fine garments, beautifully decorated. Such items were also economically valuable commodities for export.

The professional activities of women in the Near East were largely confined to women of the artisan and slave classes, who were forced to work for survival. In royal families, women practiced spinning and weaving, as well as embroidery and basket plaiting. But aristocratic women (as in the Middle Ages) performed these tasks for the domestic needs of the household, not as professional skills.

Visual Evidence

In contrast with the contemporary surviving visual evidence from Egypt (see Chapter 3), the roles in which women appear in images known to us from the ancient Near East are relatively few. Irene Winter notes the very limited number of roles performed by women in public life in Mesopotamian art. She suggests that the "general invisibility" of women does indeed reflect greater distinctions between the public and private definitions of gender roles than, for example, in imperial Roman art (see Chapter 6). With the notable exception of the priestess, women are not occupying important public roles in the surviving visual examples. This is also consistent with the few roles in which women appear in the epic literature of Mesopotamia.[4]

Seated women are most commonly presented as praying. Nudity is rare. "Working women are shown in scenes depicting weaving, harvesting, . . . creating dairy products and caring for animals."[5]

As in Crete, women made pottery. A cylinder seal from the early third millennium B.C. shows women potters making vessels in what appears to be a workshop.[6] Basket plaiting was another craft practiced by women of all classes.

PRIESTESSES

Asher Grève has catalogued the figures of clothed women in "cultic settings." Women are shown donating statues as votive offerings and carrying different emblems or symbols of the deities. Asher Grève believes that most of these images depict priestesses. Some of the seated figures found in cultic settings, such as temples, were most likely donated by women of high rank. This is suggested by the fact that some of these women are seated on elaborate stools. Such statues, presented to the temple on important religious occasions such as the temple's inauguration, could serve a variety of purposes. Women are shown in three roles in images of religious ceremonies: (1) high and middle rank priestesses, (2) queens and princesses representing the ruling family, and (3) offering bearers in religious ceremonies.[7]

• *Disk of Enheduanna*

Irene Winter has analyzed the information we can glean from this image. An inscription identifies Enheduanna as the wife of Nanna and the daughter of Sargon. She was En-priestess of the cult worship of the moon-god Nanna/su'en at Ur during the reign of her father, Sargon of Akade. On the left, a nude male figure pours a libation. The central figure of a woman, identified as Enheduanna, is facing toward the

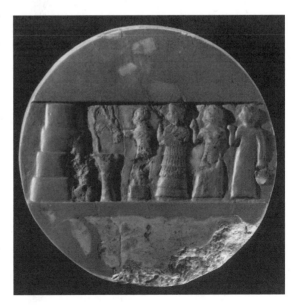

Fig. 2–1. *Calcite Disk of Enheduanna, Daughter of Sargon the Great.* (University of Pennsylvania Museum, Philadelphia)

cultic activity. Her upraised hand is a gesture of pious greeting. Her cap with a rolled brim is identified with the headgear of priestesses. As En-priestess, she does not pour herself, but stands in worship while the male functionary performs the ritual act. Her head is the only one which touches the upper edge of the border, which is a sign of her importance.

Winter suggests that the stepped architectural form on the left is a symbol of the zigurrat of Nanna. From this and other evidence, Winter concludes that the office of En-priestess predates this disk. It is assumed that Enheduanna was "placed in the service of the moon-god precisely to consolidate the Akkadian dynasty's links with the traditional Sumerian past in the important cult and political center of Ur."[8] As daughter of Sargon, her Akkadian identity is important for the political consolidation of that dynasty. Her role as priestess, then, is a means of providing divine sanction for the legitimacy of the political rule of her family.

Suggestions for Further Reading

LERNER, GERDA, *The Creation of Patriarchy* (New York: Oxford University Press, 1986).

SEIBERT, ILSE, *Women in the Ancient Near East*, trans. Marianne Herzfeld (New York: Abner Schram, 1974).

THE NATURE OF THE EVIDENCE IN IMAGES

Virtually all surviving images of women in Egyptian art occur in the context of temples, funerary monuments, and tomb art. Since all Egyptian art is idealizing, there are no portrait likenesses or deviations in anatomy from the standard, perfected types. There are two basic types for men, the slender youthful image as seen in the statue of Mycerinus (Fig. 3–1), and an older, fuller figure with enlarged breasts and abdomen. Gay Robins identifies the second type with the successful official whose sedentary lifestyle and access to ample food permitted a weight gain as a mark of status. Women had only the single, slender image with no indications of the physical changes of childbearing.[1]

A second convention that distinguishes men from women is skin color. Women's skin is usually a lighter yellowish-brown, while men's skin is a darker reddish-brown. This convention may have been a symbol for the realities of some women's lives. Since women's occupations were more frequently performed indoors, their skin may have been less colored by exposure to the sun. Light-colored skin, then, may have conveyed upper-class status since women living in wealthy families did not have to work outdoors at all. However, Robins warns that this is an artistic convention and not a reliable indicator of actual skin colors, which would most likely have varied widely in reality.[2]

REPRESENTATIONS OF ROYAL WOMEN

- *Pair Statue of Mycerinus and Queen Khamerernebty II*

The main role of Egypt's royal women was to complement the divine aspect of kingship through divine queenship. Both the "king's mother" and the "king's principal wife" played crucial roles in ritual. Based on analysis of headdress and other insignia, Robins concludes that just as kingship was considered divine, there was also a concept of "divine queenship" spanning the entire history of Egyptian civilization.[3]

However, there is evidence to dispute the position of some scholars that the

Fig. 3–1. *Pair Statue of Mycerinus and His Queen.*
From Giza. Dynasty IV, 2599–1571 B.C. Schist.
Height (complete statue): 54$\frac{1}{2}$ in. *(Harvard
University–Museum of Fine Arts, Boston, Expedition.
Courtesy, Museum of Fine Arts, Boston)*

pharaoh occupied the throne by marrying a female of the royal family. This "heiress" theory, according to Robins, simply cannot be supported by the surviving evidence since queens were frequently not of royal birth.

This statue shows a remarkably equal and balanced image of the king and queen. It is obvious that the queen is very important, even if she is not the "heiress" through which Mycerinus achieved kingship. This sculpture reveals two other consistent elements in the gendered conventions of Egyptian royal imagery. The proportions of the queen are more slender, the definition of her musculature is less developed, and her legs are longer compared with the male figure. Furthermore, her extremely form fitting clothing reveals the body beneath. By contrast, Mycerinus's loincloth does conceal his genitals.

• Funerary Temple of Queen Hatshepsut at Dier el-Bahri

In many respects Hatshepsut (1504–1483 B.C.) was an exceptional and unusual woman who, benefitting from specific circumstances in the dynastic succession, emerged as a powerful leader on her own.

She was the daughter of the Pharaoh, Thutmose I. She apparently married her half-brother, Thutmose II, since she appears on a stele with the title of "principal wife" and "God's Wife" of Thutmose II. This is a case in which succession was contained within the royal family. Robins explains this practice as a way of mimicking the behavior of the gods. For example, in Egyptian mythology, Osiris and Isis were a brother and sister who married. This distinguished the king from other mortal Egyptians, who did not marry their sisters.

The successor of Thutmose II was Thutmose III, who must have been a boy since his reign is recorded as lasting fifty-four years. Records also indicate that Thutmose III was not Hatshepsut's son.

For the first years of Thutmose III's reign, Hatshepsut served as regent, but when Thutmose III grew old enough to assume the rule independently, Hatshepsut did not relinquish power and step down as regent but, using the precedent of a co-regency, reigned as "king" jointly with Thutmose III. This joint "kingship" lasted from year 7 to year 22 in the reign of Thutmose III. At the beginning of the regency, Hatshepsut used the titles and insignia of "king's principal wife," although she preferred the title of "God's Wife." After year 7 in Thutmose's reign, she abandoned all references to her role as queen and adopted the full range of titles and insignia of a king, even appearing on monuments in the body type and costume of the king.

Hatshepsut had one daughter, Neferura, who is most frequently recorded as "God's Wife." The exceptional prominence of a daughter may be due to the unusual circumstances of her mother's rule. Hatshepsut needed her daughter to fulfill the ritual role normally played by a king's mother or king's principal wife. Hatshepsut, who

Fig. 3–2. Funerary Temple of Queen Hatshepsut, Dier el-Bahri.   *(Foto Marburg / Art Resource, NY)*

defied tradition, is clearly exceptional; no other woman in the span of 3,000 years of Egyptian history assumed such power and for such a long period of time. In fact, only four of the 200 to 300 Egyptian rulers were female.

One measure of the success of her reign is her building activities. She supervised construction of the temple to Amun at Karnak. She ordered a pair of obelisks for this temple, an act which was strictly the prerogative of the king, and had herself depicted presenting offerings directly to the gods. Most important, she had the impressive mortuary temple at Dier el-Bahri constructed. In this temple, designed for her funerary cult rituals, reliefs illustrate the achievements of her reign. Prominently featured is the successful trading mission to the land of Punt in east Africa, which was a source of incense and other valuable goods. This temple is the only example of a large-scaled stone architectural monument built by a woman ruler. It is tangible evidence of the political power wielded by Hatshepsut as "king" of Egypt.

• Stele, Altar at Amarna

Amenhotep IV, who changed his name to "Akhenaten," is well known for a major shift from the polytheism of Egyptian religion to a monotheistic worship of the single god Aten, symbolized in the sun disk.

His "principal wife" Nefertiti was extremely important in his reign since "no other queen was ever shown so frequently on the monuments, in temples, tombs and statuary."[4] Her importance in the Aten religion is documented by her appearance in the temple at Karnak, presenting offerings directly to the god Aten. This relief was part of a household altar in the palace at Amarna. Nefertiti is depicted in the same scale and as an equal partner with Akhenaten. Both king and queen are seated below the symbol of the new god, forming a triad, such as the famous example of Mycerinus between two goddesses. Other textual evidence shows that Nefertiti functioned as an intercessor, much like the Virgin Mary, between common people and the new male god, bridging the gap left by the abandonment of the traditional pantheon of goddesses.

Fig. 3–3. Stele, Altar at Amarna, Nefertiti and Ahknaten.
(© Staatliche Museen zu Berlin, Preußischer Kulturbesitz, Ägyptisches Museum)

The tall blue crown in the famous bust of Nefertiti (now in Berlin) was a unique royal insignia. Early in her reign, Nefertiti wore insignia commonly associated with queens. However, later on she was sometimes depicted wearing crowns identical to that of the king and in poses and situations borrowed, like Hatshepsut, from the king's iconography.

REPRESENTATIONS OF WOMEN IN TOMB PAINTINGS

One important function of tomb paintings was to provide a setting for the rebirth of the tomb owner in the next world. Representations of women in tomb paintings must be interpreted in this context.

- **Scene from Tomb of Menna, *Spearing Fish and Hunting Birds***

This scene, common in tomb paintings from the Old Kingdom throughout the Eighteenth Dynasty, usually combines two motifs. The tomb owner hunts birds with a throwstick and spears two fish. The marsh setting carries associations with Hathor, the cow goddess, and the primordial swamp from which it was believed the mound of creation arose. The lotus, present here in abundance, was a common symbol of rebirth. Hunting the wild fowl symbolizes the ability of the tomb owner to establish order from the chaos of natural forces. Fowling was an activity associated with the god Osiris, who was resurrected after his murder by his sister, the goddess Isis. Isis would conceive a son with Osiris, the falcon god Horus. She gave birth to Horus in the marsh of Khemmis, where wild fowl abound.

The fish, the tilapia, was also a symbol of rebirth, associated with Hathor. It was believed to accompany and protect the sun god in his journey and is invoked in the text of *The Book of the Dead*.

Fig. 3–4. *Menna with Family Fishing and Fowling,* Tomb of Menna. *(The Metropolitan Museum of Art. All rights reserved, The Metropolitan Museum of Art. 30.4.48)*

Female members of the family appear prominently in these representations. Their presence may be interpreted not merely as a genre element but as crucial to the successful rebirth of the tomb owner and here function as "representative[s] of the female generative principle of the universe."[5]

- **Tomb of Nebamun, Banquet Scene**

Banquet scenes which depict the deceased tomb owner and guests participating in a ritual meal were common tomb decorations in the Eighteenth Dynasty.

As discussed in relation to the sculpture of Mycerinus and Khamerernebty II (Fig. 3–1), the costumes of men and women were clearly differentiated in Egyptian artistic conventions. In the New Kingdom, during the Eighteenth Dynasty, the visual representations of female costumes began to change to pleated looser fitting drapery which reflects the styles in actual dresses which have survived from this epoch. Linen cloth, worn loosely, would tend to conceal the body. The "sheath" dress, then, was an artistic convention and not a reflection of the daily realities of clothing. A costume that obscures the form of the body beneath is visible in both these tomb paintings. While goddesses continued to be shown in the sheath dress, other images of women adopt this looser style.

This tomb painting is of further interest in that it contains three nude adolescent serving girls wearing only headdresses, jewelry, and a thin belt around the waist. The nakedness of young girls is very rare in Egyptian art and has no counterpart in male figures, who are never shown completely undressed. Small children of both sexes, however, were usually depicted without clothes.

In other paintings and sculptures, nude adolescents wear an amulet associated with Bes, the deity entrusted with the protection of women in childbirth and newborn infants. Robins concludes that such banquet scenes carry associations of sexual-

Fig. 3–5. Wall Painting, Tomb of Nebanum.   *(Copyright The British Museum, London)*

ity relative to birth and rebirth. The presence of these serving girls would facilitate the rebirth of the deceased tomb owner.[6]

Suggestions for Further Reading

CAMERON, AVERIL, and AMELIE KUHRT (eds.), *Images of Women in Antiquity* (London: Croom Helm, 1983).

LESKO, BARBARA (ed.), *Women's Earliest Records from Ancient Egypt and Western Asia* (Atlanta, GA: Scholar's Press, 1989).

MANNICHE, LISE, *Sexual Life in Ancient Egypt* (London: Routledge, 1987).

ROBINS, GAY, *Women in Ancient Egypt* (Cambridge, MA: Harvard University Press, 1993).

WENIG, STEFFEN, *The Woman in Egyptian Art* (New York: McGraw-Hill, 1969).

CHAPTER 4

· · · · · · · · ·

CRETE

THE NATURE OF THE EVIDENCE

Surviving archeological remains on the island of Crete are more elaborate and better preserved than other early Bronze Age civilizations. This visual evidence is connected mainly with large architectural complexes, such as the palace at Knossos. Since the vast majority of evidence comes from palaces, sites of the wealthiest elite of the society, the frescoes would clearly reflect the values and interests of this particular class. It is highly speculative to pinpoint, from the surviving archeological remains, the exact functions and purposes of the different spaces, so it is unwise to rely too much on designations such as "Queen's bedroom" attributed to certain spaces by the original archeologist who supervised the excavation, Sir Arthur Evans. One aspect of the palaces that is undeniable, however, is their chosen physical location. Vincent Scully has convincingly argued that the selection of Minoan palace sites and their architectural orientation were dependent on the relationship of the surrounding landscape to the "body" of the Earth Mother. All Cretan palaces were located in an enclosing valley and oriented to a conical hill and double-peaked or cleft mountain in the distance. The closer cone was perceived as the body of the Great Mother Goddess, and the horns of the more distant mountain created a profile evocative of a pair of horns, raised arms, the *mons Veneris* or a pair of breasts of the Great Goddess.[1] In the courtyard of Knossos, from which Mount Jouctas is visible, young men and women performed the famous bull dances, seizing the horns sacred to the goddess. Thus, locations of Cretan palaces were determined by their proximity to the center of life and the divine powers of the Earth Mother Goddess.

PALACE FRESCOES

Many of the walls of these palaces were decorated with frescoes, in which women are depicted more frequently than men. Women are included as spectators in scenes of crowds observing an event, and sometimes women occupy the front row of seats. In a famous example, the "bull-leaping" scene, one of the figures is usually identified as a woman, based mainly on the lighter color of her skin.

It is believed that this culture may have demonstrated a relatively high status for women. Minoan women had access to all professions, including the manufacture of their famous pottery, which was distributed throughout the ancient world.

- ### Snake Goddess

Further evidence of the role of women in Crete can be found in small-scaled sculptures. A number of these statuettes, made of terra cotta or faience (a glass-like material), have been located on Crete. They share some consistent elements: the women wear long skirts but reveal their breasts, their arms are outstretched, and snakes are entwined about their arms.

Ehrenberg looks at the archeological context in which such figures were found to help interpret their meaning. They were excavated within the palaces in rooms with raised structures thought to be altars. They have also been found in caves on top of certain mountains. Furthermore, similar representations have been found in fres-

Fig. 4–1. Snake Goddess, Palace at Knossos. c. 1600 B.C. Height 13½ in.   (*Archaeological Museum, Heraklion, Crete. Courtesy of Hirmer Verlag München*)

coes, sarcophagi, and other small-scale objects, in which the figure appears to be venerated by a group of people, mainly women. Ehrenberg accepts these images as either an effigy of a goddess or a priestess devoted to the worship of a goddess. She rejects their interpretation as images of the queen, perhaps in the role of priestess or goddess, due to differences between the dress and hairstyle of these sculptural figures and other visual evidence in depictions of ordinary people. These statuettes, therefore, document female participation as divinity and priestess in Minoan society.[2]

WAS CRETE A MATRIARCHY?

Despite the longings or wishful thinking of some scholars it would appear unwarranted to identify Crete as a matriarchy. Based on the archeological evidence, it is not valid to assume that Crete was ruled by a female leader or that women occupied a higher status than men. However, we can safely assume that upper-class women participated in a wide range of activities. It is likely that a female divinity was worshiped and women were predominant in the role of priestess in the cult worship of a Mother Goddess. In fact, there is no solid evidence for identifying any culture in antiquity as a "matriarchy."

Suggestions for Further Reading

EHRENBERG, MARGARET, *Women in Prehistory* (Norman: University of Oklahoma Press, 1989).

SCULLY, VINCENT, *The Earth, the Temple and the Gods: Greek Sacred Architecture*, rev. ed. (New Haven, CT: Yale University Press, 1979).

CHAPTER 5

· · · · · · · · ·

GREECE

THE NATURE OF THE EVIDENCE

Archeological evidence indicates that the Greeks practiced female infanticide and that males outnumbered females by at least two to one.[1] This smaller proportion of females surviving infancy extends from the Greek Dark Ages (1100–800 B.C.) through the classical and Hellenistic periods. By the Hellenistic era (fourth to first centuries B.C.), even fewer children of either sex were raised to maturity. A Greek girl who survived infancy was fed an inferior diet.

A wide range of visual and textual documents are extant from Greek civilization, especially dating from the classical era of the fifth century B.C. From this wealth of sources, it has been possible for scholars to formulate a more complete picture of women's lives and the relations between men and women, mainly in Athens, than from earlier civilizations.

WOMEN AND TEXTILES

- **Amasis Painter, *Lekythos***

Throughout this period in the Greek world, one of the major tasks of women was the weaving of textiles and their decoration. Women of all classes contributed to the making of cloth. Wealthy women and slaves worked in their homes, while poorer women earned wages as wool workers in the cloth industry. Spindles used to spin flax or wool into thread have been found in graves from the Dark Ages, identifying these as burial places of females.

Many female figures, including Helen and Penelope, are occupied with spinning and weaving in the *Iliad* and the *Odyssey*. Penelope, the wife of Odysseus, spends her days weaving a shroud for Laertes, Odysseus's father, and unraveling it at night to evade her suitors. This is her primary activity and can be taken as an example of the importance of weaving in the life of the Greek upper-class woman. In Athens, a robe (*peplos*) for the cult statue of the goddess Athena was woven every four years. Two young girls selected from among the noble families of Athens would spin the yarn for

Fig. 5–1. Attributed to The Amasis Painter, *Lekythos.* right
side: Women working wool. Attic vase, c. 560 B.C. Height
6³/₄ in.   *(The Metropolitan Museum of Art, Fletcher Fund,*
1931. All rights reserved, The Metropolitan Museum of Art.
31.11.10)

the cloth. Other women then assisted in the weaving and embroidering of this holy garment. The culmination of the Panathenaic procession was the presentation of the *peplos* to the statue of Athena on the Parthenon, as depicted in the Parthenon frieze. Representations on Greek vases of women spinning or weaving far outnumber the pictures of other crafts. For example, the black-figured painting on this *lekythos* (Fig. 5–1) illustrates women occupied in a variety of tasks related to the making of cloth.

Textile manufacture was a primary occupation for women throughout the ancient world. As noted before, women of all classes in the ancient Near East made textiles. Phoenician women were famous for their fine cloths. In the excavations of Troy, many weaving tools have been found.

• Dipylon Vase

Women were not only responsible for the manufacture of cloth but also for its decoration. Embroidery was an exclusively female occupation in Greece. In the decoration of textiles, women were the tastemakers of antiquity. Here, they had an outlet for their visual creativity.

Kate McK. Elderkin has built a convincing case for the influence of textile patterns and decoration on the successive stylistic development of Greek pottery design.[2] She maintains that the geometric style, as seen in the Dipylon pottery vases of the eighth century B.C. (Fig. 5–2), was derived from the ornamental patterns found in Dorian wool fabrics. Not only the specific forms, but also the use of bands is consistent with the weaving of wool fabrics. Ornamentation in bands is a noteworthy characteristic of Corinthian ware, such as the famous François Vase. In the later Archaic

Fig. 5–2. Dipylon Amphora (Geometric Style) from the Dipylon Cemetery, Athens. c. 750 B.C. Height 61 in. *(National Archaeological Museum, Athens. Courtesy Hirmer Verlag, München)*

period, i.e., the sixth century B.C., fashions changed and the less decorated linen *chiton* of the Ionians gained popularity. The painted decoration on pottery subsequently became less ornate, and the influence of weaving became less pronounced in this epoch.

Barber also confirms the close relationship between pottery designs and the weaving patterns in Archaic Greece, arguing for the decisive impact of textile decoration on contemporary vase painting.[3] Athena was the patron goddess of both weavers and potters, connecting both of these activities with women, although by the Classical era it was mostly men who made pottery. Some women did continue to practice this craft. A woman, shown decorating a vase on a Greek red-figured *hydria* from the fifth century B.C., is depicted in a workshop setting.

THE "HISTORY OF SEXUALITY" IN CLASSICAL ATHENS

For the culture of classical Athens, scholars have been able to study the earliest interpretations of the "history of sexuality." Such a concept is possible since there is a wide range of sexual behaviors tolerated, permitted, and accepted in any given culture. Sexuality, then, may be defined as a question of culture: "Sexuality is that complex of reactions, interpretations, definitions, prohibitions and norms that is created and maintained by a given culture in response to the fact of the two biological sexes."[4]

CLASSICAL SCULPTURE AND NUDITY

The Adolescent Male

- #### *The Kritios Boy*

    Michel Foucault is one of the most important scholars who has analyzed surviving written texts to study the history of sexuality in Greek and Roman culture. Foucault identifies the relationship between adult men and adolescent boys as the location or "site" of classical Athens's "problematizations" of sexual relations. There is nothing that "prevented or prohibited an adolescent from being the openly recognized sexual partner of a man . . . there is every indication that they [the Greek writers] were anxious about it."[5]

    It is this philosophical and ethical background which should be brought to bear on the interpretation of the preponderance of ideal male nudes in the classical era. Works such as *The Kritios Boy* (Fig. 5–3), the *Doryphorous*, and so forth are famous examples of the nude adolescent male body presented as objects of sexual attention in works of art created by male artists and targeted at the male viewer. As Foucault concludes: "The young man—between the end of childhood and the age when he attained manly status—. . . his youth with its particular beauty (to which every man was believed to be naturally sensitive) . . . and the status that would be his . . . formed a 'strategic' point around which a complex game was required."[6] This definition of the adolescent male as an object of sexual attraction is paralleled in the history of art with the preponderance of male nudity observable in monumental sculpture.

Fig. 5–3. *The Kritios Boy* (Young victorious athlete). c. 480 B.C. Marble. Height 34 in. *(National Archeol. Museum, Athens, Greece; Alinari/Art Resource, NY)*

The Female Nude

- ### Praxiteles, *Aphrodite of Knidos*

It is not until the fourth century B.C., outside of the culture of classical Athens, that the female nude first appears as an appropriate subject for sculpture. That extremely special case can be pinpointed to the work of the sculptor Praxiteles, who created two cult statues of the goddess of love Aphrodite. The citizens of the city of Kos selected the clothed version, while the nude sculpture was placed on the island of Knidos, in a circular temple so it could be appreciated from a full range of 360 degree viewpoints. In this sculpture, existing only in later Roman copies such as this image, Aphrodite was depicted as a bather. Female nudity was believed to have "aphrodisiac" powers, i.e., the ability to arouse sexual feelings in the viewer deriving from the power of the goddess of love. The myth of Pygmalion who fell in love with his sculpture is echoed in a story retold by Roman authors about this statue. A dark blemish on the statue was left by a youth who, locked in the temple overnight, supposedly had intercourse with the statue.[7]

Fig. 5–4. *Aphrodite of Knidos.* Roman copy after an original of c. 330 B.C. by Praxiteles. Marble. Height 6 ft. 8 in. *(Vatican Museums, Vatican State; Alinari/Art Resource, NY)*

- ## Athenian Red Figure Vase Painting,
  Procession to the Nuptial Bed

Athenian girls were married between the ages of 12 and 15; men were usually married at 30. Such young marriages forced women into early pregnancies, further threatening their survival. The shortage of women plus selective rearing also ensured that women would have multiple pregnancies. Many women did not survive the childbearing years, and women's life expectancy was five to ten years shorter than men's. One may conclude that only a fraction of the female population lived long enough to practice any profession without being pregnant or responsible for the care of small children.

The future of the bride was thus one of enforced isolation and multiple pregnancies of great danger to the woman's survival. In this context, this example of a wedding scene acquires new meaning. Wedding scenes depicted in the classical period are frequently on a ritual water jar, known as a *loutrophoros*. These vases were used to carry water for the bridal bath from a special spring. In this example, several figures of Eros are flying about the head of the bride and, according to Robert Sutton, adorning her with a wreath and a necklace. Another winged eros is zooming out from the bridal chamber. Sutton suggests that since only marriage to an Athenian woman could produce legitimate children with full citizenship rights, the acceptance of sexual relations between husband and wife carried political implications.[8] The romantic elements in this scene might have encouraged young women to accept the sexual elements of marriage, which were part of their social responsibilities in this culture.

Fig. 5–5. Athenian Red Figure Vase Paintings, *Bridal Procession* and *Father and Son Bidding Farewell.* c. 430 B.C. Height 0.753 m. Diameter (of body): 0.18 m. *(Francis Bartlett Donation; Courtesy, Museum of Fine Arts, Boston)*

• **Domestic Scene**

This vase illustrates the central roles of the upper-class married woman, i.e., bearing and caring for children and making textiles in a nonprofessional, domestic context. It is another example of the prominent association of textile manufacture with the activities and responsibilities of women, as has already been discussed.

The central figure is seated on a chair and is handing her baby to a female servant. She is flanked by an adolescent male (presumed by Dyfri Williams to be an eldest son) and a loom.[9] This vase was believed to have been found in a tomb and would therefore have been a gift for the deceased presented by a member of the family.

As in the ancient Near East, marriage and motherhood were the most widely accepted and expected roles for women to fill in the society. However, the position of wife and mother conferred varying degrees of social status on women in different periods. The position in their society of some royal women in the Bronze Age, as described in the Homeric epics (c. 1200 B.C.) was very high, and evidence also indicates that women were dominant in the religious sphere.[10] By contrast, the status of Greek women in the culture of the classical era (fifth century B.C.), especially in Athens, seems to have been very low, and this may be explained by a number of factors. Particularly among the upper classes, a sharp separation existed between the men's public world and the women's domestic one, a situation similar to that in modern capitalist cultures. While men were occupied with running the Athenian democracy and waging almost continual warfare, upper-class women rarely left their homes. They remained in segregated quarters, often on the upper story of town houses. While boys

Fig. 5–6. Painter of the Polygnotan Circle, Domestic Scene. c. 430 B.C. Red-figure ceramic, 34.6 x 24.6 cm. *(Courtesy of the Arthur M. Sackler Museum, Harvard University Art Museums, bequest of David M. Robinson)*

were taught the arts of rhetoric and other intellectual pursuits, girls learned domestic crafts from their mothers. The age discrepancy between husband and wife and the gaps between the education of men and women further intensified the isolation between the sexes in Classical Athens.[11] As we know, women were excluded from any form of political participation in the city-state or *polis*. Women were ranked with those men who, accused of a serious crime, were deprived of political rights.[12]

The Athenian woman, daughter of a citizen, always had a dowry that was meant to remain intact when she married. The dowry provided her with some degree of economic security. In the absence of sons, a daughter could legally inherit the family wealth, but the nearest male relative was supposed to marry the heiress. While women could acquire property through their dowries or by inheritance or gift, they had no legal rights. Women could not conduct business or sign contracts for major sums. Furthermore, because few women were literate, it was virtually impossible for women to conduct a business enterprise independently of men.

Greek women of all classes were occupied with the same types of work, mostly centered around the domestic needs of the family. Women cared for young children, nursed the sick, and prepared food. Wealthy women supervised slaves who did these tasks. Poorer women who could not afford to remain at home worked for wages at these jobs. There is evidence that some lower-class women sold retail goods in the marketplace.

PORNOGRAPHY

• *Madam Teaching Hetairai to Dance*

The location of the *Kerameikos*, the place where potters and painters produced their wares, was "a byword for prostitution" in classical Athens.[13] Williams suggests that a state run brothel was physically proximate to the workshops of the potters. Women who were prostitutes, or the better educated hetairai (courtesans), were most probably slaves and foreigners like the men who were employed as potters and vase painters. However, the frequent depictions of courtesans on pottery from this period may not only be due to the physical proximity of the *Kerameikos* and brothels or the similarities in social backgrounds. The market for these wares was specifically the male *symposia*, usually drinking parties that required cups and water jars. Mixing bowls were also needed since the wine was diluted with water, but not enough to prevent intoxication. Shapiro notes the market for such erotic ware was also stimulated by the tastes of the Etruscans.[14] The red-figured drinking cups are most common in the period in which these vessels were being exported to Etruscan settlements in Italy, and they have been found in Etruscan tombs. A number of vases show scenes of hetairai and madams of brothels. As in nineteenth-century French images, nudity is the sign of the class status and position of these women. The dancing lesson shown on this example is an erotic motif targeted at male users of the vessel.

Other red-figured vases depict nude women whom we can assume to be prostitutes bathing.[15] These representations of the female nude are considerably earlier than

Fig. 5–7. *Madam Teaching Hetairai to Dance.* *(Copyright The British Museum, London)*

the nudity of the monumental sculpture of *Aphrodite* by Praxiteles previously discussed.

Another group of red-figured ware, usually cups for the drinking parties, depict explicit scenes of sexual intercourse between prostitutes and male customers. These are most prevalent on drinking cups from c. 520–470 B.C. These images depict a high proportion of "rear entry couplings." One cup by the Douris painter even has a written inscription, "Be Quiet."[16] These cups were targeted at the male patrons. The female is being utilized for the sexual pleasures of the male viewer/owner of the cup.

By contrast the scenes of homosexual encounters are restrained. They most frequently fall into the category of "courting" scenes in which an older man fondles the genitals of a youth and offers him gifts. "A clear distinction had to be made from heterosexual pornography, with its emphatic dominance of one [male] partner over the other [female]. Oral and anal sex . . . conspicuous in scenes with female prostitutes, thus are absent from homoerotic scenes."[17] This is consistent with the tone and emphasis of the texts, which are concerned more with the ethics of homosexual courtship of adolescent males, discussed in relation to works of sculpture such as *The Kritios Boy* (Fig. 5–3).

WOMEN ARTISTS IN GREECE

Considering the severe restrictions on women's lives, their inability to move freely in society, conduct business, or acquire any type of nondomestic training, it is not surprising to find that no names of important artists have come down to us from the classical era. Only the poet Sappho (c. 600 B.C.) received high praise from the Greeks; Plato referred to her as the twelfth Muse. Significantly, she came not from Athens or Sparta but from Lesbos, an island whose culture incorporated a high regard for women.

While very few artists' names of either sex survive from antiquity, the earliest recorded names of women painters are found in Hellenistic texts. As in later centuries, these few women artists are mostly daughters of artists, who acquire their training from their fathers. Unfortunately, none of the works of these artists has survived. In 228 B.C., Nealkes of Sicyon had his daughter trained as a painter.[18] Another Greek painter known by name alone was Eirene, daughter of Kratinos, who was famous for painting in the city of Eleusis. Eirene is singled out for special mention in Boccaccio's *Concerning Famous Women.*[19] Boccaccio's treatise, largely dependent on the Roman historian Pliny, is a very important Renaissance source, preserving for his era the names of notable women of antiquity. Boccaccio also mentions Thamyris, or Timarete. This artist's reputation was based on a painting of the goddess Diana, guarded at the sanctuary in Ephesus. It is, of course, possible that women were painters in earlier periods and that their names, like those of their male colleagues, have simply been lost in history. To my knowledge, no evidence of women sculptors or architects in the ancient world has survived.

Long before the appearance of women painters in literary records, women had been credited in legend with the invention of this art. In both Eastern and Western cultures, the origin of the art of painting is attributed to the observation of a shadow and the tracing of that outline. By the time Pliny recorded the legend, the inventor of painting was identified as a woman, i.e., the "Corinthian Maid." The Maid traced her lover's profile on a wall. Subsequently, her father, the potter Butades, built up the work into a sculpture. The Corinthian Maid is often called "Dibutade," i.e., the daughter of Butades. A variation of this legend is recorded by Athenagoras, a Christian Athenian of the second century A.D. The first artist is now called "Core."

The legend of the Corinthian Maid was first widely used as a subject for the visual arts during the era of romantic classicism, in the late eighteenth century A.D. One art historian, Robert Rosenblum, believes that the increased popularity of the story of Dibutade at that time is related to the prominence of contemporary artists such as Angelica Kauffman and Elisabeth Vigée-Lebrun.[20] The careers of these artists will be discussed in Chapter 10.

The legend of Dibutade and the preservation of the names of these women painters from the past have immense importance for the history of women artists. Despite their limited number, these notable painters served as role models for women artists from the Renaissance through the nineteenth century. Eirene, Timarete, and the other women recorded by Pliny and included in Boccaccio's study were incorporated into many subsequent histories of women artists.[21] Even though their works were lost, their reputations remained alive, preserving the idea that women could become excellent painters.

Suggestions for Further Reading

AVERIL, CAMERON, and A. KUHRT (eds.), *Images of Women in Antiquity* (London: Croom Helm, 1983).

CANTARELLA, EVE, *Pandora's Daughters: The Role and Status of Women in Greece and Roman Antiquity* (Baltimore, MD: Johns Hopkins University Press, 1987).

FANTHAM, ELAINE, HELENE PEET FOLEY, NATALIE BOYMEL KAMPEN, SARAH B. POMEROY, and H. ALAN SHAPIRO, *Women in the Classical World: Image and Text* (New York: Oxford University Press, 1994).

FOUCAULT, MICHEL, *The Use of Pleasure: The History of Sexuality*, vol. 2, trans. Robert Hurley (New York: Random House, 1985).

JOHNS, CATHERINE, *Sex or Symbol? Erotic Images of Greece and Rome* (Austin: University of Texas Press, 1982).

KEULS, EVA C., *The Reign of the Phallus* (New York: Harper and Row, 1985).

LEFKOWITZ, MARY, *Women's Life in Greece and Rome: A Sourcebook in Translation*, 2nd ed. (Baltimore, MD: Johns Hopkins University Press, 1992).

PERADOTTO, J. (ed.), *Women in the Ancient World* (Albany: State University of New York Press, 1984).

POMEROY, SARAH B. *Goddesses, Whores, Wives and Slaves: Women in Classical Antiquity* (New York: Schocken Books, 1975).

POMEROY, SARAH B. (ed.) , *Women's History and Ancient History* (Chapel Hill: University of North Carolina Press, 1991).

RABINOWITZ, NANCY SORKIN, and AMY RICHLIN (eds.), *Feminist Theory and the Classics* (London: Routledge, 1993).

RICHLIN, AMY (ed.), *Pornography and Representation in Greece and Rome* (New York: Oxford University Press, 1992).

WALLACE-HADRILL, A. (ed.), *Patronage in Ancient Society* (London: Routledge, 1989).

ZINSERLING, VERENA, *Women in Greece and Rome*, trans. L. A. Jones (New York: Abner Schram, 1973).

CHAPTER 6

• • • • • • • • • •

ROME

THE NATURE OF THE EVIDENCE

The issues raised by feminist art historians studying the visual evidence in the Roman Empire focus attention on the weakness of thinking in terms of a public vs. private dichotomy. Roman women were not consistently confined to a private sphere while men occupied positions of political importance in the Empire. A study of the visual evidence, supported by the survival of written documents, allows for a more complete picture of the roles of women in the political, economic, and cultural life of Rome.

IMAGES OF WOMEN ON HISTORICAL RELIEFS

• Family of Emperor Group on *Ara Pacis*

Diana Kleiner is one of a number of scholars who have studied this monument. Kleiner examines reasons for the unusually prominent appearance of women and children in the processional friezes of the *Ara Pacis*.[1] Unlike the Parthenon frieze, which is clearly a visual source, family groups form an important part of this procession. Following Augustus, there are three groups of men, women, and children on the south side of the monument, and two additional groups with children on the north side. Such prominent displays of family groups are unprecedented in earlier republican art forms, although prototypes in Greek funerary stelae do exist.

The display of family groups in public sculpture should be understood in the context of Augustus's policies as documented in a series of laws intended to strengthen and preserve the nuclear family of the upper-class patricians who were citizens. The *lex Julia de adulteriis* brought adultery under court jurisdiction and out of the private sphere, reinforcing marriage bonds. Another law, the *lex Julia de maritandis ordinibut*, as well as other legal measures, removed existing restrictions on marriage and was intended to stimulate the raising of children. Many social policies favored married men with large numbers of children. For example, in the case of a tie for an electoral office, the man with the most children would be declared the winner. Celibacy

Fig. 6–1. Family of Emperor Group on *Ara Pacis*.

and childlessness, both of men and of women, were penalized financially in the existing tax structure. The exposure of girl infants and early death in childbearing resulted in fewer women than men in Roman society.[2] During both the Republican era and the Empire, virtually all upper-class women were married. In fact, Augustus made marriage almost compulsory. Girls were married early, between the ages of 12 and 15. Mother-hood conveyed great status, as well as economic benefits, on women. Unmarried women forfeited their inheritances, and childless women lost half of their inheritances.

The legendary Cornelia, who lived in the second century B.C., provided a cultural ideal for women as mothers. Cornelia was considered a paragon of virtues: "She possessed an excellent Greek education, was a master of rhetoric such as no other woman was and corresponded with philosophers, scientists and distinguished men of affairs."[3] Through her sons, the Gracchi (their father was the tribune Tiberius Sempronius Gracchus), she exerted political influence as well. Cornelia was a model figure not only for subsequent generations of Roman matrons but also for later centuries. (See Kauffman's *Cornelia Pointing to Her Children as Her Treasures*, Fig. 10–3.)

As in Sparta, the prolonged absence of men on military campaigns and the administration of a far-flung empire gave upper-class women greater autonomy. As Natalie Kampen notes, the highly visible appearance of women on the *Ara Pacis* occurs precisely when the political regime was "most uncertain about issues of reproduction, legitimacy and dynastic succession" at the very beginnings of the Roman Empire.[4]

• Relief on Column of Trajan, Provincial Town

In this portion of the Column of Trajan, the Emperor is traveling through the regions already under Roman control. Women and children form a prominent portion of the audience of townspeople observing a sacrifice. As Kampen indicates, "the

Fig. 6–2. Relief on Column at Trajan, Provincial Town. C 110 A.D.   (Courtesy
Deutsches Archäologisches Institut, Rom)

presence of women and children signified the whole 'community' and implies a happy future as well as the benefits of *romanitas* to both public and private realms."[5] For
Kampen, one of the leading scholars of this field, when women appear on public
monuments they should be interpreted as carrying the intended meaning of reflecting the political action of the Emperor and the Roman state on the domestic priva-
tized world of the family as well as on *all* the individuals living under Roman rule.
The well-being of both the family and the state are perceived as mutually interde-
pendent in the Roman Empire.

• Relief of Poultry Vendor

Kampen has studied the appearances of women of a very different class than
those on the *Ara Pacis*. This relief is one of two panels depicting retail saleswomen,
vendors in the market. The woman vendor is positioned in the center of the relief,
behind the counter. She is dressed in a simple garment associated with the working
classes and wears her hair in an unadorned style. Kampen concludes that the visual
language of position and gesture is the same for both men and women vendors in
both carved sculptural reliefs and painted images. This represents a unique situation in
the visual arts. It is "one of the very few instances when men and women were seen
doing exactly the same work in circumstances which were undeniably the same—
public and economically motivated."[6] As a rule, men and women working at the

same jobs, such as artisans or medical practitioners, are distinguished iconographically according to gender. Women working in other occupations, such as artisans, do not appear in representations. Neither do women belonging to families of a wealthier class, such as merchants. While a wide variety of images of men working has survived, there are very few visual examples of women working.

Kampen concludes that women's work was not frequently represented in visual imagery because the vast majority of patrons who could afford to commission or own a work of art operated under a class ideology in which, like Victorian England, women's work was not acceptable unless confined to the domestic realm and generated for the use of the family. Lower-class patrons, who might have been more inclined to depict women at work, could not afford figural monuments. They opted for the less expensive option of the inscription, some of which survive.

The role of the vendor is unique. Vendors occupied a social class below the aristocracy and wealthy merchants but above slaves, manual laborers, waitresses, entertainers, and prostitutes. The work performed by both men and women was identical and was seen in public. Perhaps this is why artistic representations of vendors show greater similarities between men and women than the normal conventions that generally differentiated between images of men and women in Roman art.

We know that lower-class women practiced a number of occupations. In Pompeii, there were women physicians and "commercial entrepreneurs," as well as prostitutes, waitresses, and tradeswomen. Slaves worked as domestics and, as already noted, in the clothing industry. "Freed women and female slaves worked as fishmongers, barley-sellers, silk weavers, lime burners, clothes-menders . . . as midwives and nurses . . . stenographers, singers, and actresses, among other professions."[7]

Spinning and weaving continued to be a major preoccupation of women of all classes: "The old-fashioned Roman bride wreathed the doorposts of her new home with wool. When Augustus wished to instill respect for old-fashioned virtues among the sophisticated women of his household, he set them to work in wool and wore their

Fig. 6–3. Relief of Poultry Vendor   *(Museo Ostiense, Ostia; photo courtesy of the Fototeca Unione, Rome)*

homespun results. Many women of the lower classes, slave and freed, were also employed in working wool both at home and in small-scale industrial establishments where working-class men joined women as weavers and weighers of balls of wool to be apportioned to weavers. Spinning, however, continued to be solely women's work."[8]

Iaia of Kyzikos (known as Marcia to Boccaccio) is the only name of a Roman woman artist that has been preserved. According to Pliny, "She painted chiefly portraits of women. . . . No artist worked more rapidly than she did, and her pictures have such merit that they sold for higher prices than those of Sopolis and Dionysios, well-known contemporary painters. . . ."[9]

Considering the wide variety of occupations practiced by Roman women, there may well have been other women painters whose names have not come down through the centuries. At any rate, the fact that Pliny recorded for posterity the names of a handful of women painters is a mark of the increased respect the Romans had for women of talent.

Plancia Magna

Plancia Magna was an extremely wealthy and prominent citizen of a city called Perge, now located in modern Turkey, which was then in the eastern portion of the Roman Empire.

Plancia Magna subsidized an elaborate monumental city gate and triumphal arch with a nearby "display wall" just south of the city gate. Mary T. Boatwright has reconstructed the complex building program that can be attributed to the lavish patronage of this leading citizen of Perge. In fact, from the surviving inscription it can be determined that Plancia Magna was the *demiourgos*, the leading magistrate of the city, the priestess of Artemis, and "the first and only priestess of the Mother of the Gods."[10] In one statue, Plancia Magna is depicted with her head covered with the outer cloak, or *himation*, in a reference to her functions as priestess. Her crown, or *diadem*, was ornamented with four busts of Roman emperors, identifying her priestess function with the imperial cult religion.

This statue was part of an extensive complex consisting of a large, horseshoe-shaped courtyard decorated with statues of Olympian gods and the city's mythological and historical founders. Plancia Magna's father and brother, identified through their relationship with her, are also represented. This was quite unusual, since women were most commonly identified through their relationships to their male relatives, especially their fathers, rather than the other way around.

Plancia Magna also had a huge triple arch constructed, which served as a transitional structure between the courtyard and the city streets. The arch carried a prominent inscription in which Plancia Magna dedicated the arch to her city. The arch was decorated with statues of members of the imperial family including many female members, such as the Emperor Trajan's sister, the mother of Hadrian's wife. Boatwright speculates that the number of imperial women on the arch was motivated by Plancia Magna's own gender. She was associating herself with the female members of the imperial family to acquire status and recognition in Rome. The sculpture and the marble revetement all added to the cost and magnificence of this gift to her city.

Plancia Magna's public patronage is exceptional but not unique. She is one of many women who played an active role in their communities. There were other benefactresses whose buildings have disappeared but whose generosity is documented in coins and inscriptions.

Although, legally, women could not control any money or transact business on their own, in practice women did control and bequeath their wealth. The growing bureaucracy of the Empire served to protect the rights of wives and children. A wife's dowry had to be returned intact if her husband repudiated the marriage.

> The growing custom of marriage *sine manu* enabled a woman to remain under the power of her own family rather than being transferred to her husband's on the simple condition that she live for three days of every year in her father's house. By the beginning of the third century, [the Roman jurist] Ulpian said that a woman had to have a tutor to act for her at law, to make contracts, to emancipate slaves, or to undertake civil business. But he added that a woman who had borne three children was no longer subject to this regulation. Thus, the Roman woman, entirely powerless within the public structure, could exercise very considerable power in private life as a result of the wealth and property that she might accumulate by herself or through her family.[11]

Classical scholar, Ramsay Macmullen, has studied the evidence of women's public roles in the Roman Empire. The role of priestess, which Plancia Magna occupied, was a highly prestigious and very public office. Macmullen notes that one of the largest buildings in Pompeii's forum was presented by a woman named Eumachia. Macmullen concludes that "women as benefactors should be imagined playing their part personally and visibly, out in the open."[12]

Inscriptions on coins provide us with additional evidence of the importance of the role of high priestess, like that occupied by Plancia Magna. Most often, Macmullen believes, the title was held by the wife of the high priest. For example, Menodora, living in a city in Pamphylia, was a member of the aristocracy. Her father and grandfather had been high priests before her, and she was a very wealthy individual who funded a temple and distributed money publicly to town senators. Women most probably did appear regularly in public, but were unlikely to speak in public.

DOMESTIC ARCHITECTURE: ARISTOCRATIC ROMAN VILLAS

A number of scholars have studied the archeological remains of homes of upper-class, wealthy families living in Roman cities throughout the empire. "They see this art as addressing an interlocking set of concerns of the patrons having to do with decorum, status, wealth, social privilege and obligations . . . the atrium house . . . [the *domus*] contained not only the private living quarters of the owner but also public rooms and gardens that served as the center of the owner's life of *negotium*, his civil and political activity. Both the architecture and decor of the town house were orchestrated to create appropriate settings in which the owner, his dependents and his adherents acted out their socially ordained roles."[13]

The research of Yvon Thébert and Andrew Wallace-Hadrill, among others, has clarified and expanded our understanding of the ways in which interior spaces of upper-class Roman villas mediated between the concepts of the public world of the city or empire and the private world of the family. The Roman household was the site of a wide range of social activities. The master of the house would receive any number of strangers into the house on a daily basis to conduct business affairs. Thébert tells us that political life was concentrated in the home of Caesar as much as in the Senate. Therefore, the impact of these spaces for women of this class who did not circulate as freely in the other politicized spaces of the city are significant.

Typically, Roman villas had a main entrance which was the transition from the street to the interior. The vestibule was a large space where visitors would be seen, under the observation of a slave who served as guard. Meals united the family. Men, women, and children ate together. Women and children also regularly attended banquets. The dining room, then, "played a key role in domestic socializing."[14]

Upper-class girls were educated by private tutors, but the early age of marriage limited the extent of their education. However, as was also true of the Renaissance, education and other accomplishments were considered positive attributes for women. Because women were not so completely isolated from male company as in classical Athens, a woman was expected to be able to converse intelligently with men. Large numbers of upper-class women were interested in literature, and a few were even authors and poets. Numerous orations honoring women have survived, indicating a public approval of notable women.

However, the bedroom, the *cubiculum*, was a strictly private space. Bedrooms were not open to strangers, although private homes did have guest bedrooms. The privacy of the *cubiculum* is nowhere more apparent than in the nature of the erotic paintings that were regularly placed there. Molly Myerowitz has discussed these images.[15] Most of the surviving works are from Pompeii and were located in the bedrooms of Roman villas of the wealthiest people. Their intended audience was the married couples of the upper classes. Most of these images depict anonymous, idealized heterosexual couples displayed in explicit positions of sexual intercourse.

Myerowitz interprets the presence of these scenes in the bedroom as a sort of mirror in which the real-life sexual partners could see an idealized reflection of their own behavior. She relates such an interpretation to literary texts, such as Ovid's *Ars Amatoria (The Art of Love)* in which women are instructed to manipulate their bodies for the visual effects on their male partners. This context emerges, however, from the literary evidence on the social attitudes surrounding sexual relations. The images themselves are remarkably free of the types of voyeuristic poses which we will encounter in the post-Renaissance world. They also present men and women in nonviolent and nonhierarchical depictions of sexuality.

It is tantalizing to interpret these images further in the context of Foucault's reading of Pliny and other Roman texts in which the relationship between married couples may be seen as "detach[ed] . . . from the status-determined authority of the husband . . . and take on the character of a singular relation having its own force, its difficulties, obligations, benefits, and pleasures . . . [Roman texts] . . . show that marriage was interrogated as a mode . . . of relation between two partners . . . this role was involved in a complex interplay of affective reciprocity and reciprocal dependence."[16]

This was a favorable situation for Roman women since marriage and motherhood continued to be the main occupation of Roman matrons.

WOMEN IN PUBLIC BATHS

One scholar, Roy Bowen Ward, has concluded, from the surviving evidence, that men and women customarily bathed together in the nude in Roman public baths.[17] The earliest public baths were created in the second century B.C. and may have been used only by men. Later, public baths such as those in Pompeii do have separate facilities for men and women. However, baths built after the first century A.D. have only a single set of bath rooms. Another scholar, Fikret Yegul, explains this evidence by proposing that men and women bathed at different times of the day, rather than together.[18] Ward cites evidence in literary texts from both Roman and Christian authors to support his view that women and men customarily engaged in mixed bathing and were enjoying each other's company while bathing together in the nude. Yegul will concede that prostitutes were available at the baths and did bathe with male clients.

If Ward is correct, then mixed bathing may have been occurring at a time when at least some women of the upper classes were acquiring greater personal "emancipation." This would be contemporary with the erotic paintings in the homes of the upper classes. According to Eve Cantarella, during this epoch, some aristocratic women began to use their newly acquired legal rights to "end unhappy marriages and contract new ones. They practiced birth control and abortion, formed freely chosen amorous bonds, lived outside of matrimony, and enjoyed a new liberty that had been absolutely unthinkable—sexual freedom."[19]

THE BYZANTINE EMPIRE

• Mosaic of Empress Theodora, San Vitale, Ravenna

This image of the Empress Theodora, wife of Justinian, is among the most famous visual images of a woman from the Byzantine Empire. It is one of a pair of dedicatory mosaics in the apse of San Vitale in Ravenna, and the only certain portrait of Theodora that has survived.[20] It is important, therefore, to understand the ways in which the images of Emperor and Empress are similar as well as their differences. Both Justinian and Theodora are in the center of their compositions which are of equal scale. However Justinian's image has an indeterminate setting, and he is escorted by other important males, such as the Bishop of Ravenna, Maximian. Theodora's mosaic setting is in an interior, and she appears to be passing through the space of the mosaic into yet another region screened by the curtain on the left. Justinian's crown is less ornate and imposing, while Theodora's headdress expands her physical height so she is taller than the ladies of the court and the two men in her entourage. She is wearing a purple cloak, the *paludamentum*, identified as a symbol of the imperial family. The embroidered image of the three Magi relates to the chalice she bears as a gift to the new church. This image was dedicated one year before Theodora's death in 548 and would be contemporary with Procopius's account of her in *The Secret History*.[21]

The problems with accepting Procopius's narrative concerning Theodora in this account as secure historical evidence have been clearly defined by Averil Cameron. Procopius's text was distorted by his political desire to discredit Justinian. All "facts" about Theodora are therefore called into question.[22] However, the very visible presence of Theodora in San Vitale is unprecedented and must relate to certain conditions of the time. Cameron does note that court ceremonies were giving the empress a greater ritual role, one in which other women of the court participated.[23] This is surely one element explaining this image.

Theodora was an actress and a prostitute prior to her marriage to Justinian (c. 524) and her elevation to the position of Empress. Procopius tells us that Theodora founded a Convent of Repentance for reformed prostitutes and helped women in distress. Theodora was an active supporter of a religious sect known as Monophysitism. The members of this group regarded Theodora as their champion and protectress. The Monophysites were grateful for her support and welcomed her as a reformed and penitent sinner, perhaps on the model of Mary Magdalen. Cameron sees these acts as well within the traditional roles of a "great lady," rather than as "feminist" interventions to improve women's status.[24]

It should be remembered that Theodora never ruled independently. She led a

Fig. 6–4. Mosaic of Empress Theodora, San Vitale, Ravenna. 6th century.   *(Alinari/Art Resource, NY)*

private life as queen of a traditional court, and any power she did achieve was exerted from behind the scenes, not in a public manner.

The life of Theodora does, however, document the large degree of upward mobility in social status of certain women in the elite of Constantinople. Theodora had one daughter, born illegitimately during her days as an actress. This woman married a man in the family of the Emperor Anastasius. The marriage produced three sons, Theodora's grandsons, all of whom married into the most wealthy and highest circles of Byzantine society. "The marriage alliances of Theodora's descendants conveyed wealth, position and lineage."[25] It is reasonable to view Theodora, at the least, as an intelligent woman who vastly improved her own life and those of her descendants through her marriage to Justinian.

Suggestions for Further Reading

AVERIL, CAMERON, and A. KUHRT (eds.), *Images of Women in Antiquity* (London: Croom Helm, 1983).

CANTARELLA, EVE, *Pandora's Daughters: The Role and Status of Women in Greece and Roman Antiquity* (Baltimore, MD: Johns Hopkins University Press, 1987).

CLARK, GILLIAN, *Women in Late Antiquity: Pagan and Christian Life Styles* (Oxford: Clarendon Press, 1993).

D'AMBRA, EVE (ed.), *Roman Art in Context: An Anthology* (Englewood Cliffs, NJ: Prentice Hall, 1993).

FANTHAM, ELAINE, HELENE PEET FOLEY, NATALIE BOYMEL KAMPEN, SARAH B. POMEROY, and H. ALAN SHAPIRO, *Women in the Classical World: Image and Text* (New York: Oxford University Press, 1994).

FOUCAULT, MICHEL, *The Care of the Self*, in *The History of Sexuality*, vol. 3, trans. Robert Hurley (New York: Random House, 1986).

GAZDA, ELAINE K., *Roman Art in the Private Sphere: New Perspectives on the Architecture and Decor of the Domus, Villa, and Insula* (Ann Arbor: University of Michigan Press, 1991).

JOHNS, CATHERINE, *Sex or Symbol? Erotic Images of Greece and Rome* (Austin: University of Texas Press, 1982).

KEULS, EVA C., *The Reign of the Phallus* (New York: Harper and Row, 1985).

LEFKOWITZ, MARY, *Women's Life in Greece and Rome: A Sourcebook in Translation*, 2nd ed. (Baltimore, MD: Johns Hopkins University Press, 1992).

PERADOTTO, J. (ed.), *Women in the Ancient World* (Albany: State University of New York Press, 1984).

POMEROY, SARAH B., *Goddesses, Whores, Wives and Slaves: Women in Classical Antiquity* (New York: Schocken Books, 1975).

POMEROY, SARAH B. (ed.), *Women's History and Ancient History* (Chapel Hill: University of North Carolina Press, 1991).

RABINOWITZ, NANCY SORKIN, and AMY RICHLIN (eds.), *Feminist Theory and the Classics* (London: Routledge, 1993).

RICHLIN, AMY (ed.), *Pornography and Representation in Greece and Rome* (New York: Oxford University Press, 1992).

YEGUL, FIKRET, *Baths and Bathing in Classical Antiquity* (Cambridge, MA: MIT Press, 1992).

ZINSERLING, VERENA, *Women in Greece and Rome*, trans. L. A. Jones (New York: Abner Schram, 1973).

CHAPTER 7

• • • • • • • • • •

The Medieval World

WOMEN MYSTICS AND MANUSCRIPT ILLUMINATORS

The range, variety, and power of women in the religious life of the Middle Ages has been the object of recent scholarly attention. A clearer picture of the special characteristics of female religious life and mysticism in the later Middle Ages can thus be formulated.

The role of convents or nunneries in the cultural life of upper-class women throughout these decades was crucial. Only women from the upper classes could become nuns, since a dowry was required before a woman was permitted to join a convent. Furthermore, unmarried women of the lower classes were economically productive, and their labor was useful for the family unit. The nunneries provided a socially accepted refuge for women whose only other alternative was marriage. The convent schools trained boys and girls of the upper classes. Convents also served as boarding houses for wealthy wives and widows who, for whatever reason, could no longer reside in their castles. Even though the contemplative life of a nun was an available option for only a small percentage of the female population, nunneries fulfilled an important purpose for upper-class women. Freed from male domination, some women could exercise leadership skills, powers of organization, and management of a complex estate. Especially in the early Middle Ages, between 500 and 700 A.D., nunneries not only preserved learning and maintained culture but often exercised power through their land holdings.

Prior to the end of the thirteenth century, the production and illumination of sacred books was solely confined to monasteries and convents. For the history of art, this is the most important role of these institutions. The nunnery was the only place in that society where women could be trained as painters. Consequently, women painters of the Middle Ages came from the upper classes. A limited number of women manuscript illuminators who were nuns are known from the tenth to the sixteenth centuries. The attribution of a manuscript illumination to a woman can be authenticated only by a signature or self-portrait, and many medieval artists did not sign their works. It is possible that many other women artists are simply unnamed and therefore unknown.

The first major convent scriptoria, or book-making workshops, coincided with the revived interest in manuscript creation and preservation under the reign of Charlemagne. Charlemagne's sister Gisela directed the first Carolingian convent scriptorium located at Chelles, northeast of Paris. Although one cannot firmly attribute a set of illuminations to women painters at the Chelles convent (which was part of a double institution of monastery and convent), other related manuscripts are signed by women. Also, there are literary references to illuminators who were nuns in England and Flanders in the eighth and ninth centuries.

- ### En, *Battle of the Dragon with Child of the Woman*

The earliest manuscript firmly attributed to a woman is the Gerona Apocalypse, signed "En depintrix" and produced in Spain around 975. These paintings are very fine illustrations of the Apocalypse compiled by Beatus. In the double-page painting reproduced here (Fig. 7–1), one can see a strong sense of abstract design and linear energy. The horizontal registers provide both a base line for some figures and a background for other forms. The active curvilinear shape of the dragon and the drawing of the figures demonstrates a highly competent draftsmanship. Dorothy Miner has noted "the sensitive play of sharp colors against disarmingly delicate ones . . ." as another interesting and original element of En's style.[1] Furthermore, within the tradi-

Fig. 7–1. En, *Battle of the Dragon with Child of the Woman.* (Beatus Apocalypse. Gerona Cathedral, Gerona, Spain)

tion of Mozarabic manuscript illuminations, the "longer and more active bodies, pale complexions and . . . lively silhouettes"[2] of the figures are personal stylistic elements of this talented and innovative artist.

After the Gregorian reform movement of the late eleventh century, the formerly widespread practice of the double monastery, one for men and one for women, was abolished. Convents were thus excluded from the institutional hierarchy of the Church. There was no female monastic order, despite the efforts of a few men, most notably Pope Innocent III, who wished to keep the women's religious movement within the Church organization. The existing orders, such as the Franciscans, Dominicans, and Cistercians, were not receptive to the integration of nuns into their administrative domain. It is not surprising, given this unwillingness on the part of the established Church hierarchy to accept the administration of pious women, that women formed independent, semireligious, unofficial communities. Beginning in the twelfth century, pious women known as Beguines gathered together to live in chastity and poverty. Most of these women were from the upper class, both married and single, who renounced all worldly goods to pursue a penitential life and perform charitable acts.[3]

Significant numbers of women were also attracted to heretical sects that provided a wider role for women in their orders. The Waldensians and Carthars, for example, permitted women to preach and act as priests. The Albigensians also concerned themselves more directly with the position of women in society.

At the peak of their population, in 1250 A.D., there were 500 convents in Germany. The large number of German nunneries accounts for the fact that most known female manuscript illuminators of the later Middle Ages were German nuns. A self-portrait identifies Claricia as the illuminator of a manuscript made in Augsburg, Germany, in the twelfth century. In a clever way, Claricia painted herself swinging from the body of the initial "Q." Another illuminator named Guda inserted her own image in a manuscript from Frankfurt also dating from the twelfth century. While Guda is in a nun's habit, Claricia appears in ordinary clothes. Claricia might have been an upper-class woman who was sent to a convent for schooling—a common practice. "It becomes clearer and clearer as the Middle Ages move on that miniature painting was regarded as an appropriate occupation and a becoming accomplishment for a lady."[4] The future recommendation of Castiglione in the sixteenth century, advising women of the courts to acquire painting skills, is merely a continuation of a widespread practice in the Middle Ages and not the initiation of a new set of expectations for women of the upper classes.

• Illumination from St. Hildegarde of Bingen, *Scivias*

Nunneries permitted women to pursue lives dedicated to spiritual contemplation, which was highly respected in the society of the Middle Ages, so dominated by religious concerns. Furthermore, convents provided a good education for the nuns and daughters of the nobility, although standards of education and literacy varied. The most learned women of the Middle Ages, those who made significant contributions to their culture, were nuns. Furthermore, convent scriptoria provided women with the opportunity to become artists.

The power of abbesses, rivaled only by queens, was equal to that of abbotts and even bishops. St. Hildegarde of Bingen was the abbess of a convent in Germany. She is generally regarded as one of the greatest mystics of the Middle Ages. From her position as head of a convent she became quite famous in her epoch and corresponded with the most noted contemporary religious and political figures. Although not a painter herself, St. Hildegarde was believed to be responsible for the innovative design of the imagery that illustrated her visions, the *Scivias* (Fig. 7–2).

This image illustrates one of Hildegarde's visions in which "the figure of woman" (Hildegarde's phrase) is shown receiving a dowry of Christ's blood. Below the cross stands an altar with the chalice of the Eucharist and representations of events in Christ's early life. Hildegarde heard the words "Eat and drink the body and blood of my Son to abolish the prevarication of Eve and receive your true inheritance."[5] One noted scholar of medieval female mysticism, Caroline Bynum, underscores the centrality of the image of "woman" for female mystical writers. Hildegarde also wrote, "And man truly signified the divinity of the Son of God, and woman his humanity."[6] Hildegarde argued that since Christ's body was formed by Mary, it was female flesh that restored the world. This lent women an elevated status in mystical thought.

Fig. 7–2. Illumination from St. Hildegarde of Bingen, *Scivias.*
(© 1978 Brepols Publishers Corpus Christianorum Continuatio Mediaevalis 43–43A: Hildegardis, Scivias)

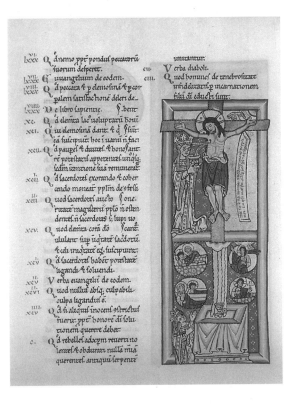

The "Lactating Madonna"

- ### Robert Campin, *Madonna and Child Before a Firescreen*

Caroline Bynum and Margaret Miles, historians of this period, both develop persuasive arguments that demonstrate the medieval association of women's bodies with food. Bynum notes that the cult of the Virgin's milk was one of the most extensive in medieval Europe.[7] This is one of the many images of the "Lactating Madonna" in the visual arts. The motif has sources in the Egyptian Goddess Isis breastfeeding Horus and in Roman antiquity in the allegorical figure of Caritas or "Charity," who was al-

Fig. 7–3. Robert Campin, *Madonna and Child Before a Firescreen.* *(Reproduced by courtesy of The Trustees, The National Gallery, London)*

ways depicted nursing a child. During the Middle Ages, this image was extended to the allegorical figure of the Church or "Eclesia."

Medieval writers believed that breast milk was the transformed blood of the mother. The analogy between God who feeds humanity with his blood in the Eucharist and the human mother who feeds her children was drawn by Christian theologians as early as the second century. Miraculous lactations, exuding fluids after death, and visions by women mystics of nursing the Christ child are recorded. "The extreme interest in physicality and the close association of woman with body and food that characterized late medieval culture seem to lie behind not only women's eucharistic piety and food asceticism but also the startling number of women's miracles that involve bodily change."[8]

The image of the "Lactating Madonna" first appears in Italy in the 1340s, for example, in works by Ambrogio Lorenzetti. The "Lactating Madonna" imagery appears historically at a time in which the cult worship of Mary was at its peak.[9] Miles notes that often the lactating Madonna is combined (as in this image) with the Madonna of Humility, who is replacing the imagery of Mary as a Byzantine empress or Queen of Heaven.

Food scarcity and famine were major problems in Tuscany, even prior to the summer of 1348 and the devastating number of deaths due to the "Black Death" or bubonic plague epidemic. Since most middle- and upper-class women did not nurse their own children but hired wet nurses, the issue of children's nourishment was a significant area for social "problematization." Miles suggests that such images might have been directed at women who had employed wet nurses. Contemporary sermons by preachers such as Bernardino of Siena warned of the dangers of employing wet nurses. Visual images might have sought to encourage women to nurse their children in emulation of the mother of Christ.

One last element of this image should be noted. The Madonna is shown in a middle-class interior with a book displayed prominently. Women as patrons and owners of books exercised a significant impact on book production in the later Middle Ages.

Secular Manuscript Illuminators

- #### Marcia, Self-Portrait from a Mirror

This image depicts a woman artist, identified as Marcia, painting her self-portrait using a mirror. Marcia was one of the outstanding women recorded by Boccaccio in his text, *De Claris Mulieribus, Concerning Famous Women*. Boccaccio revived a tradition in which men write in defense of women by noting outstanding women of the past, the "women worthies." Although the gender of the artist who painted this miniature is unknown, we do know that women were active as secular manuscript illuminators, outside the nunneries, in the later Middle Ages.

In northern Europe, unlike Italy, the art of illuminating manuscripts did not occupy a secondary place to large-scale fresco painting. This form of painting was highly valued and actively supported by the leading art patrons of the era.

Fig. 7–4. *Marcia, Self-Portrait from a Mirror.* From Boccaccio, *Concerning Famous Women.* (Bibliothèque Nationale de France)

As early as the thirteenth century, commercial book illustrators, as opposed to monks and nuns, ran businesses in the cities of Europe. While never very numerous, women painters and sculptors did exist by the late thirteenth and early fourteenth centuries, as documented by tax records. Etienne Boileau's *Livre des Métiers* (1270) refers to a guild of female book illuminators and binders.[10]

Susan Groag Bell has analyzed the impact on medieval culture of women's widespread ownership of books, especially those not written in Latin.[11] Women were not regularly given instruction in Latin, then the universal language of the Church and the universities. Latin was taught mainly to boys, not girls. Therefore, women patrons were instigators in commissioning vernacular translations of Latin texts. Based on surviving evidence, such as bequests, Bell concludes that women of the upper classes inherited books frequently. Most of the Duc de Berry's famous collection of manuscripts came into the hands of women after 1416. By the fourteenth century there are records of women who amassed libraries, and women collected, in the late fifteenth century, printed books as well as handwritten texts. Unlike this manuscript, many of the books owned by women were devotional in nature, a book of hours containing religious texts being the most common.

Books served other purposes for women in medieval society. Women were expected to involve themselves with the literary and moral upbringing of their children, especially daughters. When women had the opportunity and financial means to commission a book, they could exert a powerful influence on the contents of the volume. When noblewomen married, they often moved to an entirely new country. They became a "cultural ambassador" when they brought their manuscripts with them. This served to disseminate stylistic elements around Europe. Bell suggests that a close analysis of devotional literature and the contents of these books may reveal aspects of the relationships between mothers and daughters. A daughter of the noble classes was often married at a young age and forced to live far away from her parents. It is tempting to suppose that this version of Boccaccio's text was commissioned by an aristocratic mother to fortify the spirits and strengthen the courage of just such a young bride, removed from her family.

• *Christine de Pisan at Work*

In 1405 an extraordinary woman author, Christine de Pisan, wrote the first defense of women that was actually written by a woman. This text, *The City of Women*, thus initiates, as Joan Kelly has documented, a 400-year-long debate in innumerable texts known collectively as the "Querelle des Femmes."[12] Kelly refers to Christine de Pisan as "the first feminist," meaning that she was the first writer who understood gender as a cultural, not primarily a biological, issue. Widowed at the age of 25, Christine de Pisan was able to support herself, her children, and her widowed mother through the income derived from her writing of over thirty texts.

This scene depicts a crucial moment in the text. The author describes how she was oppressed by the massive literature on women's nature which found all women "abominable" and "the vessel . . . of all evil and all vices." In a vision, three allegorical figures, Reason, Righteousness, and Justice, appear to inspire Christine de Pisan to challenge these misogynistic dogmas. Kelly refers to this episode as a "passage of consciousness" which stimulates the writing of her unprecedented defense of women.

These arguments would be repeated over and over in the next 400 years. Gerda Lerner, in *The Creation of Feminist Consciousness*, theorizes that the lengthy period in which such arguments were repeated by women writers was characterized by "a lack of continuity and the absence of collective memory on the part of women thinkers."[13] Lerner emphasizes the disadvantages of women intellectuals who were isolated and lacked communities, which inhibited the growth of a collective feminist consciousness.

Of special importance to the subject of women artists, Christine de Pisan praises the illuminations of a contemporary artist, Anastaise, in *The City of Women*:

> . . . with regard to painting at the present time I know a woman called Anastaise, who is so skillful and experienced in painting the borders of manuscripts and the backgrounds of miniatures that no one can cite a craftsman in the city of Paris, the center of the best illuminators on earth, who in these endeavors surpasses her in any way. . . . And this I know by my own experience, for she has produced some things for me which are held to be outstanding among the ornamental borders of the great masters.[14]

Fig. 7–5. *Christine de Pisan at Work.*   *(Bibliothèque Nationale de France)*

It would seem that Anastaise specialized in the less prestigious aspects of manuscript painting, i.e., backgrounds and borders. Yet her skills were clearly impressive enough for Christine de Pisan to extol, thereby leaving a record of her existence for posterity.

Surviving records document the existence of another woman artist, Bourgot, who was actively employed by the most important patrons of her era in the decoration of manuscripts. Bourgot was the daughter of the painter Jean Le Noir.[15] Le Noir and Bourgot executed a book of hours for Yolande de Flandres, an important and active patron of the era around 1353. This "delicious and delicate" manuscript incorporated the inventive traditions of Jean Pucelle, but "infused it with a more sturdy expressionism."[16] They moved to Paris where they worked for the King of France, Charles V. Le Noir received payments from Jean, Duc de Berry in 1372 and 1375. The list of their sophisticated patrons testifies to the skills and reputations of Le Noir and Bourgot.

By the fifteenth century, women would appear to be even more active in the art of book painting. The records of the painters' guild in Bruges, which, atypically, did admit women as members, reveal that 12 percent of the guild members were female in 1454, and that the proportion had increased to 25 percent by the 1480s. As Ann Sutherland Harris suggests, such extensive participation in this field is an essential background for the emergence of Flemish miniature painters in the sixteenth century.[17]

From this account it is clear that both in convents and commercial enterprises, women formed a small but not insignificant percentage of the artists active as manuscript illuminators. While it is impossible to identify the precise contributions of these craftswomen, their existence can be either inferred from general custom in the society or documented when guild records included women and have been studied by modern historians.

MEDIEVAL EMBROIDERY

The association between women and the decoration of textiles with embroidery can be traced back to the ancient world. This time-consuming activity is usually associated with women of the upper classes who had the leisure to devote to the art. During the Middle Ages, many women were taught to embroider, and they used this skill to fashion some of the most significant but fragile works of their epoch. In many of the homes of noblewomen, embroidery was not a casual pastime but a serious occupation, an organized domestic activity.

Prior to the development of the town economies of the twelfth and thirteenth centuries, embroidery was made in convents and in the homes of noblewomen. In Carolingian convents, teams of women produced fine fabrics used for vestments or as export commodities to be sent to Byzantium in exchange for gold. Women's work thus produced one of the few marketable export items of the economy.

Many convents were occupied with the creation of elaborate embroideries used for priests' vestments or as an offering to a saint. These objects were frequently encrusted with pearls and other jewels and often sewn with gold and silver thread. The earliest reference to a woman embroiderer is St. Etheldreda, Abbess of Ely, who lived in the seventh century. She "offered to St. Cuthbert a stole and maniple, a fine and magnificent embroidery of gold and precious stones, worked, it is said, with her own hands, for she was a skillful craftswoman in gold embroidery."[18]

Convent schools taught the arts of needlework to the daughters of the landed nobility as part of their premarital education. This factor, combined with the transmission of techniques informally from generation to generation, did not merely preserve the art but helped to stimulate its practice. Noblewomen prided themselves on the skill of their needlework, lavished on clothing as well as on the decoration of church vestments. The stole and maniple worked by order of Queen Aelfflaed, wife of Edward the Elder (c. 910) have been preserved in Durham Cathedral. The work demonstrates the extreme finesse and technical excellence of the art of embroidery at this time.

In addition to the use of embroidery to decorate religious garments, we know of at least one tapestry that illustrated a narrative of the deeds of a nobleman. Around 991, a woman named Aedelfleda presented the church at Ely with a hanging embroidery illustrating the achievements of her husband. This work, although now lost, may have inspired Odo, Bishop of Bayeux, to commission the most famous embroidered work of the Middle Ages, the *Bayeux Tapestry*.

• Bayeux Tapestry

The *Bayeux Tapestry* is a unique surviving masterpiece of the medieval art of needlework.[19] Made around 1070, it depicts events surrounding the invasion of England by William the Conqueror in the year 1066. The narrative is a moral tale of the downfall of Harold, who broke his oath, sworn at Bayeux. Whether the historical account of the Norman Conquest documented in the *Bayeux Tapestry* should be considered reliable history is less important than the fact that the tapestry was almost certainly executed by teams of women, following the cartoons of a single designer of undetermined sex. Worked in brightly dyed wool on linen, the *Bayeux Tapestry* is 230 feet long. The elaborate detail, lively movement of men and animals, and sophisticated composition prove that it is a work of highest quality.

The energy and activity of the narrative in the *Bayeux Tapestry* is shown in this banquet scene (Fig. 7–6). Roasted poultry on skewers is taken off the fires and placed on a sideboard. The horn informs the company that dinner is served. Bishop Odo, seated in the center of the semicircular table, says grace; William the Conqueror is seated at his right. The scene uses green, red, and yellow thread that retains some of its original brilliance. The precision of the needlework demonstrates the exceptional technical capabilities of the workers. The decorative borders, enlivened with composite animals, provide additional scope for inventive designs.

As Roszika Parker has noted, in the Victorian era it was believed that Queen Mathilda, the wife of William the Conqueror, was the sole creator of the embroidery. Mathilda was portrayed by the Victorians as an exemplar of "wifely excellence."[20] Victorians were attached to this fiction of the individual aristocratic noblewoman embroiderer because of the survival of such images in medieval texts of courtly love. "The Victorian lady found a reassuring representation of her own curious power and powerlessness in the medieval lady of courtly love."[21]

Fig. 7–6. *Bayeux Tapestry,* detail, c. 1073–1083. Wool embroidery on linen. Height 20 in.   *(Town Hall, Bayeux, France)*

Opus Anglicanum

• *Syon Cope*

As early as the eleventh century, some lower-class women earned their living practicing the art of embroidery. By 1250 professional women embroiderers in England had an international reputation, and their creations were in great demand. The popes frequently ordered embroidered vestments from English workshops. Royalty, clerics, and wealthy persons all over Europe wanted to own examples of the now renowned *opus Anglicanum*, the term used to refer to works of embroidery created at this time in England. Around 1240 Mabel of Bury St. Edmonds was an important creator. In the early fourteenth century, Rose of Burford, received a commission from Queen Isabella of Spain to decorate a vestment intended as a gift to the Pope.

After 1250 the demand for examples of *opus Anglicanum* was so great that there was a shift from production by individuals in scattered homes to an organized commercial activity in the towns. With this shift the names of more men appear in connection with this art, although they may have been acting more as intermediaries. We do know that by the thirteenth century, a master craftsman such as a goldsmith was considered perfectly competent to supply a design for an embroidered vestment, although the actual fabrication of the garment may well have remained in the hands of women. At first, men may have restricted their role to supervision and management of female workers. "Modern scholars note a general decline in the quality of embroidery being produced by the fourteenth century but without commenting on the growing role of men in this hitherto female craft. By the fifteenth century, we hear of traveling teams of embroiderers, a situation incompatible with extensive female participation."[22] Whether one should attribute this diminished excellence to the greater participation of men or the changing methods of production remains undetermined.

One of the most famous examples of *opus Anglicanum* is the *Syon Cope* (Fig. 7–7),

Fig. 7–7. *Syon Cope*. Gold, silver, and silk thread on linen.   *(© The Trustees of the Victoria and Albert Museum, London)*

once the property of the Bridgettine Nuns of Syon Convent, located outside London. Originally a chausable, which was reshaped into its present semicircular form, the cope is a complex composition of interlaced barbed quatrefoils. The heraldic shields of the border are a later addition, and not part of its original design. The work illustrates scenes from the life of Christ and the Virgin, St. Michael slaying the dragon, and the twelve apostles. Seraphim, angels, and two priests fill the interstices of the quatrefoils. Most of the robes of the holy figures inside the quatrefoils are sewn in gold thread. A wide range of colored silk threads enlivens the work. The background colors alternate between salmon inside the panels and green as background in between.[23] The *Syon Cope* is one example of the delicacy, precision, and magnificence characteristic of the best examples of *opus Anglicanum*.

URBAN WORKING WOMEN: 1200–1600

Opus Anglicanum must be understood in the context of women's work in the later Middle Ages. Martha Howell has studied the women workers in the German cities Cologne and Leiden during the later Middle Ages.[24] She has developed a theoretical framework that helps to clarify the role of women workers in medieval embroidery. Howell asserts that when work was organized in a "family production unit" women had access to high-status jobs. This is consistent with the prominence of wives and widows of merchants such as Rose of Burford, who came from a wool merchant family and continued running the business as a widow. Howell found evidence of the strong presence of women in Cologne's commercial world as long as business and work were organized around "family production units."

Wives and daughters most often worked in the family's commercial enterprise. Many wives, not directly active in their husband's trade, would handle the retail end of the business. Because there was a surplus of women, unmarried women were forced to support themselves and often worked for wages or ran their own businesses. "Under English common law, the unmarried woman or widow, the *femme sole*— was, as far as all private, as distinct from public rights and duties are concerned, on a par with men."[25] In certain cases when women were conducting businesses of their own, even a married woman could be treated as a *femme sole* in England.

Women workers were widely employed in the manufacture and sale of food and beverages. The bread-making and brewing industries were dominated by women. Women often sold food in markets and were innkeepers. These types of employment continued the traditional identification of women with food preparation for the family.

Of greatest interest for the history of art is the wide range of craft and artisan activities practiced by women in medieval towns. In Paris by the late thirteenth century, women were working at 108 occupations of the most diverse kinds. Women were shoemakers, tailors, barbers, jewelers, goldsmiths, bookbinders, painters, and many other skilled artisans.

Another important female occupation during the Middle Ages and continuing into the seventeenth century was midwifery. However, while midwives could practice family medicine and obstetrics, they were not permitted to become professional physicians.[26]

A large number of women were occupied in the rapidly expanding textile industry. In fact, the making of wool, linen, and silk cloths was one of the major occupations of women until the eighteenth century and the Industrial Revolution. Women performed nearly all the work in the preliminary processes of cloth making—combing and carding the fibers, spinning the yarn, etc. Women holding distaff and spindle, the tools of the trade, appear frequently in the marginalia of medieval manuscripts. In England, the Netherlands, northern France, and Italy many women worked at these tasks. The term "spinster," i.e., one who spins, originally identified a person's occupation. By the seventeenth century, the term had acquired the additional meaning of "an unmarried woman," indicating the virtually total identification of spinning with women. Weaving was also a female occupation in the thirteenth century, but by the sixteenth century this craft was taken over by the all male weavers' guilds.

In addition to the wool trades, women dominated the silk-making industry in France. The women who spun the thread and made the silk cloth were paid notoriously low wages. The manufacture of silk belts and alms purses was the responsibility of women's guilds. Until the fourteenth century, dressmaking and embroidery were also female-dominated activities.

Women and Guilds

While women were very active in a wide range of crafts throughout the Middle Ages, their relationship to the guilds varied widely. Guilds were powerful trade organizations that limited membership in the professions and established regulations controlling the products.

In Paris, women could become independent members of a guild as early as the thirteenth century and were subject to the same regulations as men. Crafts monopolized by women were organized in the same way as crafts with greater male participation. Five of the 110 craft guilds that existed in Paris restricted membership to women only.

In the fourteenth century women were often members of German guilds. However, by the fifteenth century women began to be excluded more and more from membership in Italian and German guilds.

In England women were almost never admitted as full members to a guild, and there were no guilds for the female-dominated industries. Exceptions were made for widows, who were regularly admitted as full members of their husbands' guilds. Some widows carried on their husbands' businesses, documenting their active partnership in the trade.

As Kowaleski and Bennett conclude: most medieval townswomen worked in a wide variety of low-skilled, low-status, low-paid occupations that never formed into guilds.[27] Even the most skilled trades and crafts in which women were active rarely formed guilds on the continent and never in London. The women's guilds in Rouen, Paris, and Cologne were highly exceptional instances of skilled women who orga-

nized and regulated their crafts.[28] In the case of London silkworkers who did not organize their craft into a guild, men eventually took over the work and used the guild
structure to protect their economic position and exclude women. This background is
extremely important for understanding the difficulties of women in subsequent periods to become professional artists.

Howell believes that restrictions in women's access to high-status work occurred
with the shift to "market production."[29] In these different systems, labor became
more specialized, and access to training became more important. Guilds were the
main organizations that controlled training and access to the expertise needed to create goods for "market production." This is generally identified with the beginnings of
"capitalism."

Merry Wiesner, in her study of German cities, identifies the period of the mid-
fourteenth century as the time when guild ordinances begin to control, limit, and re-
strict the activities of the female members of the household workshop, especially the
master's widows.[30] Wiesner discusses the attitudes of the journeymen who were the
most vocal opponents of work by women. Since the journeymen lost work when
widows could not continue running the shop, the opposition to women members of
the master's household goes beyond economic self-interest. Wiesner believes that the
frustrations of this group increased when their opportunities to become masters were
restricted. They could raise their status and position only by differentiating their work
in the shop from "women's work."[31]

Wiesner uses two crafts, goldsmithing and textile production, to analyze the
changing patterns of women's work. In Nuremberg, women continued to work independently as "gold spinners," making gold thread used in fancy embroidery such as
the *opus Anglicanum*. This was so unusual that Wiesner concludes it was a craft especially suited to women. It could be done at home, with little workspace and few
tools.

Cloth production shows a different picture. Beginning in the fourteenth century,
the guilds controlled the production of cloth. Women were "gradually excluded from
most weavers', drapers', tailors', and cloth cutters' guilds in most cities."[32] The earliest
phases of the process, i.e., carding and spinning, and the production of cheap cloth
were left to unorganized women workers.

Clothmaking was not the only occupation taken over by men in the fourteenth
and fifteenth centuries. Men were invading many other trades that had been traditionally exercised by women, for example, wholesale brewing. At this time occupa-
tional designations, with a few exceptions, such as the food and clothing trades, were
male. By the sixteenth century, women were forbidden to become apprentices or to
take the examinations that might have enabled them to become journeymen or masters.

Natalie Zemon Davis has studied the role of women in the production of crafts
in the French city of Lyon during the sixteenth century. Her conclusions provide insight into the ways in which women's work was organized. She finds that women had
"weak work identity and high identity as a member of a family and neighborhood. . .
the female adapted her skills and work energies to the stages of her life cycle."[33] Davis
believes that this flexibility was an important component of the craft economy of the

period. While women continued to work "however and whenever they could,"[34] they were accepting of the conventions which identified the husband as "The Artisan." This would have had clear financial advantages in the trades controlled by guilds. Independent women were concentrated in textile and clothing trades and provisioning trades, such as bakers and innkeepers.

The progressive exclusion of women from full membership in professional organizations continued into the sixteenth century. "By 1600 women had disappeared almost completely from professional life."[35] In the seventeenth and eighteenth centuries, new commercial organizations that were replacing the guilds were almost exclusively male-dominated. Throughout most of Europe, women could not function on a professional basis independently of male relatives during the Renaissance era.

Given this discriminatory situation, it is not surprising to learn that the absolute number of women who were professional artists is very small in comparison with the number of male artists. In the sixteenth century, only thirty-five women are known to have been artists.

Suggestions for Further Reading

General Sources on Women

GIES, FRANCES and JOSEPH GIES, *Women in the Middle Ages* (New York: Crowell, 1978).

LABALME, PATRICIA (ed.), *Beyond Their Sex: Learned Women of the European Past* (New York: New York University Press, 1980).

LABARGE, MARGARET W., *A Small Sound of the Trumpet: Women in Medieval Life* (Boston: Beacon Press, 1986).

MOREWEDGE, ROSEMARIE THEE (ed.), *The Role of Women in the Middle Ages* (Albany: State University of New York Press, 1975).

POWER, EILEEN, *Medieval Women*, M. M. Postan (ed.) (London: Cambridge University Press, 1975).

STUARD, SUSAN MOSHER (ed.), *Women in Medieval Society* (Philadelphia: University of Pennsylvania Press, 1977).

On Female Mysticism and Religious Life

BYNUM, CAROLINE WALKER, *Jesus as Mother: Studies in the Spirituality of the High Middle Ages* (Berkeley: University of California Press, 1982).

BYNUM, CAROLINE WALKER, *Holy Feast and Holy Fast: The Religious Significance of Food to Medieval Women* (Berkeley: University of California Press, 1987).

MILES, MARGARET, *Image as Insight: Visual Understanding in Western Christianity and Secular Culture* (Boston: Beacon Press, 1985).

MILES, MARGARET, "The Virgin's One Bare Breast: Nudity, Gender and Religious Meaning in Tuscan Early Renaissance Culture," in Norma Broude and Mary D. Garrard (eds.), *The Expanding Discourse: Feminism and Art History* (New York: HarperCollins, 1992).

NEWMAN, BARBARA, *Sister of Wisdom: St. Hildegard's Theology of the Feminine* (Berkeley: University of California Press, 1987).

Christine de Pisan and the Querrelle des Femmes

JORDAN, CONSTANCE, *Renaissance Feminism: Literary Texts and Political Models* (Ithaca, NY: Cornell University Press, 1990).

KELLY, JOAN, "Early Feminist Theory and the Querelle des Femmes: 1400–1789," *Signs*, 8 (1982), pp. 4–28.

LERNER, GERDA, *The Creation of Feminist Consciousness: From the Middle Ages to Eighteen-Seventy* (New York: Oxford University Press, 1993).

Medieval Embroidery

PARKER, ROSZIKA, *The Subversive Stitch: Embroidery and the Making of the Feminine* (London: Routledge, 1984).

WILSON, DAVID M., *The Bayeux Tapestry* (New York: Knopf, 1985).

Urban Working Women

HANAWALT, BARBARA A. (ed.), *Women and Work in Preindustrial Europe* (Bloomington: Indiana University Press, 1986).

HOWELL, MARTHA, *Women Production and Patriarchy in Late Medieval Cities* (New Brunswick, NJ: Rutgers University Press, 1986).

KOWALSKI, MARYANN, and JUDITH M. BENNETT, "Crafts, Guilds and Women in the Middle Ages: Fifty Years after Marian K. Dale," *Signs*, 14 (1989), pp. 474–488.

WIESNER, MERRY E., *Working Women in Renaissance Germany* (New Brunswick, NJ: Rutgers University Press, 1986).

Women Artists

CARR, ANNEMARIE WEYL, "Women Artists in the Middle Ages," *Feminist Art Journal*, V (1976).

MINER, DOROTHY, *Anastaise and Her Sisters* (Baltimore, MD: Walters Art Gallery, 1974).

CHAPTER 8

Italy:
1450–1650

THE ABSENCE OF WOMEN ARTISTS
IN QUATTROCENTO FLORENCE

The patterns of urban working women, discussed in Chapter 7, help to explain the virtual absence of professional women artists in Florence during the fifteenth century. Florence was one of the most industrialized cities in Europe during this period. Women are largely absent from the records of the wool industry after 1350, as well as from most other work situations. Judith Brown documents this shift in the labor force from female weavers to German male weavers.[1] The well-documented power of the Florentine guilds would have been an additional factor restricting women's opportunities to become artists.

Most artists in the early Renaissance came from an artisan or working-class background and were members of guilds. Predictably, one can infer from the artists' guild regulations in Italy that women were hardly ever active. Furthermore, by the fifteenth century, the study of the human body, especially the male nude (from corpses and live models) was an essential component of the artist's training. It was absolutely impossible for women to acquire such training. Artists were also expected to travel to art centers to study contemporary production. Such freedom of movement was also totally beyond the capabilities of most women.

Brown proposes that the re-entry of women into the labor force in Florence only occurred after the 1530s when the Medici dukes had established their political control and restricted the power of the guilds. Women found work in the textile industry then, as men shifted employment to luxury crafts such as ceramics, books, jewelry, and furniture intended for export to the European aristocracy.

While women were being actively excluded from the labor force in the fourteenth and fifteenth centuries, an ideology of domestic confinement was developing. This "Cult of Domesticity" was initiated during the early Renaissance among the aristocracy. Brown notes that by the early seventeenth century, the vast majority of women weavers worked in the home and had children. In 1610 one visitor to the city noted, "in Florence women are more enclosed than in any other part of Italy;

they see the world only from the small openings in their windows."[2] By 1600, then, this gender ideology had permeated throughout all social classes of Florentine society.

QUATTROCENTO ARISTOCRACY IN FLORENCE

The Profile Portrait

- **Domenico Ghirlandaio,** *Giovanna Tornabuoni, née Albizzi*

Patricia Simons has studied profile portraits of women from the quattrocento.[3] This work is an example of a type of image which dominated the production of portraits of aristocratic women beginning in the 1440s. These images present women as objects of "the male gaze." They are painted by male artists for male patrons and are addressed, like virtually all art from this period for male viewers. As a rule, aristocratic Renaissance women were not permitted to be seen in public.

The scope of activities demanded and expected of the upper-class woman of the Renaissance was more narrowly restricted to the roles of wife and mother than it had been for the noblewoman under feudalism. "All the advances of Renaissance Italy, its proto-capitalist economy, its states, and its humanistic culture, worked to mold the noblewoman into an aesthetic object; decorous, chaste, and doubly dependent—on her husband as well as the prince."[4]

For most women of all classes, marriage and motherhood were expected roles. For upper-class women, the only other available option was the seclusion of the convent. Marriages were always arranged by parents and continued to be primarily an economic contract or an alliance between two families of the same class status. A daughter's chastity was an absolute necessity and a very high priority of the culture. Daughters were strictly supervised to ensure their virginity. Divorce was virtually unknown.

Women's legal rights throughout this era remained very limited. In general, husbands administered matters and made decisions. Women were not only excluded from holding public office, but also from participation in legal matters and law courts. For example, a law in Florence passed in 1415 forbade a married woman from drawing up her own will or disposing of her dowry to the detriment of her husband and children.[5] In Florence, women "could not adopt children, go bail for any body, act as guardian or representative of any person of minor age, except of their own children, and even for these they were not allowed to appoint a guardian."[6]

Almost all Renaissance treatises on women viewed them strictly as wives, regardless of class status. The most important virtue of the wife was obedience to the will of her husband. After obedience, chastity was an essential virtue. In a wife chastity signified sexual fidelity to her husband, and this was sometimes enforced by the "chastity belt." In addition, silence, discretion, love of her husband, and modesty are frequently cited as ideal qualities for the Renaissance woman. The gentle, passive aspects of her nature were extolled and cultivated; the more aggressive aspects of her character were repressed.

The list of virtues makes it clear that the upper-class woman in the Renaissance was subjugated emotionally to a greater extent than the noblewoman of the Middle Ages, who retained control over property and often ran the estate in the absence of her husband. One of the most important activities of the female members of the upper classes continued to be the spinning of wool and flax, although professional weavers organized in guilds actually made the cloth. Needlework was also deemed one of the most appropriate activities for women.

The education and training of the upper-class girl in the Renaissance was focused exclusively on her destined role of wife and the skills needed to maintain a household. Therefore, her education aimed primarily at ". . . suppressing all individuality, fostering both fear of offense and complete dependence upon the will of her husband for all her comforts, and contentedness to live within the orbit of the house. . . . nothing must be allowed in the training of her mind that would encourage or enable her to compete on even ground with men. This general assumption is implicit in everything that was said on the training and education of women, in the limited aim set for their education even by their most ardent supporters, in the restriction on subjects and books, and most of all in the almost total absence of reference to the professions."[7] While the Renaissance man received an education in a wide variety of subjects, Renaissance women were taught only those skills that would make them com-

Fig. 8–1. Domenico Ghirlandaio, *Portrait of Giovanna Tornabuoni, née Albizzi.* 1488. Mixed media on panel, 77 x 49 cm. *(Fundación Coleccion Thyssen-Bornemisza, Madrid)*

petent housewives, except for instruction in religious principles, which would encourage docility and obedience.

The sitter in this portrait, Giovanna Tornabuoni, died while pregnant in 1488. The work was commissioned by her husband, Lorenzo Tornabuoni, whose initial "L" is embroidered on her garment. Her expensive clothes and prominently displayed jewelry were part of the aristocratic custom of loading the bride with a "portable dowry." This practice of conspicuous consumption served as a symbol of the husband's rank and status. Within this "display culture," as Simons characterizes it, the profile painting of a wife is a "representation of an ordered, chaste and decorous piece of property."[8] This specific image was hung in the Tornabuoni family palace, "Forever framed in a state of idealized preservation, she is constructed as a female exemplar for Tornabuoni viewers and others they wished to impress with the *ornamento*."[9]

DOMESTIC ARCHITECTURE

The Renaissance Palace

There is no more obvious example of the quattrocento aristocratic taste for conspicuous consumption than the building of palaces. As Richard Goldthwaite has documented, a significant change in attitudes about private spending took place in Florence. Prior to the fifteenth century, Florentines operated under strong restraints against spending money too visibly. After 1400, however, such restraints were lifted, and Alberti, for example, believed that possessions are necessary for the happiness of the family.[10]

Prior to 1350, urban residences of the wealthy class of Florence did not constitute a distinctive architectural form. The ground floor often housed a retail shop. The second story had an open *loggia* or balcony where the family could "assemble on ceremonial occasions."[11] These structures were also defined by a tower that served as protection when needed. What Goldthwaite manages to ignore in his otherwise excellent study, *The Building of Renaissance Florence*, are the specific implications of these architectural changes for the women of the household. The open loggia would have provided a place in which women could communicate, albeit from a height, with the larger social life of the streets.

The design of the new Renaissance palaces of the fifteenth century, such as the Palazzo Medici or the Palazzo Strozzi to cite the two most famous architectural examples, was dramatic. Unlike the Roman villa, the Renaissance palace is exclusively a residential property and not a place of business. For example, the Medici bank and cloth shop where the family's business dealt directly with the public was located elsewhere. The open loggia onto the street was eliminated and replaced by a completely enclosed internal courtyard, arcaded and architecturally embellished. These enormous buildings housed, generally, a nuclear family.

The new palaces provided vastly greater areas of living space than had existed in the earlier buildings. These empty spaces demanded to be filled. As Goldthwaite notes: "The more space *he* had to fill up, the more *he* consumed, and the more conspicuous *his* consumption became, the greater was the social distance *he* put between *himself* and the ranks of ordinary *men*—a distance that *his* ancestors *probably* did not know even though they may have been every bit as wealthy."[12]

What this scholar remarkably does *not* discuss is the impact of this increased isolation and social stratification on the women of the household, confined in these huge structures. The design of the Renaissance *palazzo* would have effectively served as prisons, isolating the women from the life of the community.

- **Sandro Botticelli, *La Primavera***

This famous painting was commissioned for the wedding of Lorenzo de Pierfrancesco de' Medici to Semiramide d'Appiani. It was hung in the home of this couple, in a room adjacent to their bedroom. Lilian Zirpolo has interpreted this painting in the context of the prevailing rituals connected with marriage and the discourses on the ideal wife in this period.[13] The Graces represent the behavior and ideals appropriate to a Renaissance bride. They symbolize purity and chastity, exhibit restrained movements and lack of emotionality.

On the right, the rape of Cloris, who is then transformed into Flora, would instruct the new bride on the need for her sexual submission to her husband to ensure order, stability, and future children to continue the Medici clan. Flora's stomach is enlarged to emphasize her fertility, and her face reveals contentment as opposed to Cloris's distress. This would serve as a model for the desired response of the bride. The centrality of Venus would have underscored the importance of procreation for the Renaissance marriage. Venus is shown as a goddess of fertility by her enlarged stomach. Fertility is emphasized, as well, by the lush, fruitful garden setting.

Italian women of this aristocratic class were married at age 16 or 17, as opposed to most women in northern Europe who did not marry until 25 or 26. Italian noble-

Fig. 8–2. Sandro Botticelli, *La Primavera*. c. 1477–1480. Tempera on panel. Approx. 6 ft. 8 in. x 10 ft. 4 in.   *(Uffizi, Florence, Italy; Alinari/Art Resource, NY)*

women could expect to have three more children than would women living in northern Europe. Since they played virtually no economic role in their society, other than the transfer of property in the dowry (as discussed in the profile portraits), their reproductive capacities were enhanced in the ideology of the culture.[14]

WOMEN ARTISTS: 1550–1650

- **Sofonisba Anguissola,** *Bernardino Campi*
  Painting Sofonisba Anguissola

This portrait is an extraordinary document of the emergence of a serious and accomplished woman artist, Sofonisba Anguissola (1532/35–1625). To understand how this could occur we must look to the social background of Anguissola, not in the guild-controlled realm of work but in the context of the humanist thought of the epoch, which began to impact women of the aristocracy. It is in this cultural context that Sofonisba Anguissola achieved her status as "the first Italian woman to become an international celebrity as an artist and the first for whom a substantial body of works is known."[15]

Beginning in the fifteenth century, a few humanist scholars influenced the education of a small group of noblewomen, at first in the courts of Italy, then spreading through Europe. Some Italian women emerged as scholars in this period and wrote in most of the genres of literature of the time, letters, orations, dialogues, treatises, and poems.[16] Margaret King cites, in particular, women from the fifteenth century such as Laura Cereta and Isotta Nogarola, who achieved fame for their learning as Sofonisba Anguissola achieved fame for her painting skills. Like Sofonisba they came from elite families. Just as Sofonisba had to learn to paint from the male artist Bernardino Campi, so the women humanists were educated by men, often members of their families.

These ideals were incorporated into a "Christian humanism" in England, France, and the Netherlands, spread by intellectuals like Erasmus and Thomas More. According to the humanists, women should receive the same education as their male counterparts. Like the Renaissance men, women should study Latin, classical literature, philosophy, and history, as well as geometry, arithmetic, and astrology. This model was eventually adopted for the upper-class women of the towns as well as for the ladies at court. By the sixteenth century, under the influence of humanism, schools for girls that taught minimal literacy were widespread in northern Europe. Some women, educated in the humanist tradition, wrote lively defenses of their sex, which, as noted earlier, became known as the *Querelle des Femmes*.

These humanist ideals also affected the training of artists. Artists were expected to possess a knowledge of science, mathematics, and perspective, as well as the practical skills acquired in an apprenticeship.

The noblewoman's education was impacted by the publication of Baldesare Castiglione's *The Courtier* in 1528. This book became an enormously influential treatise not only for the education of women but also for the definition of ideal modes of

Fig. 8–3. Sofonisba Anguissola, *Bernardino Campi Painting Sofonisba Anguissola.*
c. 1549.   *(Pinacoteca Nazionale, Siena)*

conduct for upper-class men and women. Castiglione grants to the noblewoman all the virtues and potential for perfection of the male courtier. Her education is equivalent to that of men. Most significantly for the history of art, all the arts practiced at court, i.e., music, writing, drawing, and painting, are seen as positive attributes for women.

These arts are not viewed as professional skills to be executed for money, but rather as appropriate accomplishments for a refined and properly educated noblewoman. Castiglione's ideas affected many women in the upper classes, the stratum of society from which some of the most important women artists of the sixteenth century, like Sofonisba Anguissola, emerge.

Anguissola was raised in an exceptional environment that allowed her to develop her creative talents. The oldest of six daughters, she was born into a noble family in the provincial northern Italian city of Cremona. Following the advice popularized by Castiglione in *The Courtier*, her family made sure to provide their daughter with instruction in painting and music, as befitted a woman of her class. In addition to lessons in painting, Anguissola was taught to play the spinet, and in several self-portraits she shows herself playing this keyboard instrument. One can imagine that her father, Amilcare, faced with the financial burden of providing dowries for six daughters, was highly motivated to cultivate their talents. In fact, the three oldest sisters all received instruction in painting. Endowed with the fortunate circumstances of her class background and birth, Sofonisba Anguissola was in an unusually favorable position to develop her talents beyond the level of accomplished amateur to that of professional painter.

Anguissola painted more self-portraits than any other artist between Dürer and Rembrandt. These works were especially desirable. One patron wrote to her father:

> There is nothing that I desire more than the image of the artist herself, so that in a single work I can exhibit two marvels, one the work, the other the artist.[17]

What is noteworthy about this image is that Sofonisba also created a portrait of her teacher, Bernardino Campi (1522–1591). Campi was well known in the 1540s in Sofonisba's native town of Cremona, in northern Italy. According to Perlinghieri, author of the first full-length monograph on the artist, Sofonisba and her sister Elena actually lived in the Campi household as paying "guests."[18] This situation would recreate the characteristic "family production unit" of earlier periods. The Anguissola sisters would have experienced a training similar to that of male apprentices.

Campi left for Milan in 1549, and this work probably dates from around the time of his departure. It is an unusual homage to her teacher. Sofonisba had good reason to be grateful to Campi. The training she received from him, as recorded by this skillful double portrait, was unprecedented for a woman, especially from her class. Sofonisba's sister, Elena, however, gave up her career to become a nun. The third sister, Lucia, also became an accomplished painter, although very few works can be securely attributed to her.

- ### Sofonisba Anguissola, *Boy Pinched by a Crayfish*

Sofonisba Anguissola studied with another Cremonese artist, Bernardino Gatti (c. 1495–1576), for about three more years. However, the opportunities to develop her skills in Cremona were limited. In 1554 she traveled to Rome, and Perlinghieri believes that Anguissola created this drawing in Rome. Vasari mentions that Tomasso Cavalieri, a friend of Michelangelo's, sent the drawing to Duke Cosimo de' Medici of Florence in 1562. Documents exist which confirm that Sofonisba was in direct contact with the most important living artist of the time, Michelangelo.[19]

From surviving letters, it is known that Sofonisba sent Michelangelo a drawing she had made of a smiling girl, and asked for the master's criticism and advice. Michelangelo admired the work, but challenged her to depict the more difficult subject of a crying boy. In response to this challenge, Anguissola created a drawing that cleverly juxtaposes the two subjects. This work, *Boy Pinched by a Crayfish* (Fig. 8–4), demonstrates Anguissola's ability to represent a range of emotions. The features of the boy were based on those of her young brother (the seventh sibling in the family). This drawing was presented to the duke of Florence, Cosimo de' Medici, and had widespread influence. It was seen by other artists, including Vasari, and copies were made of it. It has been suggested that Anguissola's drawing inspired Caravaggio's *Boy Bitten by a Lizard*.[20]

Fig. 8–4. Sofonisba Anguissola, *Boy Pinched by a Crayfish*. 1554. Drawing.
(Galleria Nazionale de Capodimonte, Naples)

Despite this contact with the renowned Michelangelo, the main influence on Anguissola's painting style derives from the local environment of Cremona. Surrounded by Milan, Brescia, and Parma, Cremona's painters were exposed to several strands of "verist" or naturalist styles prevalent in these art centers. Artists from this region of northern Italy retained an almost Flemish taste for the precise description of nonidealized forms, in religious painting as well as in portraiture. The stylizations of Mannerism, so dominant in central Italy, never completely overwhelmed this local tradition. Thus, Sofonisba's talents for realistic description and anecdote seen in her drawing of the crying boy reflect the style of her native city. By 1555 the artist was back in Cremona.

Paintings from the first period of Anguissola's career, prior to 1559, are mostly portraits of her family. One of the most interesting of these works, *Three of the Artist's Sisters Playing Chess* (1555), is an inventive composition for a group portrait. While the older sister on the left looks directly at the viewer, the younger player with hand raised appears to be speaking to her. The third sister and a servant are spectators to the interchange. This painting may be the first "conversation piece," a type of group portrait that would gain wide popularity in subsequent centuries.[21]

In 1559 Anguissola was invited to join the court of King Philip II of Spain. The governor of Milan had mentioned Anguissola to the duke of Alba, an emissary of the Spanish court. Anguissola's position as one of Spain's court portraitists fits into a pattern of artistic links between Spain and Italy in the mid-sixteenth century. There was a tradition of importing foreign artists to Spain as well as of sending native Spanish artists to Italy for training. In 1567 Philip II hired six Italian artists to work as fresco decorators on the huge palace-mausoleum-monastery complex, the Escorial. The most famous artist working in Spain at this time, El Greco, was trained in Italy. From the 1560s through the eighteenth century many Italian artists worked on royal projects for the Spanish monarchy.

Anguissola remained at the Spanish court through the 1560s. She painted several portraits of Queen Isabella, one of which was sent to Pope Pius IV. In 1569 she married a Sicilian nobleman, Fabrizio de Moncada, with a dowry that had been provided in the queen's will. King Philip of Spain gave her in marriage and presented her with numerous gifts. Through her talents as a painter, Anguissola achieved both fame and fortune, and her example was emulated by other aspiring women artists.

Anguissola's renown rests primarily on her pioneering position as the first professional Italian woman painter. Aside from her artistic talents, which were exceptional, she altered the conventions of portrait painting. She injected an innovative liveliness and range of emotion into her intimate portraits of members of her family. Her art anticipates the more overt emotional content of much Baroque imagery.

- **Lavinia Fontana, *The Visit of the Queen of Sheba***

Compared to Sofonisba Anguissola, Lavinia Fontana (1552–1614) as the daughter of an artist acquired her training in a manner that was much more characteristic for women artists of future centuries. Her father, Prospero Fontana, was one of the leading painters of Bologna. "Lavinia Fontana is the first woman to have had what might be called a normal successful artistic career. Although many of her works are lost or disputed, she still has the largest surviving body of work by any woman artist active before 1700."[22] Many of her works consist of large scaled multifigured religious paintings, executed on commission as altarpieces. She also painted many commissioned portraits, a practice which was quite exceptional for a woman artist.

Her early portrait style is believed to have been influenced by that of Sofonisba Anguissola "whom Lavinia knew and admired."[23] By the 1570s her fame as a portraitist was well established. According to Eleanor Tufts, this painting is, in fact, a group portrait of the Gonzaga family, the Duke and Duchess of Mantua, who were famous and generous art patrons. The Duke, Vincenzo I (1562–1612), and the Duchess, Leonora de' Medici, might have sat for this work on their way to Florence for the wedding of Maria de' Medici in 1600.[24] Tufts connects the appropriateness of depicting this noble couple as Solomon and Sheba to one of their treasures, an onyx vessel believed to come from the temple of Solomon. Holbein had used this analogy in a miniature for a gift from Henry VIII to one of his wives. A literary source is found in Tasso's 1582 discourse on Feminine Virtue, which the poet dedicated to Vincenzo's mother. In that work, the woman who does not seek love from unbridled desire is likened to Sheba coming to Solomon.

Entrusting Lavinia Fontana with such a major commission testifies to her repu-

Fig. 8–5. Lavinia Fontana, *The Visit of the Queen of Sheba.* c. 1600.   *(Courtesy of the National Gallery of Ireland)*

tation among cognoscenti of her period. This group portrait would then date from the period of 1595–1600 when she was at the height of her artistic powers. The work combines naturalistic observation of the heads in the portrait likenesses with the Flemish precision of the costume textures. The work exhibits all the conventions demanded by court portraiture of the period.

Lavinia Fontana received an important commission from Cardinal Girollamo Bernerio in May 1599, for the chapel in Santa Sabina decorated by Federico Zuccari. The *Vision of Saint Hyacinth* was selected to illustrate an episode from the life of a recently canonized saint. Fontana followed this work to Rome and is known to have been living in Rome by 1604. She painted another large altarpiece, a *Martyrdom of Saint Stephen* in the palace of Cardinal d'Este for the basilica of San Paolo Fuori Le Mure. (This work was destroyed in a fire in 1823.) During the last decade of her life she continued to be in great demand as a portraitist. She survived eleven pregnancies and died in 1614 at the age of 62.

- ### Artemisia Gentileschi, *Susanna and the Elders*

Artemisia Gentileschi (1593–c.1652) developed a forceful personal style that placed her among the leading artists of her generation who worked in the style of Caravaggio. She traveled a great deal and helped spread the Caravaggesque mode through Italy. The dispersal of her own paintings further extended her influence.

Like Lavinia Fontana, Artemisia was the daughter of an artist, Orazio Gentileschi. Artemisia therefore had the advantage of being raised in an environment where she could acquire the basic technical skills necessary for a professional artist. Because Orazio was among the first artists to adapt Caravaggio's style in the first decade of the seventeenth century, it is not surprising that Artemisia would also develop a Caravaggesque style. One of her earliest paintings, *Judith with Her Maidservant* (Pitti Palace), was copied from her father's version of this theme as a learning exercise.

Orazio must have recognized his limitations as a teacher for his talented daughter because he arranged for her to study perspective with Agostino Tassi, a successful artist and collaborator who was receiving major commissions for fresco decorations of Roman palaces. Tassi seduced and raped Artemisia and then promised to marry her. When it became clear that Tassi, a disreputable character with a prior criminal record, had no intentions of marrying the girl, Orazio sued Tassi. The trial took place in 1612 and lasted several months.[25] One can only wonder at Orazio's motivation in bringing Tassi to court and publicizing the mortification of his daughter. Artemisia was tortured on the witness stand with thumbscrews, a seventeenth-century lie detector. Tassi was imprisoned for eight months, but the case was ultimately dismissed, leaving Artemisia publicly humiliated.

We are indebted to Mary Garrard for our insights into the earliest signed and dated painting by Gentileschi, *Susanna and the Elders* (Fig. 8–6). If we accept the inscribed date of 1610 as authentic, this work demonstrates Gentileschi's highly developed technical expertise by the age of 17 and her ability to paint a convincing female nude. Iconographically, the work differs markedly from male artists' versions of this theme. "The expressive core . . . is the heroine's plight, not the villains' anticipated pleasure."[26] The artistic source for the pose of Susanna is not the usual Venus prototype, but a figure from a classical Orestes sarcophagus (also used, in reverse, by Michelangelo for the figure of Adam expelled from Eden on the Sistine ceiling). This pose suggests the anguish of the heroine and the punitive consequences of the event. The whispering, conspiratorial collusion of the two males is another unique factor in Gentileschi's image. Garrard explains this as an allusion to sexual harassment, the threat of rape which Artemisia probably experienced for some time before her actual rape by Agostino Tassi, in 1611.

As Mieke Bal notes, the attribution by Garrard of this work to Artemisia is based on the gendered nature of the theme as presented in the image. The issue of "the gaze" and voyeurism is at the core of the interpretation of this work. "Gentileschi's *Susanna* refuses visual intercourse not only with the two elders, but with the viewer as well."[27] This image is especially fascinating because it works against the western tradition of voyeurism in which the viewer is gendered as a male and the image of the female is consistent with that voyeuristic position. In traditional versions of this theme, painted by men, the viewer is encouraged to identify with the male elders. This can be seen quite clearly by comparing Gentileschi's *Susanna* with a more typical version of the theme by Tintoretto (Fig. 8–7). Susanna's anguish as depicted by Gentileschi breaks the implied complicity of depicted subjects and male viewers owning the gaze.[28]

Fig. 8–6. Artemisia Gentileschi,
Susanna and the Elders. 1610.
*(H. Langer/Graf Von Schönborn'sche
Schlossverwaltung Pommersfelden)*

Fig. 8–7. Jacopo Tintoretto, *Susanna and the Elders.* c. 1556.   *(Kunsthistorisches
Museum, Vienna)*

- ## Artemisia Gentileschi, *Judith Decapitating Holofernes*

Shortly after the trial, Artemisia married a Florentine and went to live in Florence. There was little Caravaggist painting in that city, and Gentileschi's presence stimulated Florentine artists to investigate the new expressive possibilities of Caravaggism.

One of her most impressive paintings from the Florentine period of her career is the dramatically baroque composition *Judith Decapitating Holofernes* (Fig. 8–8). Judith, the Old Testament heroine, stole into the enemy camp of the Israelites, murdered the tyrant Holofernes, and then escaped with his head. This story was a popular subject among the Caravaggists because it provided a biblical anecdote that could serve as a genre theme of violence or suspense.

Artemisia was especially fascinated with the Judith story and painted at least six different versions of it. One can understand why this theme appealed to her. Through the daring deed of Judith, Artemisia was avenging her own betrayal and all the wrongs she had suffered. Judith was an ideal subject for Artemisia—a female hero with whom she could identify as a woman.[29]

When one compares Gentileschi's *Judith Decapitating Holofernes* with Caravaggio's version of the theme (Fig. 8–9), one can see both the extent of Gentileschi's assimilation of Caravaggio's style and the differences that reveal her own vigorous sense of drama and originality. Like Caravaggio, Gentileschi positions large-scale figures in the foreground and uses highlighted forms that emerge from a dark background. The women in both works are not idealized and details are realistic. Both artists have selected the gory moment of decapitation.

However, Gentileschi designed a composition that is much more dynamic and energetic. In Caravaggio's painting, the figures are positioned across the picture surface. Gentileschi's composition places the figures in depth and is much more compact, therefore more dramatic. Caravaggio's old maidservant is peripheral to the action while Gentileschi's maid actively participates in the murder, holding Holofernes down. In Gentileschi's painting, the arms of all three figures intersect in the center of the canvas, fixing the viewer's attention inescapably on the grisly act. The position of Caravaggio's rather pretty, elegant Judith seems frozen; she is not exerting physical force to cut off the tyrant's head. By contrast, one can acutely sense the intensity of the physical effort that Judith and her maid bring to this act. The powerful, monumental, and robust anatomy of Gentileschi's women make this decapitation seem much more convincing than Caravaggio's version.

One notable characteristic of Gentileschi's talent is her excellent knowledge of female anatomy. Perhaps being raised in the home of an avant-garde painter, she had the opportunity to study the female nude in private, using a servant or even her own body as a model. Her knowledge of male anatomy was understandably less sophisticated. The drapery covering Holofernes's torso masks this weakness.

In 1621 Gentileschi returned to Rome where she found the situation of the Caravaggists considerably different than when she had left the city almost a decade earlier. The Bolognese followers of Carracci were winning most major commissions,

Fig. 8–8. Artemisia Gentileschi,
Judith Decapitating Holofernes.
1615–20. Oil on canvas, 46$\frac{3}{4}$ x
37$\frac{1}{4}$ in.   *(Pitti Palace, Florence)*

Fig. 8–9. Caravaggio, *Judith and Holofernes.* c. 1598. 144 x 195 cm.   *(Galleria Nazionale D'Arte Antica, Palazzo Barberini, Rome)*

and Artemisia Gentileschi was now one of the few major Caravaggist painters living in Rome.

• Artemisia Gentileschi, *Self-Portrait as the Allegory of Painting*

The story of Judith was not the only subject in which Gentileschi invented new compositions or discovered new layers of meaning based on her identity as a woman. In an extremely unusual painting, Gentileschi painted herself as the living embodiment of "Painting." In *Self-Portrait as the Allegory of Painting* (Fig. 8–10), Gentileschi depicts herself bearing the widely recognized attributes that identify the allegorical figure "Painting" in this era: on the gold chain hangs a mask standing for imitation; her unkempt hair symbolizes the divine frenzy of the creator; and her multicolored dress demonstrates the painter's talents. The artist is not actually painting but is poised facing the light flooding her from an unknown source. She is waiting for inspiration or summoning her mental energies: "Without recourse to complex personification, Artemisia evokes the contrast between Theory and Practice in her *Self-Portrait*. She has posed herself with one arm raised upward, the hand stretched toward its invisible target, suggesting the higher, ideal aspirations of painting, with the other arm resting firmly on a table, the hand holding the brushes and palette which are the physical materials of painting."[30]

Fig. 8–10. Artemisia Gentileschi, *Self-Portrait as the Allegory of Painting*. 1630s. Oil on canvas, 38½ x 29½ in. *(St. James Palace, London. Copyright reserved; photo Rodney Todd-White & Son)*

Unlike male artists, who were forced to depict themselves accompanied by an idealized female figure symbolizing Painting, Artemisia, as a woman artist, could combine her image with the iconography of the allegorical personification of Painting and create a deceptively simple composition of great iconographic originality.

Unwilling to abandon her personal style of Caravaggism to accommodate the changing tastes of Roman patrons, Gentileschi traveled to Naples in 1630. Except for a brief visit to London to assist her ailing father on a commission, she lived in Naples for the rest of her life. The selection of Naples as her next residence was logical because more artists worked in a Caravaggist style there for a longer period of time than in any other Italian city. In fact, between 1600 and 1630, Caravaggism was the only advanced painting style practiced in Naples. However, this situation was to change during the 1630s when the influence of the Bolognese school, especially the art of Guido Reni, became increasingly important, even in Naples. Accepting the inevitable, Gentileschi now adapted her style to the more brightly illuminated, idealized mode of the Carracci followers. In the process she lost some of the intensity of her personal style. Scholars generally agree that the works created in her original Caravaggist mode are her finest paintings.

In addition to her paintings a few letters written by Gentileschi survive. Some reveal her attitude about being a woman artist quite clearly. In a letter from 1649 to one of her patrons, Don Antonio Ruffo, she writes:

Most Illustrious Sir and My Master,
    By God's will, Your Most Illustrious Lordship has received the painting and I believe that by now you must have seen it. I fear that before you saw the painting you must have thought me arrogant and presumptuous. But I hope to God that after seeing it, you will agree that I was not totally out of line. In fact, if it were not for Your Most Illustrious Lordship, of whom I am so affectionate a servant, I would not have been induced to give it for one hundred and sixty, because everywhere else I have been I was paid one hundred *scudi* per figure. And this was in Florence, as well as Venice and Rome, and even in Naples when there was more money. Whether this is due to [my] merit or luck, Your Most Illustrious Lordship, a discriminating nobleman with all of the worldly virtues, will [be the best] judge.
    You think me pitiful, because a woman's name raises doubts until her work is seen. Please forgive me, for God's sake, if I gave you reason to think me greedy. As for the rest, I will not trouble you any more.[31]

The sheer formal beauty and power of many of Artemisia Gentileschi's paintings serve to rank her with the best artists of her generation. Never a mere imitator of Caravaggio, she adapted some of that artist's devices to forge an original style of strength and beauty. Her inventive adaptations of existing subjects are another aspect of her originality. She harnessed her formal energies to the expression of a personal iconography, expressing her identity as a woman and as an artist.

Suggestions for Further Reading

BROUDE, NORMA, and MARY D. GARRARD, *The Expanding Discourse: Feminism and Art History* (New York: HarperCollins, 1992).

FERGUSON, MARGARET, M. QUILLIGANS, and N.VICKERS (eds.), *Rewriting the Renaissance: The Discourse of Difference in Early Modern Europe* (Chicago: University of Chicago Press, 1986).

GOLDTHWAITE, RICHARD A., *The Building of Renaissance Florence: An Economic and Social History* (Baltimore, MD: Johns Hopkins University Press, 1980).

HERLIHY, DAVID, and CHRISTIANE KLAPISCHE-ZUBER, *The Tuscans and Their Families: A Study of the Florentine Castasto of 1427* (New Haven, CT: Yale University Press, 1985).

KELSO, RUTH, *Doctrine for the Lady of the Renaissance* (Urbana: University of Illinois Press, 1956).

LABALME, PATRICIA (ed.), *Beyond Their Sex: Learned Women of the European Past* (New York: New York University Press, 1984).

Anguissola

PERLINGHIERI, SONDRA ILYA, *Sofonisba Anguissola: The First Great Woman Artist of the Renaissance* (New York: Rizzoli, 1992).

Fontana

The Age of Correggio and the Carracci: Emilian Painting of the 16th and 17th Centuries (Washington, DC: National Gallery of Art, 1986).

TUFTS, ELEANOR, *Our Hidden Heritage: Five Centuries of Women Artists* (New York: Paddington Press, 1974).

Gentileschi

GARRARD, MARY D., *Artemisia Gentileschi: The Image of the Female Hero in Italian Baroque Art* (Princeton, NJ: Princeton University Press, 1989).

MOIR, ALFRED, *The Italian Followers of Caravaggio* (Cambridge, MA: Harvard University Press, 1967).

CHAPTER 9

• • • • • • • • •

NORTHERN EUROPE: 1600–1700

WOMEN ARTISTS AND STILL LIFE PAINTING

Holland secured its independence from Spain in 1581 and by the seventeenth century was the major maritime power of Europe, with a far-flung colonial empire. Because Holland was a Protestant country, the Church was not an active arts patron as it remained to some extent in neighboring Catholic Flanders. However, the Dutch middle class was wealthy and purchased paintings on a regular basis. This provided a strong incentive for Dutch artists to paint the kinds of works that would appeal to the merchants of the middle class—their only source of patronage.

Because these works of art were intended to adorn the burghers' homes, the vast majority of Dutch paintings are small in scale, suitable for hanging in private houses. With the exception of portraits, paintings were sold on the open market, creating a competitive situation that kept prices low. In this context, painters developed precise areas of specialization, such as still life painting, flower arrangements, landscapes, seascapes, and genre paintings, in an effort to secure a steady market. The unifying factor in all these categories was a dependence on precisely observed natural phenomena. Dutch art is characterized stylistically by its realism. Painting schools were flourishing in Utrecht, Haarlem, Amsterdam, Leiden, Delft, and other cities in Holland.

The competitive art market created an advantageous situation for women artists. Artists could paint what they liked and when they liked, rather than painting only when commissioned, and artists could accept as many pupils as they wished. Although the guilds were the primary artists' organizations, there were considerably fewer restrictions on who could become an artist in Holland than in other parts of Europe. Furthermore, with the development of the new painting specialties there was no need to study the nude; in fact, there are very few nudes in Dutch art.

The careers of the three artists discussed in this chapter demonstrate the level of excellence that may be achieved by women artists when the expectations for women in their culture do not conflict with a measure of equality of opportunity and access to training.

Still life and flower painting did not require knowledge of anatomy or extensive travel to Italy to study the High Renaissance masters. Throughout Europe, women were in the forefront of still life painting in the early 1600s. Only a still life attributed to Caravaggio is known to predate the works of Fede Galizia in Italy. In France, Louise Moillon painted a series of impressive still lifes, and four women painters of still lifes were elected to the French Academy during the seventeenth century. However, the most noteworthy women still life painters were Flemish and Dutch, since these schools were the most active and suffered least from the French Academy's low esteem for this genre.

Painters incorporated into their works the new floral species that were brought back to Europe from the voyages of discovery around the globe. The East and West India Companies were expanding the Dutch colonial empire at this time. The introduction and cultivation of exotic species, not native to Europe, further stimulated contemporary interest in flower painting. As the prosperity of the merchant class increased, there was widespread interest in gardening and the cultivation of flowers, including new and familiar types. By 1600 the cultivation of flowers as a commodity had become an important component of the Dutch economy. A highly speculative market developed and huge sums were paid for rare tulip bulbs. Prices became so inflated that the market crashed in the 1630s. (The term "tulipomania" is still used today to designate a highly speculative commodity market.) All these factors combined to create an especially strong interest in the Netherlands for paintings of flowers.

Another way to account for the widespread interest in flowers is that these fragile objects, which bloom and die so quickly, are universal symbols of life's transience. Whether combined with other objects, associated with the vanity of earthly existence, or standing alone, flowers express in a gentle, beautiful manner the connotations of imminent mortality.

- ## Clara Peeters, *Still Life with Flowers, a Goblet, Dried Fruit and Pretzels*

Recent scholarship has thrown into question the reliability of almost every known fact about the life and career of this artist, a member of the "first generation" of still life painters. E. de Jongh notes the absence of documents to secure Peeter's birth and death dates and to verify the location of her work activity.[1] Even the presumed location of her early life in Antwerp cannot be verified by any guild records, although as has been noted in connection with earlier practices, women were not usually guild members.

What can be verified is the existence of a unified group of works that can be attributed to Peeters either through a monogram signature or very close stylistic affinities to those signed works.

We do not know how Peeters acquired her skills. It is possible that she studied with Osias Beert, fourteen years her senior, who was a noted still life painter in Antwerp. Her works relate to those of Beert in the combination of different types of objects: flowers, fruits, tall decorative metal goblets, and flat dishes of fruits. Peeters, however, uses a lower viewpoint than Beert or other Flemish colleagues. With this lowered viewpoint, she employs more accurate perspective to situate the objects firmly in space. The illusion of the arrangement is thus enhanced. Compositions also differ from those of her immediate contemporaries in that she groups her objects closer together, permitting a certain amount of overlapping. These elements anticipated the subsequent development of the banquet pieces of artists such as Pieter Claesz and Willem Claesz Heda.

Peeters's innovations are evident in *Still Life with Flowers, a Goblet, Dried Fruit and Pretzels* (Fig. 9–1). This painting is part of a series of four complex works, each focused around a different theme: a fish piece, a game piece, a dinner arrangement, and the work illustrated here. This painting is typical of every known work by Peeters in its use of a simple stone ledge set against a dark background. An elaborate goblet defines the center of the composition. The central focus is underscored by the low dish filled with dried fruits and nuts. The vase of flowers on the left is counterbalanced by a plate of pretzels, a pewter pitcher, and a glass. The placement of these objects results in a balanced composition that is not symmetrical or monotonous. Each object is rendered in a precise style that conveys clearly the diverse textures of the objects.

The inclusion of a vase of flowers in this work was consistent with Dutch tastes for flower paintings. Flower painters regularly juxtaposed blossoms that could never bloom simultaneously in nature. Each flower was studied individually. Assembling these studies in the studio, the painter created imaginary bouquets.

One of the most important artists to continue the tradition of the independent flower painting was Jacques de Gheyn. Born in Antwerp, he lived and worked in various cities in Holland. In 1606 the Dutch government commissioned a flower piece from him for the large sum of 600 guilders, to be presented to Marie de' Medici,

Fig. 9–1. Clara Peeters, *Still Life with Flowers, a Goblet, Dried Fruit and Pretzels.* 1611. Oil on panel, 19 1/16 x 25 5/16 in.   *(Prado Museum, Madrid)*

queen of France. This placed de Gheyn among the best paid artists of his time and indicates the high level of esteem for this type of painting. It is easy to see, then, that when Clara Peeters included bouquets of flowers in her still life pictures, she was both demonstrating her versatility and increasing the marketability of her canvases.

The emergence of Clara Peeters early in the seventeenth century anticipates the extremely successful careers of other Dutch women artists, such as Maria Van Oosterwyck and Rachel Ruysch.

- ## Rachel Ruysch, *Fruit, Flowers, and Insects*

Rachel Ruysch (1666–1750) and Jan van Huysum were the two most prominent and successful painters specializing in flower pictures in the late-seventeenth and early-eighteenth centuries. Ruysch's complex paintings of flowers, fruits, and fauna were widely admired during her lifetime, and her reputation has not diminished since her death. One indication of the esteem in which her talent was held were the high prices her contemporaries regularly paid for her paintings. Ruysch sold her works for 750 to 1,250 guilders as compared with Rembrandt, who rarely received more than 500 guilders for his canvases.

Ruysch was born into a highly distinguished family, which encouraged her talents. Her father, an eminent professor of anatomy and botany in Amsterdam, had an extensive collection that Rachel could study up close and draw upon for her compositions. In fact, the lizards and insects she included in some of her paintings might very well have been observed among the specimens in her father's collection. Her mother was the daughter of the noted architect Pieter Post, who designed the royal residence near The Hague. Given this stimulating intellectual and artistic milieu, Rachel's talents were bound to thrive.

Ruysch studied painting with the finest contemporary still life painter in Amsterdam, Willem van Aelst. An innovator in flower compositions, Aelst's arrangements were very open and asymmetrical. Like Aelst, Ruysch favored a baroque, diagonal composition, quite different from the compact and symmetrical arrangements of Peeters and other early seventeenth-century flower painters.

Ruysch married an undistinguished portrait painter named Jurien Pool in 1693. They were married over fifty years, and Rachel bore ten children. Despite this large family and the burdens of domestic responsibilities, about a hundred authenticated works are attributed to her. The family moved to The Hague in 1701, and over the next years Ruysch developed an international reputation. From 1708 to 1716 she was court painter to the Elector Palatine, Johan Wilhelm von Pfalz, whose court was located in Düsseldorf. During these years most of her paintings were kept in the Elector's collection. One of her most brilliant and complex works, *Fruit, Flowers, and Insects*, was presented to the grand duke of Tuscany, another mark of the extremely high esteem in which her art was held.

Fruit, Flowers, and Insects demonstrates the power and precision characteristic of her paintings. A cornucopia of fruits and plants cascades in a diagonal from upper right to lower left. The curving stems of the wheat create a dynamic countermovement, filling the upper-left corner. This work is an innovative type of still life picture.

Fig. 9–2. Rachel Ruysch, *Fruit, Flowers, and Insects*. 1716. Oil on canvas. *(Palazzo Pitti, Firenze)*

Although other artists had pioneered the use of a wooded setting and had created equally complex arrangements, only Ruysch combined the wooded setting with a still life so large that it fills the foreground almost completely. The landscape location is indicated but its description is minimal. Thus, the depicted space remains quite shallow and the viewer's attention rests firmly on the objects in the foreground; there is no escape back into deep space. Each type of fruit, flower, insect, or animal is botanically accurate, demonstrating Ruysch's close study of natural phenomena. Nevertheless, the painting is a wholly artificial construction. Despite the wooded setting, these objects could never be found juxtaposed in this manner in nature. Ruysch's choice of colors, delicate brushwork, and precise description of object textures are aspects of her highly appreciated technique. Ruysch also bathed her compositions in an enveloping atmosphere that heightened the illusionism of her works. de Jongh notes that this type of image was influenced by the painter Otto Marseus van Schrieck (deceased in 1678), whose works Ruysch might have known through van Aelst.[2]

On a symbolic level, Ruysch's paintings, like those of many of her contemporaries, are *vanitas* images. The ripening fruit, grain, and blooming flowers all retain their symbolic associations with the transience of earthly existence, the passing vanities of the temporal world. Lizards were seen as creatures of decomposition, awaiting the end of the body's brief existence. This lizard is devouring an egg—a clear reference to the life cycle, birth and death. Butterflies were common symbols of the resurrected soul in the afterlife. However, these somber symbolic associations do not interfere with the purely sensual pleasure one can take in the accuracy and variety of the depicted objects.

Ruysch's position in the history of art is clear and secure. She was the last of the great Flemish and Dutch flower painters. Towering over her contemporaries, she enjoyed a highly productive and successful career. Her works are never monotonous. She maintained a consistently high level of excellence in paintings that reveal a range of dynamic compositional formulas. Using a wide variety of plants, insects, fruits, and so forth, she created monumental paintings of widely recognized and enduring quality.

PORTRAITURE AND GENRE SCENES

• Judith Leyster, *Self-Portrait*

Like Sofonisba Anguissola's *Bernardino Campi Painting Sofonisba*, this painting by Judith Leyster (1609–1660) combines both a portrait, in this case of the artist, and a painting. The image on the easel is a fiddler, which appears in another one of Leyster's known paintings, *The Merry Company*. Unlike the category of the portrait, the fiddler is typical of the kinds of images in which she specialized. Known in Leyster's time as "modern figures," today they are called "genre scenes."[3]

Due to the efforts of scholars, led by Frima Fox Hofrichter, and a recent exhibition catalogue, we now have a much fuller picture of Leyster's life and milieu than of any other Dutch woman artist. Like Sofonisba Anguissola, Leyster was not born into a family of artists. Her parents were both involved initially in the local textile industry in Haarlem. In 1618 her father purchased a brewery; however, this business venture was ultimately disastrous and in 1624 he was forced to declare bankruptcy. It is quite probable that Leyster first studied painting with one of the leading portrait painters in Haarlem, Frans Pietersz de Grebber. De Grebber's daughter Maria was also in the studio. However, there are no strong traces of de Grebber's style in any of Leyster's known paintings. In Leyster's earliest paintings, as well as in this image, it is the influence of Frans Hals that is most pronounced. There are no documents which link Leyster with Hals or his household, however.

In 1633, when Leyster was about 24, she became a member of the painter's guild, the Guild of St. Luke in Haarlem. This membership enabled her to establish an independent studio, and she accepted pupils to supplement her income.

The date of this self-portrait is uncertain. Leyster's known and firmly attributed works include only one other portrait. During the years 1633 to 1636 there were a number of strong competitors for the portrait market in Haarlem. In addition to Hals and De Grebber and his family, there was Leyster's future husband, Jan Miense Molenaer. This would have been a highly competitive portion of the art market, and Leyster apparently could not secure portrait commissions regularly. Her works, therefore, aim at a different market of collectors, mostly merchants who were Flemish refugees.[4] In 1636, the year of their marriage, the couple left Haarlem for the larger art market of Amsterdam.

The purpose and intended market for this unusual self-portrait may very well be, as Hofrichter proposes, Leyster's presentation piece to the Haarlem painter's guild. Hofrichter notes that the artist's artistic prowess is indicated by the eighteen paint brushes in her hand and the absence of a mahlstick, frequently used to steady the hand. The new charter for the Guild of St. Luke, passed in 1631, required that a master present a painting to the guild upon admission. "A self-portrait as presentation piece would have emphasized the significance of her acceptance as the first woman member of the Haarlem Guild of St. Luke."[5]

Leyster's technique is quite precise and linear. While she does use visible brushstrokes in her lace cuffs and skirt, she generally does not allow the texture of the paint to intrude upon the description of the variety of textures included in her image. Twentieth-century tastes, trained by exposure to Impressionism and subsequent avant-garde art movements, tend to place a higher value on the spontaneous, sketch-

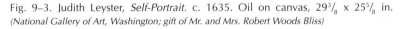

Fig. 9–3. Judith Leyster, *Self-Portrait*. c. 1635. Oil on canvas, $29^3/_8$ x $25^5/_8$ in. *(National Gallery of Art, Washington; gift of Mr. and Mrs. Robert Woods Bliss)*

like style of her contemporary, Franz Hals. However, Leyster's technique would have been at least equally valued in her own time. In fact, the popularity and skill of an artist was measured in large part by the technical ability to depict a wide range of objects and textures.

- **Judith Leyster, *The Proposition***
  or *Man Offering Money to a Young Woman*

This fascinating genre painting has been the focus of much scholarly attention because its interpretation resists clear-cut and unequivocal meaning. The painting depicts a man in a fur hat, leaning over a woman who is sewing. He is offering her gold coins, possibly as payment for her sexual favors. The bare interior focuses the viewer's attention on this scene, which is illuminated by a single candle. One point which seems certain is that Leyster is sensitive to the woman, who is very likely resisting or simply ignoring the advances of an older man. Hofrichter first drew attention to this image and, as indicated in the title by which it is most well known, interpreted it as a "proposition." However, there is no doubt that this image differs dramatically from other "propositions," which are clearly brothel scenes.

When one compares Leyster's *The Proposition* with Dirck van Baburen's *The Procuress* (Fig. 9–5), a wholly different content is immediately apparent. The woman in Baburen's image is a willing prostitute exchanging her favors for the gold coin offered by the male customer. Her low-cut dress reveals her physical attributes. The musical instrument, especially the lute, is a familiar prop in themes of prostitution since music is always associated with Venus and love-making. The old procuress on the right holds out her hand, waiting for payment for the prostitute's services. The mood is clearly jovial and animated.

By contrast, the modestly dressed woman in Leyster's image fixedly concentrates on her sewing. Her feet rest on a footwarmer, further emphasizing the immobility of her pose. As Hofrichter notes, "she is not entertaining the man, nor is she drinking, smoking, singing, or wearing a provocative gown. Leyster's work may be considered a critical response to those of her predecessors and stands apart in iconography even from the copies or variants of it."[6] From her simple dress one may deduce that the seamstress is possibly a domestic servant. Her concentration on her sewing would be viewed as avoidance of idleness, a Dutch virtue. Needlework was considered to be an important domestic skill.

Other scholars have proposed that the man's intentions are more honorable. He may actually be trying to encourage the woman to marry him, using the money as a form of persuasion for courtship and marriage. The woman is concentrating on her sewing and avoiding his advances. The fact that this encounter takes place at night, by candlelight, may refer to the emblem by Jakob Cats, "No pearl should be bought at night/no lover should be sought by candlelight."[7] Other images in which a younger woman resists the sexual advances of an older man do exist but as the recent catalogue demonstrates, no example can match the powerful image presented by Leyster. The psychological tension of the scene is unique for the period.

Leyster, as a woman, could realize more clearly than her male contemporaries that not every solicitation occurs between willing participants. The restrained, quiet

Fig. 9–4. Judith Leyster, *The Proposition*. 1631. Oil on panel, 11$^{11}/_{16}$ x 9$^{1}/_{2}$ in. *(Mauritshuis—The Hague)*.

Fig. 9–5. Dirck van Baburen, *The Procuress*. Oil on canvas, 101 x 107.5 cm.   *(M. Theresa B. Hopkins Fund; Courtesy, Museum of Fine Arts, Boston)*

mood of *The Proposition* may have influenced the next generation of genre painters, including Vermeer and Metsu. In several works, Metsu explores the theme of a sensitive woman victimized by a coarser man, while Vermeer became a master in the intimate domestic scene in which men interrupt women at their work. Both themes are anticipated in Leyster's painting.

Judith Leyster's works demonstrate her ability to combine influences from the Utrecht Caravaggists with her local Haarlem traditions, epitomized by the art of Hals into a personal style of variety, beauty, and iconographic originality.

While only one image can be securely attributed to Leyster after her marriage, one suspects that she did not stop working. Although she did bear three children, it seems highly unlikely that she would simply exit herself from the "family production unit" of the Leyster/Molenaer household.

ANNA MARIA VON SCHURMAN
AND THE DUTCH *QUERELLE DES FEMMES*

Leyster's career was quite unusual. Most other women painters acquired their skills through direct family connections. Also, the majority of the other known Dutch women artists were amateurs and did not establish themselves as independent professional artists. Among these amateurs was Anna Maria von Schurman, who made a significant contribution to the literature of the *Querelle des Femmes*. She is best known for her essay, first published in Latin, and translated into English as "The Learned Maid or Whether a Maid May also Be a Scholar" (1659).

Simon Schama argues that only in Holland could such an intellectually bold feminist statement be made in the 1650s. Compared with Catholic and Puritan societies, Dutch women lived with a greater degree of freedom and equality with men. Schama identifies an ideology of affection which stood at the core of marriage. Love and companionship were the expected goals of marriage.

While excluded from political offices, women managed to assert their presences in public life in charitable institutions. From the Middle Ages, women retained certain rights over their property before and after marriage and were allowed to bequeath and inherit property rights. They could go to court to protect their property against irresponsible husbands. Since Dutch women could form commercial contracts, they "had all the formal qualifications needed for active commercial or business dealings."[8] Apparently many women were active in business, although mainly in the context of the "family production unit." Given this cultural context, it is perhaps less surprising to find outstanding women painters such as Leyster and Ruysch in Holland.

Suggestions for Further Reading

Women in Holland

SCHAMA, SIMON, *The Embarrassment of Riches: An Interpretation of Dutch Culture in the Golden Age* (Berkeley: University of California Press, 1988).

Still Life, Peeters and Ruysch

DE JONGH, E., *Still Life in the Age of Rembrandt* (Auckland, New Zealand: Auckland City Art Gallery, 1982).

GRANT, MAURICE H., *Rachel Ruysch: 1664–1750*. (Leigh-on-Sea, Essex: F. Lewis, 1956).

MITCHELL, PETER, *European Flower Painters* (London: Adam and Charles Black, 1973).

Leyster

HOFRICHTER, FRIMA FOX, *Judith Leyster: A Woman Painter in Holland's Golden Age* (Doornspijk, The Netherlands: Davaco, 1989).

WELU, JAMES A., and PIETER BIESBOER, *Judith Leyster: A Dutch Master and Her World* (Worcester Art Museum, Yale University Press, 1993).

ROCOCO PORTRAITURE

It was impossible for women artists to acquire training or develop a market for their works in seventeenth-century France. As opposed to the situation in Holland, where the Dutch middle classes were avid consumers of paintings, virtually all commissions in France during this period came from the monarchy. There was little diversity or scope for personal styles. Louis XIV believed that the arts, like the sciences, industries, and other activities, should serve the glory of France and her king. Through a reorganization of the Paris Academy in 1663, the fine arts were brought under the direct control of the state bureaucracy. Early in Louis's reign, he decided to create a magnificent setting for himself and his court at Versailles. Most of the efforts of French artists of this era were directed toward the embellishment of this enormous palace. Only male painters were permitted to receive the training necessary to create the large-scale history paintings that decorated the walls and ceilings at Versailles. Control over artists was easily maintained because all artists working for the king had to be members of the Academy.

Given the inflexibility of this system of education and patronage, it is not surprising to find no women artists of major significance in France during the seventeenth century. Denied access to the training essential for a professional artist, the highly structured, state-controlled art world of Louis XIV effectively prevented any women from achieving excellence. Because there was no real market for other types of paintings, few artists specialized in those genres popular in Holland, such as flower painting, still life, and small-scale portraiture, types of art in which women often excelled.

The decentralization and loosening of state control over the arts that occurred in France following the death of Louis XIV in the period known as the "Rococo" created a more favorable environment for women artists. However, women artists continued to function under highly discriminatory conditions throughout the eighteenth century. They were denied access to the major art academies, where their male colleagues studied the anatomy of the male nude and acquired training in the composition of multifigured history paintings. Therefore, it is not surprising that only one of the five artists included in this chapter, Angelica Kauffman, was able to build a career around the exhibition of history paintings as well as portraiture. Three of the five, Rosalba Carriera, Elisabeth Vigée-Lebrun, and Adélaïde Labille-Guiard, were outstanding specialists in portraiture. Anne Vallayer-Coster was a noted still life and flower painter. Also not surprisingly, three of these five artists were daughters of artists and first learned to paint at home. Rosalba Carriera, a Venetian, did not suffer severely from a lack of proper training, since she worked in two media, pastel portraiture and miniature painting on ivory, in which she invented the techniques. The fifth artist, Labille-Guiard, learned to paint by apprenticing herself to a series of masters who specialized in miniature painting, pastel portraiture, and finally, the technique of oil paint.

Despite the difficulties and obstacles, these women artists managed to achieve tremendous success and recognition for their achievements. All five painters received the highest levels of rewards for their talents in their respective cultures.

- **Rosalba Carriera, *Portrait of Louis XV***

Carriera (1675–1752) rose from very humble origins to become one of the most successful artists of her epoch. She was born in Venice; her father was a clerk and her mother, a lacemaker. Harris suggests that she began her career by learning the art of lace making and when this industry declined, shifted to the decoration of ivory snuffboxes.[1] These inexpensive items were produced in mass quantities for the tourist trade. From this initiation, Carriera became familiar with painting on ivory in a small scale, and she began to create miniature portraits.

As a miniature painter, Carriera possessed great skill in rendering detail and in applying the paint in a range of thicknesses. Her active brushwork revolutionized the style of miniature painting and certainly contributed to her success. Miniature painting has suffered from low esteem in the history of art, despite the fact that miniaturization requires an especially precise technical control. Because they are small, miniatures are often seen as inherently less "significant" than large-scale paintings. Clearly, painting in miniature is a difficult task to perform because the small size of the image forces the artist to exercise extraordinary manual control. The eyestrain that this work inevitably involved may well have contributed to Carriera's loss of sight in 1746. She spent the last years of her life blind and in seclusion, suffering from periods of depression.

Although Carriera's first professional successes were in the medium of miniature painting, she achieved international recognition for her pastel portraits. Colored chalks, known as pastels, had been invented in the late fifteenth century, yet no artist before Carriera had explored their formal possibilities. Employing pastels in an unprecedented way, she skillfully created a naturalistic range of textures.

As early as 1716, Carriera had met Pierre Crozat, a wealthy banker and one of the most important art patrons in Paris.[2] Crozat had assisted Watteau in building his career. Crozat's home was the center of early Rococo activities in Paris. Crozat had met Carriera on a trip to Venice in 1716. In the spring of 1720, at his invitation, Carriera traveled to Paris. Her surviving diary records a constant sequence of sitters and social commitments.

One of her first portraits created in Paris was of the young French king Louis XV (Fig. 10–1). The portrait was greeted with widespread admiration. This image reveals a detailed, highly finished, and almost oil-paint-like treatment of the face combined with a more spontaneous technique in the jacket, cravat, and hair. In these sections, one can actually see the individual marks of the chalk. This precision, combined with a freedom of touch not achievable in oils, amazed her audience in Paris. In recognition of her achievements, she was invited to become a member of the French Academy—a great honor for any artist, and an unprecedented one for a foreign woman. Despite her warm reception in France, Carriera decided to return to her native Venice in 1721, where she lived with her mother and sisters.

As a portrait artist, Carriera's talents were widely appreciated by an international clientele. Europe's aristocracy demanded portraits by her hand. The king of Denmark and many members of England's upper classes were among her patrons, while Augustus III, Elector of Saxony and King of Poland, collected more than 150 of her works.

Carriera possessed a refined color sense. She often used bright, fresh colors for a

Fig. 10–1. Rosalba Carriera, *Louis XV as a Boy*. 1720. Pastel on paper, 19 x 14 in.   *(Forsyth Wickes Collection; Courtesy, Museum of Fine Arts, Boston)*

brilliant, luminous effect. This specific aspect of her style relates her art to that of her Venetian contemporary, Tiepolo. Tiepolo also worked for foreign patrons, but unlike Carriera, Tiepolo regularly executed large-scale mural decorations.

A special flair of Carriera's was her ability to make a flattering image of her sitter without losing his or her individual likeness. This ability was essential for an eighteenth-century portraitist, when a portrait often served the purpose that a photograph does today. The duke of Modena, aware of Carriera's success in Paris, commissioned the artist to paint portraits of his three marriageable daughters. These portraits were circulated to attract eligible suitors who could form advantageous political alliances with the duke.[3] Clearly, a flattering image was not merely a matter of vanity but, as in this case, a political strategy as well.

Carriera's extensive correspondence is an excellent source for reconstructing the course of her career and the scope of her patronage. Her own letters and many letters from her patrons have survived. Carriera's travels, necessitating separations from her family, also stimulated correspondence. In addition, a few brief essays concerning issues of interest to the artist have also survived in her papers.

In her surviving documents, Carriera even made a contribution to the *Querelle des Femmes*. In her text, Carriera recognizes and rejects the defense of women based on the argument of the "women worthies." She places the reasons for the differences between the sexes squarely on the gender constructions of her culture, especially in the opportunities for education.[4]

That Carriera was a Venetian is not simply an accident of birth. Patricia Labalme suggests that women in Venice lived in a culture in which they had learned to challenge gender restrictions.[5] Women of the aristocracy retained rights over their dowries, which often were substantial fortunes. Lucrezia Marinelli wrote on "The Nobility and Excellence of Women," published in Venice in 1600. Another Venetian woman, Elena Lucrezia Cornar Piscopia, was the first woman to be awarded a doctorate from the University of Padua, in 1678. Despite the objections of the bishop of Padua, and the substitution of the degree of philosophy for theology, the ceremony, attended by a great crowd, did take place. Labalme asserts that in Venice, despite enormous constraints and inequities, Venetian women retained power through family connections, resisted sumptuary laws, insisting on the privilege of wearing jewelry and other forms of family wealth, occasionally found the courage to resist the ideology of misogyny to write in defense of women, and acquired an unprecedented level of knowledge which, in this case, was recognized by the award of a university doctorate.

Carriera's name resounded through the eighteenth century, and she paved the way, as a role model if not as a direct influence, for other portrait painters. Masters of pastel portraiture, such as Maurice Quentin de la Tour and Jean-Baptiste Perroneau, are among the inheritors of her invention. Contemporaries of Vigée-Lebrun and Labille-Guiard regularly compared these artists, active later in the eighteenth century, with Carriera. Theresa Concordia Mengs, Suzanne Giroust-Roslin, and Labille-Guiard's pupil, Gabrielle Capet, are among the many women who followed Carriera's example to become successful pastel portraitists in the eighteenth century.

NEOCLASSICISM

- **Angelica Kauffman, *The Artist Hesitating Between Music and Painting***

Like other artists discussed in this and preceding chapters, Angelica Kauffman (1741–1807) was the daughter of a painter. Born in Switzerland, she received her early training from her Tyrolean father. During her childhood, the Kauffmans traveled about in Switzerland, Austria, and northern Italy, executing commissions for religious murals and portraits. Angelica's precocious talents were recognized and encouraged from an early age.

Kauffman was also a talented musician. According to her biographer, Giovanni de Rossi, the artist felt that she had to choose between a career in music and one in painting, while still in her teens. Her commitment to painting is given visual form in this image, painted over thirty years later when the artist had established a European reputation.

Kauffman adapted the iconography of the story "Hercules at the Crossroads Between Fame and Luxury" to illustrate an episode in her own youth when she had contemplated embarking on a career as an opera singer. This composition demonstrates the artist's ability to combine a specific portrait likeness (in this instance, a self-

Fig. 10–2. Angelica Kauffman, *The Artist Hesitating Between the Arts of Music and Painting.* c. 1794. *(Lord St. Oswald, Nostell Priory, England)*

portrait) with the idealized neoclassical features of the two allegorical personifications. As Angelica gently presses the hand of Music on the left, her body inclines toward Painting, who points to the temple of fame, symbolically positioned on the summit of a distant mountain. The drapery is painted in warm, glowing colors and the whole composition is bathed in a painterly atmosphere.

As Wendy Wassyng Roworth notes, "Music" stands for sensual pleasure, "Painting" for Virtue. The necessity for such a choice connects Kauffman with what was usually a masculine decision of commitment to a single art form and a professional career track. Other women artists, such as Sofonisba Anguissola, painted a self-portrait as a musician, but her musical skills are amateur ones, an appropriate feminine accomplishment of aristocratic women. Kauffman distinguishes herself from this tradition with the self-discipline of a conscious choice.[6]

This decision carried immense implications for Kauffman's life. In 1762 Angelica and her father arrived in Florence, and the following year they settled in Rome. Kauffman had the fortuitous opportunity to make contact with all the leading figures of the neoclassical movement at a very early phase in its development. Under the influence of Winckelmann, Mengs, and Hamilton, Kauffman developed a sophisticated neoclassical style that placed her in the forefront of this movement.

- ### Angelica Kauffman, *Cornelia Pointing to Her Children as Her Treasures*

In 1766, Angelica Kauffman arrived in London where she quickly established herself as one of the leading artists of the English school. She became friendly with Sir Joshua Reynolds, and when the Royal Academy was founded in 1769, she and a flower painter, Mary Moser, were the only two women members. At this time, the vast majority of paintings produced in England were portraits commissioned by the aristocracy. Although she was forced to paint portraits to earn a steady income, Kauffman was one of the few artists working in England and one of the few women artists of any period who produced a steady stream of paintings with themes derived from classical and medieval history. Between 1766 and 1781, she contributed significantly to the widespread vogue for neoclassicism in England.

As Roworth notes: "What distinguished Kauffman from most artists active in England during the eighteenth century, and from virtually all woman artists before the twentieth century was her ambition to achieve standing as a history painter. Much of her success in England must also be attributed to this choice to become not just an artist, but specifically a history painter."[7]

In addition to the recognition she received for her history paintings, Kauffman's portraits were widely admired, and she attracted many patrons among the English aristocracy. Her talents were held in such high esteem by her peers that she was asked to contribute to the decoration of the new residence of the Royal Academy in 1778.

Unfortunately, her professional successes were not matched by domestic happiness. In 1767 she married a man she believed to be a Swedish count but who turned out to be an imposter. After the scoundrel's death, she married a painter, Antonio Zucchi, who remained forever loyal and supportive of his more famous wife's career.

In 1781, following their marriage, the couple returned to Italy. Refusing an offer to become resident court painter to the King of Naples, Kauffman settled in Rome in 1782. Some of her best paintings were created during these years.

Cornelia Pointing to Her Children as Her Treasures (Fig. 10–3) is one of the history paintings from her mature Roman period. Cornelia was a real matron in ancient Rome whose reputation as a paragon of virtue had come down through history. This painting illustrates a didactic anecdote in which a materialistic Roman woman, seated at the right, shows off a necklace, while Cornelia displays her three children as her "jewels." The stylized faces of the women, the severely simplified costumes, and the austere architecture are all characteristic of Kauffman's neoclassical style. The rich, glowing colors of the robes and the warm tonality of the light show her assimilation of the stylistic achievements of the Venetian school.

Cornelia is contemporary with Jacques Louis David's *Oath of the Horatii.* A comparison between these two works reveals certain stylistic and compositional similarities as well as thematic differences. Both Kauffman and David arrange their figures in a simple, shallow space like a stage in a theater. Both use idealized classical figure types with legible gestures so the viewer can read the narrative. While both paintings depict an example of moral virtue, the virtues expressed are totally different in content. Cornelia is the admirable Roman matron who prizes her children above all worldly goods and devotes her life to raising them to serve the state. David focuses on the sacrifices of war, with emphasis clearly placed on the virile sons energetically

Fig. 10–3. Angelica Kauffman, *Cornelia Pointing to Her Children as Her Treasures.* 1785. Oil on canvas, 40 x 50 in.   *(Virginia Museum of Fine Arts, Richmond, VA. Purchase: Williams Fund, 1975)*

dedicating their lives to defend the Roman Republic. While Kauffman has selected her didactic message to illustrate the behavior of a female role model, David's painting illustrates a male world of military heroism and patriotism. The women in the *Oath of the Horatii* are wilted, weak, limp, and tearful. They are clearly excluded from the male sphere and their role is confined to passive mourning.

This painting was executed for George Bowles, an Englishman who owned fifty of Kauffman's works.[8] It was first exhibited at the Royal Academy in 1786 and received rather negative responses from English critics.[9] Despite this, versions were painted for Prince Poniatowsky, nephew of the King of Poland, and for Queen Caroline of Naples.

Kauffman's achievement places her in the forefront of neoclassicism, as one of its original exponents and disseminators. By the 1760s she was creating convincing history paintings in a neoclassical idiom, anticipating David's paintings of the 1780s. She was one of the most highly respected artists of her era. Some measure of the admiration and esteem she earned during her lifetime may be appreciated when one learns that all the members of the Roman Academy of St. Luke marched in her funeral procession. The funeral ceremonies were modeled after the services conducted for Raphael.

FRENCH STILL-LIFE PAINTING

- ### Anne Vallayer-Coster, *The White Soup Bowl*

Anne Vallayer-Coster (1744–1818) was one of the most talented, versatile, and productive still life painters of the late eighteenth century. Within this genre she painted a wide variety of works, ranging from simple groups of humble kitchen objects to elaborate compositions of exotic things, as well as hunting trophies and arrangements of fruits. She was especially renowned for her paintings of bouquets of flowers.

Vallayer-Coster's technical skills were widely recognized and appreciated by her contemporaries. She was elected to the Royal Academy in 1770. The following year, in 1771, the influential critic Diderot wrote that no other artist possessed an equal force of color and assurance. Among her patrons were the Marquis de Marigny, Minister of Arts under Louis XV, the Comte d'Angiviller, who held the same position under Louis XVI, and Marie Antoinette. Through royal decree, she was permitted to live in one of the apartments reserved for artists, a mark of special esteem that had also been accorded to Chardin, her more famous colleague who also specialized in still life painting. The official rewards and successes enjoyed by Vallayer-Coster during her lifetime attest to both the quality of her art and the esteem in which naturalistic still life painting was held.

Anne Vallayer was born into a family of artisan-craftsmen. Her father was a goldsmith who worked for the Gobelins tapestry factory. Eventually, he established an independent shop, which his wife ran after his death. Thus, Vallayer was raised in an environment that cultivated and encouraged her talents. We do not know how she acquired her painting skills, but she was an accomplished artist by her early twenties.

Vallayer's successful professional career enabled her to raise her social status. In 1781, at the relatively late age of 37, she married a wealthy lawyer and member of parliament, Jean Pierre Silvestre Coster, a match that represented a definite advance in class status for the daughter of a goldsmith.

Although Diderot was appreciative of Vallayer-Coster's talents, he was the first writer to compare her works with those of Chardin, and to some extent her reputation has suffered from this comparison ever since. One cannot deny that there are similarities in subjects and compositions betwen some of the still-lifes of the two. However, one would find such constants in the works of almost any other eighteenth-century French still-life painter. They are only the most general characteristics of national and period style in this category of painting. This does not indicate that Vallayer-Coster was less talented or less innovative than Chardin.

Vallayer-Coster painted a number of works depicting simple objects set on a stone ledge, like this remarkable painting, *The White Soup Bowl*, one of her most sensitive and beautiful still-lifes of this type. This painting is a study in shades of white. The artist precisely and sensitively describes the different tones and textures of the porcelain bowl, the linen cloth, and the translucent steam rising from the soup. The composition is deceptively simple. There is a subtle play of horizontal, vertical, and

Fig. 10–4. Anne Vallayer-Coster, *The White Soup Bowl*. 1771. Oil on canvas, 19¹¹/₁₆ x 24¹/₂ in.   *(Private collection)*

diagonal linear accents that achieve a satisfying balance. The economy of the arrangement is consistent with the restrained color scheme. *The White Soup Bowl* displays a technical ability of extreme control and finesse. The convincing depiction of something as intangible and evanescent as steam is quite remarkable, yet as a whole the image conveys tangibility and immediacy. The soup is steaming and soon someone will come to lift the ladle and serve the broth and bread to hungry people.

Vallayer-Coster's talents were not limited solely to the realm of still-life painting. She also painted miniatures, portraits, and arrangements of fruits and flowers. Her paintings of flowers received widespread recognition and success, continuing the tradition of Peeters and Ruysch. Her flower compositions vibrate with color and freedom of touch, more characteristic of the nineteenth century than of the eighteenth. Both in flower paintings and still-lifes, her precision and taste for reproducing exact detail served her purposes well. These talents were less appreciated in the realm of portraiture where, as noted in connection with Carriera's success in this field, the artist was expected to beautify the sitter's appearance.

Anne Vallayer-Coster was one of the leading French still-life painters of her generation. She was a versatile artist with a sophisticated sense of composition and sensitivity to color combinations. Her paintings, like those of Chardin, are a realistic alternative to the erotic fantasies of the late Rococo painters, such as Boucher and Fragonard.

PRE-REVOLUTIONARY ARISTOCRATIC PORTRAITURE

• Elisabeth Vigée-Lebrun, *Marie Antoinette and Her Children*

Elisabeth Vigée-Lebrun (1755–1842) was among the most talented and successful aristocratic portrait painters of the late eighteenth and early nineteenth centuries. She was elected to the French Royal Academy in 1783, simultaneously with Adélaïde Labille-Guiard. These were the last two women to be admitted to the prestigious institution before its dissolution in the Revolution, in 1790.

As official portraitist for the Queen of France, Marie Antoinette, she achieved one of the highest positions in her society. After the French Revolution, as she traveled around Europe, she continued to experience a series of international triumphs. Her output was prodigious: She produced about 800 paintings during her lifetime. Like Carriera, to whom she was frequently compared by her contemporaries, Vigée-Lebrun had the capacity both to reflect and to formulate the esthetic tastes of her aristocratic clientele.

The daughter of a pastel portrait painter, Vigée-Lebrun recalled in her memoirs that her father and his colleagues gave her instruction and encouraged her talents. She also studied the paintings in the Louvre, especially Rubens's Marie de' Medici cycle. In this active, supportive environment, her talents developed precociously. When she was twenty, she commanded hgher prices for her portraits than any of her contemporaries.

In 1778 Vigée-Lebrun was summoned to court to paint her first portrait of

Marie Antoinette. Thus began a relationship that would dominate the career and reputation of the artist. An ardent royalist until her death at the age of 87, Vigée-Lebrun was called upon to create the official image of the queen. The painting that best exemplifies Vigée-Lebrun's role as political propagandist is the monumental and complex *Marie Antoinette and Her Children* (Fig. 10–5).[10] This work was commissioned directly from the funds of the state to defuse the violent attacks on the queen's moral character then circulating in France. It was painted only two years before the cataclysm of the French Revolution, the imprisonment of the royal family, and their subsequent execution. This official image was designed as an aggressive, if ultimately ineffective, counterattack to the political opponents of the monarchy.

Lynn Hunt has studied the erotic and pornographic literature focused on Marie Antoinette during these years. The Queen was accused of all manner of sexual improprieties and misconduct, including promiscuity and homosexual liaisons. She was also accused of poisoning the heir to the throne. Of direct relevance to this painting is the slander identifying the queen as a "bad mother." During the period of imprisonment of the royal family, the queen was accused of sexual activities with the 8-year-old Louis-Charles, resulting in an injury to one of his testicles. Although the accusation would occur a few years after this painting, the nature of Marie Antoinette as a mother was at the core of the popular rage targeted against her during the pre-Revolutionary period in the 1780s.[11]

Fig. 10–5. Elisabeth Vigée-Lebrun,
*Marie Antoinette and Her
Children.* 1787. *(Musée
National de Versailles)*

Vigée-Lebrun placed the queen in the imposing and easily recognizable setting of the Salon de la Paix at Versailles. The famous Hall of Mirrors is visible on the left side of the painting. The royal crown on top of the cabinet on the right is the ultimate symbol of the power and authority of the kings. The figure of the queen herself dominates the composition. Her features have been ennobled and beautified, while the enormous hat and full, voluminous skirts create an impression of superhuman monumentality. Her luxuriant costume, the immense blue velvet robe, and hat convey the grandeur of the French monarchy. Vigée-Lebrun wanted her painting to express not only the sanctity of divine right monarchy but also the bourgeois, Enlightenment concept of "Maternal Love."[12] The triangular composition is derived from High Renaissance images of the Madonna and Child by Leonardo and Raphael. Like Kauffman's *Cornelia Pointing to Her Children as Her Treasures* (see Fig. 10–3), Marie Antoinette displays her children as her jewels. The Dauphin stands on the right, slightly apart from the group, as is only appropriate for the future king of France (although events were to alter the dynastic succession). The eldest daughter gazes up at the queen with filial adoration. The empty cradle to which the young Dauphin points originally contained the queen's fourth child, an infant girl, who died two months before the painting was to be exhibited at the Salon opening. On that day, August 25, 1787, anti-monarchist feelings were running so high that Vigée-Lebrun refused to display the painting for fear that it might be damaged.

Her close association with the queen made it dangerous for Vigée-Lebrun to remain in France after the imprisonment of the royal family. In 1789 she traveled first to Italy, then Vienna, eventually arriving in St. Petersburg, Russia. There, no political revolution had dispersed the aristocratic clientele upon whom she depended for commissions.

Vigée-Lebrun was permitted to return to Paris in 1802, in response to a petition signed by 255 fellow artists, but the era in which she had risen to fame had passed into history. She lived another forty years, sadly out of place in Napoleonic France and neglected during the subsequent Bourbon restoration.

Her career is of great historical interest because she was one of the foremost painters of her era. High prices, prestigious commissions, and critical attention document her position in the society of the *ancien régime*. Unlike David and Labille-Guiard, who adapted their talents to the successive governments of France, Vigée-Lebrun was both emotionally and professionally attached to the monarchy. While the portrait of *Marie Antoinette and Her Children* found a sympathetic audience during the restoration of the Bourbons at the Salon of 1817, its creator never regained the preeminent position she had held before Marie Antoinette was guillotined.

- ### Adélaïde Labille-Guiard, *Self-Portrait with Two Pupils*

Although she was six years older than Vigée-Lebrun, Labille-Guiard's (1749–1803) public career is contemporaneous. Unlike Vigée-Lebrun, the daughter of a painter, Labille-Guiard was born into a *petit-bourgeois* family with no obvious connections to the arts.[13] Her skills were developed over a period of many years, and it was only in 1780, when the artist was over 30, that she exhibited her first oil paintings. Following the example set by Carriera, she learned the art of miniature painting during her adolescence from François-Elie Vincent. She then studied pastel technique with the preeminent pastel portraitist of the age, Maurice Quentin de La Tour. She only developed her skills in oil painting later, from François-André Vincent, her miniature teacher's oldest son and her future husband. She married Louis-Nicolas Guiard in 1769, lived with him for about ten years, and divorced him in 1792.

Although she had mastered the full range of techniques for portraiture by 1780, she struggled to develop a clientele. Between 1780 and 1783 she executed an uncommissioned series of portraits of preeminent Academicians, such as Vien, the teacher of David. This tactic proved to be an effective political lobbying technique to establish her abilities. She was admitted to the Academy in 1783, simultaneously with Vigée-Lebrun.

Labille-Guiard is remarkable not only for her successful career, but also for her concern and active interest in the education of women artists. After 1780, she accepted into her studio a small group of young women whom she trained. Several of her pupils continued to pursue active professional careers as portraitists. Her *Self-Portrait with Two Pupils, Mlle. Marie-Gabrielle Capet and Mlle. Garreaux de Rosemond* (Fig. 10–6), exhibited at the Salon of 1785, is remarkable for its inclusion of two of her most capable students. Contemporary critics noted the appearance of these, as yet unknown, women artists. This painting constitutes a public introduction of the aspiring painters.

Labille-Guiard has presented herself in the costume and coiffure of the aristocracy. Documents survive indicating that, despite her Salon success of that year, she was experiencing financial difficulties. Therefore, one must interpret this proud image as a form of self-advertisement, an appeal to potential aristocratic patrons on their own terms, rather than as documentation of the artist's actual social status. This painting is characteristic of Labille-Guiard's taste for muted color harmonies, as opposed to the more highly saturated colors often used by Vigée-Lebrun. Also unlike Vigée, who favored very simplified costumes and hair arrangements, Labille-Guiard took pleasure in delineating precisely all details of the fashionable styles of her time.

According to the authoritative study of the artist, this painting was widely praised by the critical press of the day and helped to establish her reputation as a master painter in oils. The same year this work was exhibited she was awarded a substantial stipend from the king, although she was denied a studio in the Louvre due to the presence of her young female pupils. The following year she received major commissions from the royal family and worked on portraits of the "Mesdames," the aunts of the king. Her full-length *Portrait of Mme. Adélaïde* was hung as a pendant to Vigée-Lebrun's *Marie Antoinette and Her Children* (see Fig. 10–5) in the Salon of 1787. Such obvious proximity encouraged critics to compare the two artists and helped establish a "rivalry" which continued to exist, at least as a critical premise, for the remaining years of the *ancien régime*.

Unlike Vigée-Lebrun, Labille-Guiard did not leave France during the years of the Revolution. With the obvious disintegration of her clientele, her resourceful abil-

Fig. 10–6. Adélaïde Labille-Guiard, *Self-Portrait with Two Pupils, Mademoiselle Marie Gabrielle Capet (1761–1818) and Mademoiselle Garreaux de Rosemond (died 1788)*. Oil on canvas, 83 x 59½ in.   *(The Metropolitan Museum of Art, Gift of Julia A. Berwind, 1953. All rights reserved, The Metropolitan Museum of Art. 53.225.5)*

ity to develop patronage again surfaced, and in the Salon of 1791, she exhibited fourteen portraits of deputies, representatives of the new political elite of France, including Robespierre and Talleyrand. As in her campaign for admission to the Academy, she was again successful in courting a new clientele. She received the same commission from the Constitutional Assembly as Jacques Louis David, *The King Showing the Constitution to the Prince*. Subsequent political events prevented the funding of these paintings, and neither was executed.

Labille-Guiard shrewdly used the political upheavals of the Revolution to lobby for an improved position for women artists. In September, 1790, she addressed the Academy and argued for lifting the quota of four women academicians. In another motion she pressed for an honorary distinction to recognize women, since they could not assume positions as professors or officeholders. She was unsuccessful in effecting these reforms. The following year, Talleyrand presented her proposal for a school for impoverished girls to learn art skills suitable for careers in the art industries. Such a school was eventually established in 1805. Her ability to weather the political storms of her day is documented in her finally receiving a studio in the Louvre in 1795 and the large number of portraits she exhibited in 1798.

Both Vigée-Lebrun and Labille-Guiard were widely admired by their contemporaries and recognized for their talents by their peers in the Academy. These ambitious artists outshone those male colleagues who also specialized in portraiture. One may surmise from both artists' determination to achieve excellence that, had the opportunity existed, they would gladly have competed in the realm of history painting as well. Their confinement to portraiture was determined not by talent or ability but by their gender in the state-controlled art establishment of the French *ancien régime*.

WOMEN SALONNIÈRES AND THE ENLIGHTENMENT

That the two most prominent portrait painters in late eighteenth-century Paris were women is not accidental but can be seen as related to the dominant role of women in the cultural world of the *ancien régime*. Roseanne Runte has discussed the extensive roles of women in this epoch centered in the "Salons": "It is not an exaggeration to say that literary and artistic fame and fortune depended on the judgement of women."[14] Women exercised influence in political ways, helping to elect writers to the Academy. They provided financial aid, both as private benefactors and in dispersals of funds from the royal treasury. Mmes. De Pompadour and du Barry and Marie Antoinette were responsible, collectively, for 258 pensions paid to writers and visual artists. Aristocratic women provided sources of inspiration for both literary and visual artistic production both directly and indirectly as Muses and as models. This cultural milieu was characterized in the 1830s by Vigée-Lebrun in this way:

> It is so difficult today to explain the urbane charm, the easy grace, in short all those pleasing manners which, forty years ago, were the delight of Parisian society. The sort of gallantry I am describing has totally disappeared. Women reigned supreme then; the Revolution dethroned them.

Suggestions for Further Reading

Women in Early Modern Europe

DAVIS, NATALIE ZEMON, *Society and Culture in Early Modern France* (Stanford, CA: Stanford University Press, 1975).

TILLY, LOUISE A., and JOAN W. SCOTT, *Women's Work and Family* (New York: Holt, Rinehart and Winston, 1978).

Women in Eighteenth-Century France

HUNT, LYNN (ed.), *Eroticism and the Body Politic* (Baltimore, MD: Johns Hopkins University Press, 1991).

SPENCER, SAMIA I. (ed.), *French Women and the Age of Enlightenment* (Bloomington: Indiana University Press, 1984).

Carriera

COLDING, TORBEN HOLCH, *Aspects of Miniature Painting: Its Origins and Development* (Copenhagen: Ejnar Munksgaard, 1953).

SANI, BERNARDINA, *Rosalba Carriera: Lettere, Diari Frammenti* (Florence: Leo S. Olschki, Editore, 1985). (Italian)

Kauffman

Angelika Kauffman und ihre Zeitgenossen (Bregenz: Vorarlberger Landesmuseum, 1968). (German)

ROWORTH, WENDY WASSYNG (ed.), *Angelica Kauffman: A Continental Artist in Georgian England* (Brighton: The Royal Pavilion Art Gallery and Museums and London: Reaktion Books, 1992).

Vallayer-Coster

ROLAND-MICHEL, MARIANNE, *Anne Vallayer-Coster* (Paris, 1970). (French)

Vigée-Lebrun

BAILLIO, JOSEPH, *Elisabeth Louise Vigée-Lebrun: 1755–1842* (Fort Worth, TX: Kimbell Art Museum, 1982).

The Memoirs of Elisabeth Vigée-Le Brun, trans. Sian Evans (Bloomington: Indiana University Press, 1989).

Labille-Guiard

PASSEZ, ANNE-MARIE, *Biographie et Catalogue raisonné des oeuvres de Mme. Labille-Guiard* (Paris: Arts et Metiers Graphiques, 1973). (French)

CHAPTER 11

● ● ● ● ● ● ● ● ● ● ●

The United States: 1830–1900

In antebellum culture in the United States (1830–1860) women were largely absent from the public cultural arena as both patrons and artists. Women were not involved in any major art institutions, such as galleries, academies, or art unions, which were dominated by men. However, there were a few exceptions to the absence of women in formative positions in the art institutions of the period. Sarah Worthington King Peter opened the first school of design for women in 1848 in Philadelphia, and another school in Cincinnati.[1]

The prevailing cultural ideology of the epoch, the "Cult of True Womanhood," isolated and limited women's art activity to the category of decorations intended for the home. Professional women artists suffered from the association of women's activities with amateur, household pastimes, predominantly needlework.

During the first half of the nineteenth century, women in the United States who aspired to become professional artists had limited opportunities to acquire skills through apprenticeship to male artists. In a cultural structure similar to that in Holland, both Sarah Miriam Peale and Lilly Martin Spencer, the first two women painters discussed in this chapter, learned their craft in these more informal ways. These two painters became outstanding practitioners of the arts of portraiture and domestic genre scenes, respectively, in the era prior to the Civil War.

"Women artists often labored in professional isolation, shielded and encouraged by their fathers, brothers and husbands . . . but denied many of the collegial connections these men enjoyed."[2] This generalization is most appropriate for the painters Sarah Miriam Peale and Lilly Martin Spencer. Peale was born into a family of artists and Spencer's husband ran the household, although Lilly's paintings were the only source of income for the family.

Kathleen McCarthy has described the ways in which women artists were isolated from any existing female support networks: "Relegated to the periphery of men's professional networks by popular prejudices and the invisibility of their working lives, women artists were equally estranged from female support networks by virtue of their secular, unconventional careers."[3]

PORTRAITURE AND GENRE PAINTING

- ### Sarah Miriam Peale, *Portrait of Congressman Henry A. Wise*

Like Artemisia Gentileschi, Angelica Kauffman, and other women artists discussed in preceding chapters, Sarah Miriam Peale (1800–1885), the daughter of an artist, was in a highly favorable position to develop expertise and talent as a professional portrait painter in Victorian America. Born into a family of outstanding artists, she was among the few women of her era to build her career on the execution of full-sized portraits. The daughter of James Peale, a miniature painter, and niece of the noted artist Charles Wilson Peale, Sarah acquired training in painting both at home and in the studios of her cousins. Her two sisters, Anna Claypoole and Margaretta Angelica, were also noted artists.

Born in Philadelphia, Sarah Miriam first learned the techniques of painting miniatures on ivory from her father. By 1825 she had moved to Baltimore where her cousins Rembrandt and Rubens Peale operated a museum modeled after that of their father, Charles Wilson Peale, in Philadelphia. Sarah Miriam had already learned more sophisticated painting techniques for flesh tones and fabric textures from Rembrandt. For more than twenty years she lived and worked in Baltimore, creating over one hundred full-scale portraits of the socially prominent of that city and the elected representatives of the nation living in nearby Washington, D.C. The *Portrait of Congressman Henry A. Wise* (Fig. 11–1) falls into the latter category. Peale painted this

Fig. 11–1. Sarah Miriam Peale, *Henry A. Wise.* c. 1842. Oil on canvas, 29½ x 24½ in. *(Virginia Museum of Fine Arts, Richmond, VA. Gift of the Duchess of Richelieu in memory of James M. Wise and Julia Wise. Photograph © Virginia Museum of Fine Arts)*

work when Wise was a Democratic congressman from Virginia. He would later be elected governor of the state in the years prior to the Civil War, and eventually served as a general in the Confederate army.[4]

This portrait is a characteristic example of Peale's commissioned works. The isolated sitter is presented half-length, in three-quarter position, confronting the viewer directly. Peale's style is linear, precise, and realistic. The detailed and well-modeled face, set off against the brilliant white shirt and cravat, and the unmodeled black suit forces the viewer inescapably to focus on the features of this handsome man. The barely indicated column on the left, swagged with a dark red drapery, enlivens the otherwise bare background, while the drapery establishes an echoing diagonal to the sitter's left shoulder.

In Baltimore, Peale had a very large clientele, but also direct competitors in the portrait market, such as Thomas Sully and John Vanderlyn. Perhaps this explains her eventual relocation to St. Louis in 1847. The city must have appealed to her, because she remained there for thirty years, returning to Philadelphia to live out her remaining years with her two sisters. A few still-life paintings as well as portraits have survived from her years in St. Louis.

Sarah Miriam Peale capitalized on her birthright to develop her talents in order to pursue a long, productive, and one may assume prosperous career as a professional portrait painter in nineteenth-century America. She was the most accomplished and outstanding woman artist in this field during her era.

• Lilly Martin Spencer, *War Spirit at Home*

Lilly Martin Spencer (1822–1902) was one of America's most important genre painters in the years before and after the Civil War. In the extensive catalogue, published in 1973, for a major exhibition of the artist's works organized at the National Collection of Fine Arts, she is characterized as "this country's most noted mid-nineteenth-century female artist."[5]

Spencer's parents were born in France and arrived in the United States with their young daughter in 1830. Her parents were liberal thinkers, probably affected by French Utopian intellectual movements, and were to be active supporters of reform movements ranging from Abolitionism to women's suffrage. After settling in Ohio, Lilly and her siblings were raised on a farm and educated at home. Her talent for art emerged in her teens, and, accompanied by her father, she traveled to Cincinnati in 1841 to acquire some training in painting. Cincinnati was in these years a thriving, wealthy port city, which supported many portrait painters and an active cultural life. Lilly Martin lived in this city for seven years, studied with several portrait painters, and married Benjamin Rush Spencer. Her marriage was productive and prolific. Seven children survived, and more pregnancies were endured by Lilly. Benjamin would eventually abandon any independent career activities to facilitate his wife's production of works of art. He assumed most of the domestic responsibilities of their household.

Lilly was able to develop her talents to the extent that she exhibited still-life and genre paintings at the newly established Western Art Union in Cincinnati. However, chronic poverty plagued the couple. After selling a work to a New York collector and exhibiting a work at the prestigious National Academy of Design, the Spencers decided to move to New York in 1848, seeking the wider opportunities and broader patronage base of the large city. The artist arrived in New York when enthusiasm for Düsseldorf-school genre painting was at its height. Characterized by defined outlines, crisp details, and bright colors, Spencer worked to acquire a personal style of similar precision and realism.[6] Her subjects reflect the tastes for genre of the largely middle-class patronage of the era, which supported the successful careers of such male genre painters as William Sidney Mount. After developing her skills further, her genre paintings met with wide critical approval. *Peeling Onions* (1852) shows her newly acquired expertise in combining a kitchen genre scene with a realistically rendered still life. Another famous painting, *Fi! Fo! Fum!*, used her own family as subject for an intimate domestic moment of storytelling. During the 1850s and 1860s Spencer exhibited her works along the Eastern Seaboard and gained popularity through the distribution of hand-colored lithographs based on her compositions, printed in France. By 1858, the year the couple moved to a home in Newark, New Jersey, Lilly Martin Spencer had established herself as one of the leading domestic genre painters in America. Yet the family, still growing in size, continued to experience financial pressures. The lower cost of living in Newark was surely the main motivation for the move, and the Spencers even planted a vegetable garden for a source of food in lean times.

McCarthy notes that the Spencer household was constantly in debt and Lilly was often searching for commissions. In 1856, she had not sold a painting or received a portrait commission for over seven months.[7] In 1860, she was reduced to coloring photographs, a menial task. By contrast, William Sidney Mount never suffered from poverty. He roamed the countryside for subjects, socialized with a circle of professional male colleagues, and was supported financially by male patrons.

In the immediate aftermath of the Civil War, Spencer created several major compositions reflecting this traumatic national experience. *War Spirit at Home* (Fig. 11–2) provides the viewer with an image of the domestic life of women and children during the war. This image depicts a fatherless household celebrating Grant's 1863 victory at Vicksburg, as recorded in the *New York Times*, displayed by the mother, a self-portrait, on the far right of the composition. The lighthearted energy of the children, ignorant of the realities of the conflict, is contrasted with the sober expressions of the mother and servant. The obvious absence of the father leads one to project a scenario in which the strength and determination of the women's sphere is a complement to the heroism of the soldiers on the battlefield. The sharply focused light, painterly rendering of the mother's dress, and dramatic foreshortening of the infant are all noteworthy formal elements of this image. Spencer's ability to invent a convincing domestic genre subject on such a serious issue as the Civil War demonstrates her talent for thematic innovation.

Following the War, artistic tastes began to change. The artist attempted to accommodate the new patronage demands and worked on an over-life-sized allegory, *Truth Unveiling Falsehood* (1869). It remained unsold throughout her life, and there is no evidence that it improved her financial situation. This change of direction marks

Fig. 11–2. Lilly Martin Spencer, *War Spirit at Home.* 1866. Oil on canvas, 30 x 32³/₄ in.   *(Collection of The Newark Museum. Purchase 1944 Wallace M. Scudder Bequest Fund)*

the end of the most fruitful period of the artist's career. Lilly Martin Spencer lived until the age of 80 and died after a morning spent painting an image of a family reunion, convened to celebrate the 100th birthday of her aunt.

NEOCLASSICAL SCULPTURE

- ### Harriet Hosmer, *Zenobia in Chains*

When Horatio Greenough left America and traveled to Italy in 1825, he initiated the exodus that created the first significant American school of sculpture. Prior to this time, Americans who created three-dimensional objects were largely craftsmen, although Patience Lovell Wright (1725–1786) had been active as a maker of wax images in the eighteenth century. In addition to Greenough, Thomas Crawford and Hiram Powers are the most important neoclassical sculptors of the second quarter of the nineteenth century. Powers's *The Greek Slave* (see Fig. 11–4) became the most famous sculpture produced by an American in the nineteenth century.

Italy retained its attraction for American sculptors both male and female during the third quarter of the nineteenth century. In addition to Randolph Rogers, William

Wetmore Story, and William Henry Rinehart, a number of women sculptors established studios in Rome during the 1850s. Harriet Hosmer (1830–1908) and Edmonia Lewis are among the artists of the "White Marmorean Flock." This group set a historical precedent for the ability of women to become successful professional sculptors. Henry James coined the name the "White Marmorean Flock" in 1903, and this disparaging phrase has remained attached to these artists ever since. As Jane Mayo Roos convincingly argues, the implication of the appellation is that these women are "tiny, anonymous, hapless creatures who traveled *en masse* and whose accomplishments were diminutive in scale."[8]

Harriet Hosmer had begun her training in America. She studied anatomy at the Saint Louis Medical College, following the same course as Hiram Powers. She was one of the first women to settle in Rome, arriving in 1852. In the 1850s and 1860s, Louisa Lander, Emma Stebbins, Anne Whitney, and Edmonia Lewis established neighboring sculpture studios in Italy.

On her arrival in Rome, Hosmer continued her studies with the English sculptor John Gibson. During her first year abroad she wrote to her best friend and biographer Cornelia Carr:

> Don't ask me if I was ever happy before, don't ask me if I am happy now, but ask me if my constant state of mind is felicitous, beatific, and I will reply "Yes." It never entered into my head that anybody could be so content on this earth, as I am here. I wouldn't live anywhere else but in Rome, if you would give me the Gates of Paradise and all the Apostles thrown in. I can learn more and do more here, in one year, than I could in America in ten. America is a grand and glorious country in some respects, but this is a better place for an artist.

Female sculptors were attracted to Rome for the same reasons as their male colleagues: the access to the famed statues of antiquity and the abundance of fine marble and of skilled artisans to work it. Furthermore, they also found in Rome an international community of artists who respected their unusual choice of profession. In Italy members of the "Flock" were released from the cultural restrictions imposed on women by Victorian American society. This freedom, combined with inexpensive living costs, made Rome especially attractive to these American sculptors.

Hosmer's most famous statue is *Zenobia in Chains* (Fig. 11–3), depicting the queen of Palmyra, who was marched in chains through the streets of Rome following the defeat of her army in 272 A.D. Hosmer does not present Zenobia as a powerful warrior who, according to the historian Gibbon, conquered Egypt and parts of Asia Minor, but rather as a noble captive who accepts her defeat with dignity and reserve. Like Cornelia, Zenobia was a woman of outstanding talents and abilities whose reputation survived through history and made her a female role model from the classical past.

Hosmer's conception of Zenobia is dependent on the written account of this legendary figure by Anna Jameson, a noted English authority on art and a vocal advocate of women's rights. Hosmer apparently consulted with Jameson during the genesis of the statue. Thus Hosmer's *Zenobia* was clearly and self-consciously developed as a role model of courage and wisdom for contemporary women, challenging

Fig. 11–3. Harriet Hosmer, *Zenobia in Chains*. 1859. Marble. Height 49 in. *(Wadsworth Atheneum, Hartford. Gift of Mrs. Josephine M. J. Dodge)*

Fig. 11–4. Hiram Powers, *The Greek Slave*. Marble. Height 65½ in. *(Collection of The Newark Museum. Gift of Franklin Murphy, Jr., 1926. Photo by Armen)*

prevailing Victorian ideals of femininity. The original statue was monumentally scaled, seven feet tall. The drapery was derived from the authoritative classical model of the Golden Age *Athena Giustinini* and the crown inspired by the *Barberini Juno*.[9]

A comparison of Hosmer's *Zenobia* with Powers's *The Greek Slave* reveals important differences in attitude toward the portrayal of the female image that existed between two artists of the same neoclassical movement, one a man, the other a woman. Powers made *The Greek Slave*'s nudity acceptable to prudish Victorian American society by the literary references surrounding the work. On one level, the figure was meant to evoke pity rather than lust, since she has been captured by the Turks during the Greek War of Independence. She is naked because she is about to be sold into slavery. But this motif was merely a respectable pretext because the statue is clearly designed to titillate the Victorian male viewer, and the chains emphasize the captive's passivity and vulnerability. By contrast, Zenobia, although chained, is clothed and retains her dignity and integrity as a woman. In this work, Hosmer provided an alternative to the sexual objectification of women so evident in *The Greek Slave* and chose, instead, to depict an individual woman of antiquity, worthy of deep respect and admiration on several levels.

- **Edmonia Lewis, *Old Indian Arrowmaker and His Daughter***

One of the most interesting artists in this group was Edmonia Lewis (1843–c.1911), who was half black and half Indian. The subjects of her sculpture reflect her mixed racial heritage. In 1867, as a monument to the recent emancipation of the American slaves, Lewis created a two-figure group, *Forever Free*. The white marble sculpture presents a black woman kneeling in a gesture of prayer beside a standing black man who displays his broken chains.

Lewis was raised as a Chippewa Indian. *Old Indian Arrowmaker and His Daughter* (Fig. 11–5) is one example of her ability to create sculptural images of Native Americans of great dignity and symbolic force. This work contains some very realistic details. Object textures of the fur garments are articulated, and the Old Arrowmaker has a sharply defined face with prominent cheekbones. He holds a flint and stone, while his daughter plaits a mat. This work is one of several created by Lewis that were directly inspired by Longfellow's famous poem "The Song of Hiawatha," and thus we can identify the daughter as Minnehaha. The slain deer could be the one killed by Hiawatha, implying his presence. In this sculpture Lewis has developed an original and expressive symbol of generational transmission and preservation of unique cultural values.[10]

Fig. 11–5. Edmonia Lewis, *Old Indian Arrowmaker and His Daughter*. 1872. *(George Washington Carver Museum, Tuskegee Institute)*

The achievements of the sculptors of the "Marmorean Flock" were widely recognized in their era, and many of these women received commissions for monumental works to be placed outdoors. Although in retrospect their works may seem stylistically conservative, this should not affect our appreciation of the historical position and achievement of these artists. Their statues were highly regarded in their day and were extremely popular. The works of the "Flock" embodied an idealism and optimism that reflected American aspirations and expectations of the mid-nineteenth century. The critical success and widespread recognition of this group is significant not only historically but also because it set a precedent for the many important women sculptors of the twentieth century.

The largest collection of neoclassical sculpture ever assembled was exhibited at the Philadelphia Centennial Exposition in 1876. By this date, however, Neoclassicism was no longer a viable stylistic mode for American sculptors. Post–Civil War America, disillusioned with earlier ideals of America as the new Eden and absorbed in rapid industrialization, could no longer sustain a movement in sculpture that focused so resolutely on past models.

THE EDUCATION OF WOMEN ARTISTS

• Alice Barber Stephens, *Female Life Class*

This painting depicts the advanced class taught by Thomas Eakins at the Pennsylvania Academy of Fine Arts. It was created to illustrate an article "The Art School of Philadelphia" scheduled to appear in the September 1879 issue of *Scribner's Monthly*. Its monochromatic palette surely was determined by the intended publication of the work as a black and white illustration in the popular press. Seated prominently in the left foreground is Susan Macdowell, a portrait painter who would marry Eakins in 1884. Alice Barber (1858–1932) went on to become "one of the most successful illustrators, male or female, of the late nineteenth century."[11]

It is no accident that the nude model is a woman. The male nude was outside the limits of even the supportive and liberated environment of Eakins's life class. Previously, women had studied the anatomy of a cow. The male nude was firmly excluded from the art production of women artists.

In 1873 Stephens enrolled in the Philadelphia School of Design for Women, founded by Sarah Worthington Peter in 1848 to train women for acceptable forms of employment consistent with the "Cult of True Womanhood." Stephens transferred to the Pennsylvania Academy in 1876. Upon graduation, she supported herself through illustrations that appeared in many popular periodicals of the era such as *Harpers'*, *Colliers*, and *The Ladies Home Journal*. She illustrated books as well, including Louisa May Alcott's *Little Women*. She was a professor at the School of Design from 1883 to 1893 and continued to create illustrations until 1926.

The Pennsylvania Academy of Fine Arts was the first art school to permit women to draw from plaster casts, in 1844. By 1860, women were enrolled in the anatomy class and a separate life-drawing class was established in 1868. That this was

Fig. 11–6. Alice Barber Stephens, *The Women's Life Class.* c. 1879. Oil on cardboard, 12 x 14 in. *(Courtesy of the Philadelphia Academy of the Fine Arts, Philadelphia. Gift of the artist. 1879.2)*

still a curiosity over a decade later can be inferred by the interest of Scribner's in documenting the women's class.

The educational options for artistic training in the United States available to women remained limited and discriminatory throughout the nineteenth century. For the ambitious woman seeking professional artistic training, Paris was a magnet, since the courses of study back home were fewer and less extensive than those open to men.[12]

DOMESTIC IDEOLOGY: THE "CULT OF TRUE WOMANHOOD" AND AMERICAN PIECED QUILTS

• *Log Cabin, Barn Raising Quilt*

Scholars have documented the central importance of quiltmaking and other forms of needlework in many aspects of the lives of women throughout the nineteenth century. Girls were taught to sew by age 5, and sewing occupied a central role in girls' education. Needlework created and used within the sphere of the home was "one area in which women were encouraged to give their imaginations free reign . . ."[13] The "Cult," then, is a key component of a cultural context in which quilt making could flourish.[14] Sewing reinforced the dominant ideology of the "Cult of True Womanhood," which defined women's role as domestic and maternal.

Quilts served many different purposes in the lives of women in this era. In practical terms, they covered beds and kept the sleeper warm. However, quilts were also a conspicuous demonstration of the skills of their creators. Pride, care, and effort were lavished on them. Long after the invention of the sewing machine, quilts were sewn by hand. Women made quilts as part of their dowry, and mothers made a quilt for each child. The creation of quilts was intertwined with the cycle of women's lives. Furthermore, quilts marked off major events in the lives of a family. Crib quilts were made for new babies, engagement and bridal quilts were created, and widow's or mourner's quilts were also created. Quilts traveled west with the pioneer migrations, protecting children and furniture and lining wagons for insulation. Sadly they were used as shrouds in which to bury the dead along the trail. Quilting parties in the newly opened frontier territories were essential opportunities for the socialization for women living in great isolation. All in all, quilts played an important part in women's lives.

Women also used quilts for public and political purposes. "Women used their quilts to register their responses to and also their participation in the major social, economic, and political developments of their times."[15] The Women's Christian Temperance Union used quilts as fund-raising vehicles, for example.

The women artists selected for discussion in this book overcame a variety of cultural and institutional obstacles to acquire the skills necessary for a career in the "fine arts," i.e., painting and sculpture. The vast majority of women did not have that opportunity. But like photographers, women have found outlets for their visual creativity in ways which did not require specialized training. Sewing was one skill that all women have learned since antiquity. In the nineteenth and early twentieth centuries, many American women designed and fabricated quilts pieced from scraps of cloth. Many of these quilts are remarkably beautiful and original creations, worthy of consideration as works of art. These mostly anonymous women created visual images in cloth that demonstrate a high level of sophistication, anticipating some of the developments in twentieth-century abstract painting. One such example is the anonymous quilt created with the pattern known as "Log Cabin, Barn Raising" (Fig. 11–7).

Quilts are made with geometric shapes because straight edges are the easiest to sew together. From scraps of fabric left over from clothing, square units of uniform size were stitched together. These individual squares were then arranged to form the overall design of the quilt. Some quilts used identical blocks creating a repeating pattern, while others, such as the example illustrated here, used differing blocks. The cutting of each piece to be fitted into the patchwork quilt had to be extremely accurate so the blocks would fit together precisely.

This "Log Cabin, Barn Raising" quilt employs a broad sampling of late nineteenth-century cotton calico fabrics. Most are printed in small, closely spaced patterns popular at this time. The lighter tones are mostly from fabrics used for men's shirts. After cutting, the bits of fabric were sewn into the basic unit, known as the "Log Cabin." Each individual square or block contains strips of fabric usually cut into

Fig. 11–7. "Log Cabin, Barn Raising" Quilt.   *(Dechert Price &*
Rhoades, Philadelphia, PA)

right angles or pieced into this shape from smaller scraps. The sections of fabric fit together into a telescoping pattern until there is a small square in the center. Each of
the units is divided diagonally into a dark and a light-toned triangle. The individual
blocks are then assembled so that the light–dark modulations create an overall pattern
of diamonds called the "Barn Raising." The term is derived from the resemblance of
the pattern to the sections of a barn wall laid flat on the ground before it is built.
Thus, the main design elements of this quilt are abstracted from vernacular architecture. One may even see the corner blocks as the "cornerstones" of the quilt.

Despite these references to architecture, the quilt functions visually as a two-dimensional "painting." The patterns of the fabric emphasize the flat surface of the
quilt. The light–dark transitions are carefully modulated to avoid a forceful effect of
movement forward and backward in space. The color scheme is dominated by cool
blues, greens, and earth tones. The border is a dark midnight blue. The combinations
of different fabrics indicate a refined sensitivity to color.

Once the top layer of the quilt was stitched together, it was joined to a solid
backing, and a filler of cotton or wool was sandwiched in-between. The three layers
were joined by the quilting technique itself. This final quilting was often accomplished at a social gathering known as a "quilting bee." Quilting bees were a valid
pretext for a party, breaking the often oppressive isolation of rural life.

From the perspective of the twentieth century, we are prepared to appreciate these quilts with their geometric designs as works of art in their own right. The anonymous creator of this quilt did not possess the specialized training available to the painters discussed in this book. She used a readily available and economic technique, i.e., sewing bits of leftover fabric, as the means to create a beautiful, abstract image that expresses an individual visual sensibility.

The outstanding achievements of America's quiltmakers warns against the validity of maintaining any strict, a priori value distinctions between the fine arts, i.e., painting, sculpture, and architecture, and the "crafts," i.e., all other art forms. Craft objects were often made by women without access or ambition to develop the skills needed for the execution of paintings or sculpture. As we will see in Chapter 16, the art versus craft controversy has been reopened since 1970 with a modern, feminist-inspired appreciation of craft objects such as quilts. Contemporary artists have realized the expressive potential of china plate painting and needlework, for example in Judy Chicago's monumental *Dinner Party* (Fig. 16–3), while the "pattern paintings" of Miriam Schapiro have led to a renewed appreciation for the decorative possibilities of fabric (Fig. 16–4).

THE PHILADELPHIA CENTENNIAL EXPOSITION (1876) AND THE DECORATIVE ARTS MOVEMENT

Led by a formidable organizer, Elizabeth Duane Gillespie, great-granddaughter of Benjamin Franklin, funds were raised to construct a Women's Pavilion for the Philadelphia Centennial Exposition. Six hundred exhibits organized by state and foreign women's committees were displayed in over an acre of enclosed space. Displays ranged from embroidery and other needlework, to paintings and other forms of "art," to a steam engine that powered six looms and a printing press. Some women artists were unwilling to exhibit their works in this unjuried and diverse display. Others, like Emily Sartain, showed works in both the official art exhibition and at the Women's Pavilion. Radical suffragist feminists like Elizabeth Cady Stanton objected to the absence of works by women in factories, while the building's organizers pointedly refused to participate in the most important feminist protest of the Centennial, the reading of the Declaration of the Rights of Women on July 4.[16]

Sparked by interest in the decorative arts exhibits at the Philadelphia Centennial Exposition, Candace Wheeler spearheaded the decorative arts movement, "the first major artistic crusade created, managed and promoted under female control."[17] The New York Society of Decorative Arts was founded in 1877. Wheeler attracted society leaders as well as artists and collectors to the organization. Its purpose was at least twofold. Wheeler sought to broaden women's career opportunities through the decorative arts. Therefore, one primary goal was to market the products of middle-class women so they could earn a viable living through their handicrafts. Another goal was to enlarge women's cultural authority. The success of this venture was witnessed by the establishment of several chapters across the country. Lending libraries helped upgrade the level of women's taste as decorators of the home environment. The Decorative Arts Movement employed a separatist strategy. Wheeler accepted women's general exclusion from the realm of the "fine" arts and concentrated women's efforts on the areas deemed more appropriate to women, the "minor" arts.

As laudable as these achievements were, there was a negative impact on women artists. ". . . the ambitions that inspired the decision to become an artist often challenged the domestic ideologies that legitimized women's public, philanthropic roles. Women artists did not want charity, they wanted public recognition and acceptance on a par with men—ideas that often ran counter to the separatist dictum that women should cleave to their own distinctive cultural sphere."[18]

McCarthy notes that by the 1890s women began to play a more prominent role as collectors and connoisseurs. Louisine Havemeyer, guided by her artist friend Mary Cassatt, is one obvious example, and Isabella Stewart Gardner, advised by Bernard Berenson, built an impressive collection which she eventually turned into a museum bearing her name in Boston. But urban museums, like orchestras and research universities, were largely run by men. Women did not participate on the boards or make large financial contributions to the new museums. Only a handful of women secured jobs as curators, often in the field of the "decorative arts."

THE WOMAN'S BUILDING, WORLD'S COLUMBIAN EXPOSITION, CHICAGO, 1893

Seventeen years after the Philadelphia Centennial the World's Columbian Exposition in Chicago included an impressive "Woman's Building." Led by Bertha Palmer, wife of one of Chicago's wealthiest financiers, the Board of Lady Managers selected as the building's theme, "The Progress of Women." When completed, a vast array of displays from around the world, including a library of 7,000 volumes written by women, were housed in the structure. Unlike the Philadelphia Women's Pavilion of 1876, examples of work from the women's industrial labor force were shown and women's contributions to the fine arts also were highlighted. One hundred thirty-eight prints by women printmakers were exhibited. This was "probably the first woman's art survey of its type."[19] Designed by a woman architect, Sophia Hayden, the building was decorated with murals by Mary Cassatt and other noted women painters.

The Board of Lady Managers supervised construction of a women's dormitory that provided shelter for over 12,000 women during the four months of the fair. A children's building provided child care for fair visitors. Women speakers from around the world were invited to participate in the "Congresses," which addressed a vast array of topics. The work of the Board of Lady Managers in Chicago in 1893 served to highlight the full range of women's achievements in a manner unprecedented in the history of world's fairs.[20]

Suggestions for Further Reading

General Works

MCCARTHY, KATHLEEN D., *Women's Culture: American Philanthropy and Art, 1830–1930* (Chicago: University of Chicago Press, 1991).

RUBENSTEIN, CHARLOTTE STREIFFER, *American Women Artists: From Early Indian Times to the Present* (Boston: G.K. Hall, 1982).

RUBENSTEIN, CHARLOTTE S., *American Women Sculptors* (Boston: G.K. Hall, 1990).

TUFTS, ELEANOR (ed.), *American Women Artists: 1830–1930* (Washington, DC: The National Museum of Women in the Arts, 1987).

Lilly Martin Spencer

BOLTON-SMITH, ROBIN, and WILLIAM TRUETTNER, *Lilly Martin Spencer: The Joys of Sentiment* (Washington, DC: Smithsonian Institution Press, 1973).

Neoclassical Sculpture

CARR, CORNELIA (ed.), *Harriet Hosmer, Letters and Memories* (New York, 1912).

CIKOVSKY, NICOLAI, *The White Marmorean Flock: 19th Century American Women Neoclassical Sculptors* (Poughkeepsie, NY: Vassar College Art Gallery, 1972).

GERDTS, WILLIAM H., *American Neoclassical Sculpture: The Marble Resurrection* (New York: Viking Press, 1973).

LEACH, JOSEPH, "Harriet Hosmer: Feminist in Bronze and Marble," *Feminist Art Journal* (Summer 1976).

ROOS, JANE MAYO, "Another Look at Henry James and the 'White Marmorean Flock'," *Woman's Art Journal*, 4 (Summer 1983).

WALLER, SUSAN, "The Artist, the Writer, and the Queen: Hosmer, Jameson, and Zenobia," *Woman's Art Journal*, 4 (Summer 1983).

Quilts

FERRERO, ELAINE HEDGES, and JULIE SILBER, *Hearts and Hands: The Influence of Women and Quilts on American Society* (San Francisco: Quilt Digest Press, 1987).

HOLSTEIN, JONATHAN, *Abstract Design in American Quilts* (Published for an exhibition at the Whitney Museum of American Art, New York, 1971).

HOLSTEIN, JONATHAN, *The Pieced Quilt: An American Design Tradition* (Greenwich, CT: New York Graphic Society, 1973).

MAINARDI, PATRICIA, "Quilts, The Great American Art," in *Feminism and Art History: Questioning the Litany*, ed. Norma Broude and Mary D. Garrard (New York: Harper and Row, Icon Editions, 1982).

The Women's Buildings, 1876 and 1893

CORN, WANDA M., "Women Building History" in Eleanor Tufts (ed.), *American Women Artists: 1830–1930* (Washington, DC: The National Museum of Women in the Arts, 1987).

WEIMANN, JEANNE MADELINE, *The Fair Women: The Story of the Women's Building, World's Columbian Exposition, Chicago, 1893* (Chicago: Academy Chicago, 1981).

CHAPTER 12

VICTORIAN ENGLAND: 1850–1890

THE DEVELOPMENT OF A FEMINIST CONSCIOUSNESS

During the second half of the nineteenth century there was an enormous increase in the number of practicing professional women artists in England. In 1841 fewer than 300 women identified themselves as artists in the census; by 1871 there were 1,000 women artists. The middle third of the century saw this growing body of women artists become more vocal and visible. As Deborah Cherry notes, "Women artists' claims for public recognition collided with hegemonic definitions of bourgeois femininity as dependent and domestic, while their bids for professional status contested emergent codes of masculine professionalism."[1] In 1856 the Society of Female Artists was established.

- ### Emily Mary Osborn, *Nameless and Friendless*

    The following year, in 1857, Emily Osborn (1834–c. 1909) exhibited *Nameless and Friendless* at the summer exhibition of the Royal Academy. In this painting, the woman artist stands in the center. Her clothing, a simple black dress and plaid shawl, identify her as belonging to the middle classes. However, she has entered a picture shop, a commercial place of work, to engage in an economic transaction. This activity was not compatible with the ideology of bourgeois femininity which polarized masculine and feminine identities and spheres. Like the contemporary "Cult of True Womanhood" in America, gender roles were very sharply differentiated in Victorian England. While men were involved in paid, professional work and ran the world of industry, business, and government, women's lives were viewed as centered around the home, domesticity, family, and financial dependence on men.

    Osborn appeals to her viewers by portraying this woman artist as a "distressed gentlewoman," a character familiar to her audience, since it had already been disseminated in other texts of the epoch. The distressed gentlewoman was a needy lady—a respectable, middle-class woman forced to earn money for survival, due to the death of a male provider. Osborn helped the Victorian viewers to "read" this image by supplying a quote from Proverbs 10:15 for the exhibition catalogue: "The rich man's wealth is his strong city." The black dress, then, is a symbol of mourning, and the lack of a wedding band would have helped viewers understand that this woman is unmarried, and now an orphan. She has traveled some distance through the rainy weather to sell her work.

Cherry identifies the story behind this image with a complex of meanings that have to do with issues of "looking" and "being looked at." The young artist avoids the gaze of both the owner of the picture shop and the viewer. The avoidance of a forthright stare was another sign of respectable femininity. The forthright gaze, as in Manet's *Olympia*, is the sign of the prostitute. This "distressed gentlewoman" is, however, the object of attention of both men on the far left, who have interrupted their viewing of a print of a ballerina. The ballet dancer was an obvious sexual object in this period, due to the exposure of her arms and limbs and her performance in public. Just as the men stare at her, the dealer looks critically and unenthusiastically at the painting he holds, which we presume to be the artist's work.

Sexual difference, then, is apparent in the different nature of "the gaze." Men are looking. Women, whether real or as images, are looked at and sexually consumed, as the leers of the "gentlemen" in the top hats indicate. Linda Nochlin notes that the empty chair in the right foreground and the standing position of the young woman further indicate her loss of status in this situation: ". . . had she been a wealthy lady

Fig. 12–1. Emily Mary Osborn, *Nameless and Friendless.* *(Private collection; photo courtesy of Courtauld Institute of Art)*

client rather than a nameless and friendless woman painter, she would naturally have been sitting down rather than standing up."[2]

However, this is a painting by a woman artist. Emily Osborn was encouraged to paint by her mother, who herself had aspirations to become a professional artist. Over the objections of her father, a clergyman, Osborn's mother was her first art teacher. Osborn remained unmarried but lived with a woman, whom she characterized as "her great friend, Miss Dunn."[3]

Lady Chetwynd purchased this work in 1857. Queen Victoria purchased another work by Osborn, and the commission for a portrait of Lady Sturgis enabled Osborn to acquire her own studio. The financial support of other women was crucial for Osborn's career and testifies to the existence of networks of "matronage" (Cherry's term) for the financial support of women for women artists. A few years later, in 1860, Osborn addressed the plight of the governess in another painting, which, like Charlotte Bronte's novel *Jane Eyre*, elicited sympathy for this category of "distressed gentlewoman," which was one of the few paid occupations for respectable, middle-class women.

WOMEN ARTISTS AND THE PRE-RAPHAELITE MOVEMENT

The Case of Elizabeth Siddall

The standard histories of the Pre-Raphaelite movement are focused on the formation of the all-male brotherhood led by Dante Gabriel Rossetti in 1848. Women are present in these accounts as the subjects of the male artist's visions, as images or as muses of inspiration. However, as Jan Marsh and Pamela Gerrish Nunn have documented, women artists were present in numbers at all stages of the movement from 1850 to 1900.[4]

The complexities of understanding the life and work of Elizabeth Siddall (1829–1862) have been addressed by Pollock and Cherry in a fascinating essay, "Woman as Sign in Pre-Raphaelite Literature."[5] From their research, a few basic facts about the life of Elizabeth Siddall can be established with some degree of certainty. Born in July 1829, one year after Rossetti, she died at age 32, in 1862. She came from a working-class family—her father worked in the cutlery and ironmongering trades in Sheffield and London. Two of her sisters worked in the clothing trades, as did so many other working-class women of this era.

Siddall's relationship with Rossetti is consistent with the patterns of other male artists in the Pre-Raphaelite circle. These men sought out working-class women as models, lovers, and wives, "desiring them for their difference,"[6] perhaps as a form of rebellion consistent with their avant-garde artistic practices. Siddall did make art, however, as this drawing documents, and in fact she produced over 100 works. "There is evidence that Siddall was caught up in the cult of art as expressive genius unfettered by formal training which was proclaimed by Rossetti and Ruskin."[7]

Siddall's first works were illustrations. She developed a series of illustrations of Sir Walter Scott's poems, including *Clerk Saunders*, to be published in a book edited by William Allingham.

Marsh and Gerrish Nunn emphasize that the awkwardness of proportions and perspective in her images are consistent with the "deliberate Primitivism" of "Pre-Raphaelitism" in this period.[8] These formal elements should not be interpreted as "incompetence" based on academic standards of realism or "accuracy."

Siddall's relationship with Rossetti was difficult and discontinuous. In 1858 their engagement was broken when Rossetti refused to honor his promises of marriage. Marsh and Gerrish Nunn believe that it was following this rupture, in the spring of 1858, that Siddall became addicted in laudanum, an opiate drug. In 1860 Rossetti, who believed Siddall was dying, did marry her. She became pregnant, but her baby daughter was stillborn in May 1861. In February 1862 "she. died of a massive overdose of laudanum, which the coroner judged accidental."[9]

"Her display of drawings to Mr. Deverell, . . . her work as a model to the PRB (possibly her only access to the studio), her choice of Rossetti as instructor, her acceptance of Ruskin's allowance, her participation in the Russell Place Exhibition and her attendance at Sheffield Art School should all be interpreted as the actions of an artist aspiring to professional status."[10]

VICTORIAN PHOTOGRAPHY

- **Julia Margaret Cameron, *Portrait of Mrs. Herbert Duckworth***

Because photography was not regarded as an art in the late nineteenth and early twentieth centuries, the field was open to everyone without restrictions. Anyone who wanted to could make photographs, and no official schools controlled the dissemination of the technical knowledge necessary to practice photography. This made it possible for a number of women to achieve the first rank of excellence in the new medium. Women photographers, like women active in the fine arts, have created impressive images of a wide variety of subjects in many different photographic styles. As in the fine arts, women photographers were active participants in many avant-garde groups. The Englishwoman Julia Margaret Cameron (1815–1879) was one of the most famous photographers of the late nineteenth century.

Julia Pattle was born in Calcutta, India. Her father was a wealthy merchant in the East India Company. After being educated in France and England, Julia returned to Calcutta at age 19. A few years later she met Charles Hay Cameron, an upper-class Englishman, and they were married in 1838. Cameron, twenty years older than Julia, was an eminent jurist who codified the Indian statutes. In 1848 the couple returned to England, and in 1860 they settled on the fairly isolated Isle of Wight. Julia Cameron took up photography at the age of 48 as a diversion because her six children were grown and her husband was frequently away on business. Although she had no formal training and her knowledge of photography came from popular manuals and trial and error, she attacked the new medium with characteristic energy and enthusiasm.

In her time, Cameron was best known for her romantic, unfocused photographs. She often recorded sentimental allegories, influenced by the subjects of Pre-Raphaelite paintings. Today, however, her portraits are considered her best works. The Camerons were part of Britain's social and intellectual elite, friendly with many of

Fig. 12–2. Julia Margaret
Cameron, *Portrait of Mrs. Herbert
Duckworth*. 1867. Silver print,
$12\frac{1}{2}$ x $10\frac{1}{4}$ in.   (Collection B.
and N. Newhall, The George Eastman
House, Rochester, New York)

the most notable Englishmen of the era, who often visited the family on the Isle of
Wight. Among her illustrious sitters were the painters George Watts and William
Holman Hunt, the poets Alfred, Lord Tennyson and Robert Browning, and the scientist Charles Darwin. She also used family members as sitters.

The photograph of her niece, Julia Jackson, taken in April 1867 (Fig. 12–2) is a
typical example of her portrait style. Julia Jackson, wife of Herbert Duckworth, was
the mother of Virginia Woolf, one of the most important writers of the twentieth
century. The eminent art critic Roger Fry has termed this portrait "a splendid success,"
noting further that "the transitions of tone in the cheek and the delicate suggestions
of reflected light, no less than the beautiful 'drawing' of the profile, are perfectly satisfying."[11] In a tribute to Cameron written in 1926, Fry asserts the validity of considering
photography an art form and refers to her as the "most distinguished" artist–photographer who ever lived.

THE ROYAL ACADEMY AND ISSUES OF PROFESSIONALISM

• Elizabeth Thompson Butler, *The Roll Call*

Elizabeth Thompson (1846–1933) was born into a family that nurtured her talents. Her mother was a landscape painter and her father personally tutored his two
daughters. They lived abroad for much of their youth. Thompson's sister, the poet, es-

sayist, and critic Alice Meynell, became famous in her own right. In 1866, aged 19, Elizabeth Thompson began her studies at the Female School of Arts in South Kensington, where she remained until 1870.

Influenced by the contemporary French military paintings of artists such as Alphonse de Neuville, Edouard Detaille, and J. L. E. Meissonier, whose works Butler had seen in the Parisian Salon of 1870, her realistic, detailed image is a closeup view of the Crimean War from the point of view of the soldier. This subject was radically innovative. For the first time in British painting, a realistic, serious image from a past war is combined with the sensitive portrayal of individuals typical of Victorian genre paintings.[12]

Matthew Lalumia has convincingly argued that *The Roll Call* must be understood within the reformist climate of the early 1870s, specifically the "Cardwell Reforms" enacted following the election of the Gladstone ministry in 1868. In a series of bills, practices in effect in the British army for 200 years were abolished. The legislation introduced a merit system for promotions, reduced the enlistment period, and improved barracks life.[13]

The phenomenal success of *The Roll Call* (Fig. 12–3), exhibited in 1874, catapulted Butler to fame. She was nominated as an Associate of the Royal Academy in 1879, but failed to be elected by a narrow margin. Unlike many other Victorian women artists, whose paintings often addressed the female world as defined by Victorian discourses, Butler's ambition and urge for professionalism eschewed traditional female subjects for themes of war. That her sympathies were not with the generals but the foot soldiers is not surprising given her own highly marginalized position as a professional woman artist. Her success, perhaps, can also be attributed to her rejection of "women's subjects." However, her exclusion from admission to the Royal Academy merely underscores the enormous difficulties encountered by even the most brilliant, ambitious, and talented woman artist in the face of the masculine-dominated art institutions of Victorian England.

Fig. 12–3. Elizabeth Thompson Butler, *The Roll Call: Calling the Roll after an Engagement, Crimea.*   *(The Royal Collection © 1995 Her Majesty Queen Elizabeth II)*

Thompson's submission to the next Salon of 1875, *Quatre Bras*, enjoyed almost as extensive a reception. In fact, her successes encouraged a number of male artists to try to exploit the new market that Thompson's imagery had defined. Her preparation for *Quatre Bras*, recorded in her diary, emphasizes her attention to detail and desire for authenticity. The painting was hung in a dark central room, the "Black Hole" of the Royal Academy galleries. Despite this, Thompson writes: "They make a pet of me at the Academy." Usherwood suggests that the poor hanging of *Quatre Bras* was due to the fear that further concessions toward women artists, in particular Thompson's election to the Academy, might be expected. Although she lost her bid for election by only a few votes, the artist never stood for reelection. By the 1880s, the liberal, reformist climate and the Women's Movement itself had lost the zeal and momentum of the 1870s. Thompson's success within the Academy itself was a case of "tokenism" that failed to make any permanent changes in the bastion of patriarchal privilege that was the Royal Academy in Victorian England.[14]

After her marriage to William Butler in 1879, several factors influenced the course of her career: her change of name, her transient life as an officer's wife obliged to follow her husband to far-flung geographic locales, and the bearing and raising of six children. These circumstances interfered with her ability to paint as a professional. The artist also adopted many of Butler's liberal political views. However justified it may seem to us today, his mistrust of the motives of imperialist colonial policies was not popular in the conservative political climate of the 1880s. As Lady Butler selected topics consistent with her husband's unorthodox political positions, her reputation suffered.[15]

Suggestions for Further Reading

General Works

CASTERAS, SUSAN, *Images of Victorian Womanhood in English Art* (Rutherford, NJ: Associate University Presses, 1987).

CHERRY, DEBORAH, *Painting Women: Victorian Women Artists* (London: Routledge, 1993).

GERRISH NUNN, PAMELA, *Victorian Women Artists* (London: The Women's Press, 1987).

GILLETT, PAULA, *Worlds of Art: Painters in Victorian Society* (New Brunswick, NJ: Rutgers University Press, 1990).

MARSH, JAN, and PAMELA GERRISH NUNN, *Women Artists and the Pre-Raphaelite Movement* (London: Virago, 1989).

Cameron

The Cameron Collection/Julia Margaret Cameron, introduction by Colin Ford (New York: Van Nostrand Reinhold, 1975).

GERNSHEIM, HELMUT, *Julia Margaret Cameron: Her Life and Photographic Work* (Millerton, NY: Aperture, 1975).

Lady Butler

LALUMIA, MATTHEW, "Lady Elizabeth Thompson Butler in the 1870s," *Women's Art Journal* (Spring/Summer 1983), pp. 9–14.

USHERWOOD, PAUL, "Elizabeth Thompson Butler: The Consequences of Marriage," *Women's Art Journal* (Spring/Summer 1988), pp. 30–34.

USHERWOOD, PAUL, and JENNY SPENCER-SMITH, *Lady Butler (1846–1933): Battle Artist* (London: National Army Museum, 1987).

Chapter 13

• • • • • • • • • • • •

France:
1850–1900

The French Revolution extended legal rights and privileges to many more men than had previously enjoyed them, but it left women largely unaffected. Women remained perpetual legal minors. Despite this, women did make some gains toward improved rights during these upheavals. Marriage was deemed a civil contract. Women won legal protection for their property and inheritance rights. A leading champion of equality of education for women was the Marquis de Condorcet. Inspired by the American Declaration of Independence, Condorcet demanded increased educational and social opportunities for women as well as civil equality. In fact, the National Convention passed laws in 1794 and 1795 providing free and compulsory education for girls as well as boys. Unfortunately, the instability of the time prevented the implementation of these plans.[1]

The Napoleonic Code of 1804 reversed any gains women may have achieved. The Code strengthened the patriarchal authority of the husband and father, inspired by the Roman model of the *pater familias*. The right to divorce was abolished in 1815, not to be reinstated until 1884. When a French woman married, she forfeited virtually all of her legal rights.

In addition to legal and civil discrimination, women were also prevented from developing other options in their lives by the restrictions imposed on their educational and professional training. Lower-class women received virtually no education. In France, only after 1850 were towns required to provide primary education for girls. Middle- and upper-class women received a rudimentary education either in convent schools or with tutors in the home. As in the Renaissance, a woman's education tended to reinforce her predetermined life roles as wife and mother, rather than providing practical skills that might lead to financial self-sufficiency. Instruction in drawing and watercolor painting was part of this bourgeois curriculum because "Art" was considered an appropriate hobby for women, if forbidden as a professional career.

Slowly, during the second half of the nineteenth century, a few women entered European universities. In France the first woman enrolled in medical school in 1868; the law faculty admitted its first woman in 1884. University education remained a potential option for only a tiny percentage of women throughout this period.

The general tendency for women to be excluded from professional careers of all types explains the low absolute numbers of professional women artists at the beginning of the nineteenth century. However, during the course of the century, more and more women (as well as men) became practicing artists. In the French Salon of 1801, 28 women participated. By 1878, 762 women were exhibiting.[2] By 1900 thousands of women all over Europe were regularly displaying their works in official exhibitions.

More women turned to art due to increased access to training in public and private schools and artists' studios during the nineteenth century, although women's art education still remained discriminatory. The implementation of Labille-Guiard's idea (see page 105) occurred in 1805, when the first free drawing school for women was founded in Paris. In 1849, after the death of her father, Rosa Bonheur assumed the directorship of this school. By 1879 there were twenty such schools in Paris solely designed to train women for positions in the art industries, although such jobs were scarce and underpaid. In the first half of the nineteenth century, women could also study privately in the studios of established artists. During the 1870s there was a separate women's class at alternative schools such as the Académie Julian in Paris, where women worked with a model. As noted in Chapter 11, these studios attracted many American women aspiring to become professional artists. In 1896 the most prestigious art academy of France, the *Ecole des Beaux-Arts*, officially admitted women, thus removing the most obvious institutional barrier to equality of artistic training. This feminist victory was achieved only after seven years of sustained political pressure by the *Union des Femmes Peintres et Sculpteurs* (UFPS), the first professional organization of women artists in France, whose activities are discussed in this chapter.

REALISM

- ### Rosa Bonheur, *The Horse Fair*

Rosa Bonheur (1822–1899) was one of the most famous and popular French painters of her epoch. She devoted her entire career to painting animals, both domesticated and wild, in outdoor settings. Her style was based on a complete dedication to precise observation and the thorough study of animal anatomy characteristic of Realism. Many Romantic artists, such as Eugène Delacroix, Antoine-Louis Barye, and George Stubbs, chose to depict violent attacks of predatory animals when they selected subjects from the animal realm. Bonheur, by contrast, avoided bloody encounters between animals, preferring more peaceful situations that she could observe directly. Her innovative animal subjects, depicted with naturalism of detail, were greatly appreciated by her contemporaries. Numerous engravings after her compositions were circulated in Europe and America, ensuring her widespread popularity and fame. One indication of this success is her absence from the Salons. After 1853 she did not exhibit her paintings in those large exhibitions. She was able to maintain her financial independence from the proceeds of private sales and the income produced from engravings of her compositions.

Bonheur has the distinction of being the first woman artist to be honored with the highest award of the French government, the Cross of the Legion of Honor. Empress Eugenie of France presented the medal to Bonheur in her studio in 1865.

Born in Bordeaux, Bonheur received her initial training, along with the other children of the family, from her father. All four Bonheur siblings became competent *animaliers*, i.e., artists who specialized in animal subjects. She is the first woman artist in the nineteenth century whose upbringing was directly affected by the beliefs of the utopian philosophical movement known as St. Simonianism. Bonheur's father, Raymond, was an active member of the St. Simonians, who believed that both women and artists had special roles to play in the creation of the future perfect society. The St. Simonians prayed to "God, Father and Mother of us all."

While women gained a much higher status in this ideal, utopian community, it was assumed that the leaders of the group would be male. One can understand Raymond Bonheur's attraction to St. Simonianism since male artists were given an important leadership role: "It was taught that the religious side of the sect would be directed by the man of the most artistic nature, who would be the supreme priest."[3] Armed from childhood with a belief in the innate superiority and religious mission of both women and artists to transform society, Bonheur developed her talents to the fullest extent possible. Her dedication to her art was total and unequivocal.

Bonheur regularly proclaimed the superiority of the female sex. Late in her life, she told her biographer:

> Why would I not be proud to be a woman? My father . . . told me many times that the mission of women was to elevate the human race, to be the Messiah of future centuries. I owe to these doctrines the great and proud ambition I maintain for the sex to which I have the honor to belong. . . . I am certain that to us belongs the future.[4]

The deep emotional attachments of her life were only with other women. Bonheur never married, but lived for over forty years with a female companion, Natalie Micas. However, while Bonheur idealized women, she regularly wore male clothing, usually identified with the masculine point of view, and often referred to herself in masculine terms, such as "brother."[5] As Albert Boime has so perceptively noted, Bonheur's beliefs and lifestyle were an expression of revolt against the rigid polarizations of gender roles in her society. In place of the stereotypical male and female roles defined by her culture, she substituted a belief in an ideal androgyne, symbolizing a mystical union of the sexes. This revolt against social mores was paired with political views which were quite conservative. Bonheur's subjects were more acceptable to the Second Empire than the more overtly leftist political images of Courbet.

On many levels, Bonheur rejected her own society in favor of the animal kingdom, which she valued higher than that developed by mankind. Bonheur did not perceive a clear-cut separation between the animal and the human realms. She believed in metempsychosis, the migration of souls into animal forms. Thus, she could easily identify with animals and even referred to herself, on occasion, as an animal. Like the blurring of sexually defined characteristics, the blurring of distinctions between the animal and human worlds formed a fundamental part of her intellectual makeup. Although Bonheur acquired the rudimentary principles of painting from her father, the true basis upon which she built her images came from her studies of animals.

A Realist urge toward accuracy is clearly apparent in Bonheur's masterpiece *The Horse Fair* (Fig. 13–1). This large painting (over 16 feet wide) won immediate critical and popular acclaim for its creator, firmly establishing her reputation. It attracted large crowds when it was displayed in France, England, and America. Widely reproduced in engravings, this work became one of the most famous paintings of the nineteenth century. Bonheur said that *The Horse Fair* was originally inspired by the frieze of horsemen on the Parthenon. The even distribution of the horses across the picture surface and the processional movement from left to right do recall the Parthenon frieze. One can even see an echo of a Parthenon horseman in the man with an upraised arm, riding the rearing black horse in the center of the composition. However, instead of the classical restraint, simplicity, and slowly measured pace of the Parthenon frieze, Bonheur has presented an image of forceful energy, in which men and horses strain against one another. Another interesting comparison may be made with a painting by Theodore Gericault. Bonheur manages to endow her image with the same romantic spirit and energy that Gericault gave both his horse and rider in *Mounted Officer of the Imperial Guard* (1812).

In actuality, *The Horse Fair* was the result of a conscientious study of horses at a market that was located on the outskirts of Paris. Both the realism of details, the large scale, and the unified composition contribute to the powerful impression the work makes on the viewer. Bonheur has designed an unprecedented scene of great excitement, vividly portrayed, which places the viewer in the midst of the action as the horses are displayed in a circle. Her beliefs in the superiority of animals is evident in this composition by the dominant role played by the horses. In comparison, the humans look puny and insignificant.

Fig. 13–1. Rosa Bonheur, *The Horse Fair.* Oil on canvas, 96¼ x 199½ in. *(The Metropolitan Museum of Art; Gift of Cornelius Vanderbilt, 1887. All rights reserved, The Metropolitan Museum of Art, 87.25)*

James M. Saslow has identified the figure in the exact center of the composition, the only figure looking out at the viewer, as a self-representation of Bonheur in masculine guise. He argues for understanding Bonheur's cross-dressing as "an attempt to claim male perogatives and create an androgynous and proto-lesbian visual identity."[6]

Bonheur regularly worked in trousers and a loose smock throughout her life. Wearing male clothes or "transvestitism" was illegal and Bonheur needed to obtain repeated police permits to continue to wear pants, not just for the immediate necessity of frequenting the slaughterhouses for the preliminary studies for this painting. When control of dress falls into the realm of legal issues, we can see a clear example of the Second Empire's efforts to control and regulate deviant gender behavior. Social control operated through a number of channels, such as the popular press, in which a highly unflattering caricature of the artist appeared in 1899.[7] When we contrast Bonheur's image in *The Horse Fair* with equestrian portraits of Queen Victoria riding sidesaddle in elegant and obvious "feminine" costume, we can begin to appreciate the masculinized image Bonheur projects of herself in this work. Yet the presence of the self-portrait is overwhelmed here and in Bonheur's entire career by the depiction of animals.

As Whitney Chadwick notes, Bonheur's work was very popular in England. When Bonheur traveled to England with *The Horse Fair* in 1856, a private viewing of the painting was arranged for Queen Victoria. The work was engraved and widely distributed in that country. English patrons were Bonheur's strongest financial supporters, and Great Britain is the country in which she enjoyed her greatest fame in the 1860s and 1870s.

According to Chadwick, *The Horse Fair* should be situated with the public debate on animal rights and vivisection. There was a close identification between women and animals in Victorian culture. Anna Sewell's *Black Beauty*, published in 1877, is one example of this comparison between the plight of animals and women. "*Black Beauty* is, in fact, a feminist tract deploring the cruel oppression of all creatures, especially women and the working class."[8] The practices of the new medical science of gynecology in which women's bodies were placed under the control of "medical science" was paralleled by the use of animals in vivisection experiments.[9] Chadwick notes the use of terms identified with horses, in the language of Victorian pornography, and also in gynecology. For example, referring to the footrest on gynecological examination tables as "stirrups" is still common today.[10]

After 1860 Bonheur lived with Natalie Micas in relative isolation near Fontainebleau, where she continuously studied the natural beauty of the forest and surrounding farms. On the extensive grounds of her chateau, she kept a personal menagerie to permit her to observe a variety of animals.

Bonheur remained faithful to her form of Realism throughout her life, keeping her vision fresh and direct in all her works. Her intense powers of observation and her humility before the wonders of nature impressed her contemporaries, who frequently compared her art to the Dutch painters of the seventeenth century who set the standards for realistic description.

FEMINISM AND WOMEN ARTISTS

- ### Marie Bashkirtseff, *The Meeting*

Born into a family of minor Russian nobility, Marie Bashkirtseff (1859–1884) spent much of her youth in France, first in Nice, then Paris. This emigré status was, no doubt, due to her parents' separation when she was 11. Precociously bright, she had taught herself Greek and Latin by the age of 13. A career as a singer was contemplated, but the idea was abandoned with the onset of tuberculosis, the disease that would eventually lead to her premature death. In 1877 she decided to become an artist, entering the Atelier Julian. At that time, the segregated class at Julian's provided the most complete training in the visual arts available to women, though inferior to the training available to men at the *Ecole des Beaux-Arts*. Between 1877 and her death in 1884, Bashkirtseff created several hundred paintings, drawings, and pastels. She exhibited paintings at the Salons of 1880, 1881, and 1883. In 1884 she received a medal for her most famous painting, *The Meeting* (Fig. 13–2). Bashkirtseff aligned herself with the Naturalist school led by Jules Bastien-Lepage. The similarities in theme and technique between *The Meeting* and Bastien-Lepage's work were obvious even to Bashkirtseff's contemporaries.[11] However, the painting does demonstrate her ability to organize a large-scale, multifigured composition of a psychologically engaged group, realistically delineated. Like that of Bastien-Lepage, her style treads a middle ground between the more detailed, linear, conservative academic style and the looser, more visibly painterly surfaces of Impressionists like Morisot and Monet.

As early as the summer of 1882, she expressed interest in using subjects derived from the working-class street life in urban Paris. In the lives of these young boys, Bashkirtseff perceived "a liveliness and freedom from the artifices which she as a woman of the upper class experienced as restrictions on her life."[12] Her impatience and frustrations about her lack of autonomy and independence are clearly expressed in her journal entry, dated January 2, 1879:

> What I long for is the freedom of going about alone, of coming and going, of sitting on the seats in the Tuileries, and especially in the Luxembourg, of stopping and looking at the artistic shops, of entering the churches and museums, of walking about the old streets at night; that's what I long for; and that's the freedom without which one can't become a real artist. Do you imagine I can get much good from what I see, chaperoned as I am, and when, in order to go to the Louvre, I must wait for my carriage, my lady companion, or my family?
>
> Curse it all, it is this that makes me gnash my teeth to think I am a woman!

The Meeting was purchased by the French government and reproduced in engravings and lithographs. Two paintings by the artist were shown posthumously at the Salon of 1885. That year the *Union des Femmes Peintres et Sculpteurs*, the major organization of professional female artists in France, mounted an extensive retrospective of her works, which included over 200 paintings, drawings, and pastels, and five pieces of sculpture.

Bashkirtseff's fame resides in the posthumous publication of her journal. Her

Fig. 13–2. Marie Bashkirtseff, *The Meeting.*   *(Musée d'Orsay,
© photo R.M.N.)*

eighty-four handwritten notebooks were edited by her mother and first published in
France in 1887. Her ambition and self-absorption represented an entirely new phe-
nomenon to appear in print in her epoch. The diary was widely read and created a
sensation. Upon its translation and publication in English in 1890, one reviewer,
Marion Hepworth Dixon, wrote: "It is this Journal with which the world is now
ringing, and which it is hardly too much to say is likely to carry the fame of Marie
Bashkirtseff over the face of the civilized globe."[13]

THE *UNION DES FEMMES PEINTRES ET SCULPTEURS* (UFPS)
AND THE ADMISSION OF WOMEN TO THE *ECOLE DES BEAUX-ARTS*

In 1881, led by a powerful sculptor, Mme. Leon Bertaux, a group of French women
came together to form the first professional organization of women artists in France.
They called themselves the *Union des Femmes Peintres et Sculpteurs* (UFPS). From 41
founding members the organization grew to 450 members by 1896. This group led
the campaign to admit women into France's most prestigious art school, the *Ecole des
Beaux-Arts* in Paris. The sustained political pressure needed to achieve this victory has
been detailed by Tamar Garb.

The UFPS annual Salons were large exhibitions, which document the existence of a sizable population of women artists and the discriminatory conditions that existed regarding exhibiting their works. In the 1896 UFPS Salon, 295 women showed nearly 1,000 works. As Garb notes, quality was not the main criterion for including works in these exhibitions, since they existed as well to bring the awareness of women's art to public attention. Critics judged works by their "capacity to express an essential femininity, to encapsulate Woman."[14] Issues of quality were subsumed under other concerns of the "woman question." This contemporary discourse affected the critics' responses more than political affiliations. Portraits were the most plentiful genre of painting at the UFPS Salons, followed by flower studies, landscapes, still-lifes, genre scenes, and animal scenes. Paintings tended to be fairly small-scale, and history paintings were largely absent. Furthermore, most of the two-dimensional works were drawings, watercolors, and pastels. The predominance of these media was "used repeatedly as concrete evidence of women's propensity and skill in certain types of art and as tangible demonstration of their unsuitability for others."[15]

The art education available to women was a prime concern of the UFPS. After seven years of sustained political lobbying, this organization, now led by Virginie Demont-Breton, achieved an important victory, the admission of women in 1896 to France's most prestigious art academy, the *Ecole des Beaux-Arts.* The Union did uphold the gender ideology which defined women's "nature" as that of wife and mother. The leadership of the UFPS perceived the creation of art as compatible with women's family responsibilities. Feminists, from a broad range of political positions, could champion the rights of women artists.

Mme. Bertaux was inspired by a Utopian dream to use the art of women for the redemption of a decadent France: "The flowering of an *art féminin* was . . . a Utopian vision which entailed the valourising of women's talent and the flowering of a feminine culture long stifled by men's selfish monopolisation of resources and arrogant self-aggrandisement."[16]

IMPRESSIONISM

• Berthe Morisot, *Lady at Her Toilette*

Berthe Morisot (1841–1895) was one of the founding members of the avant-garde group known as the Impressionists. Like the other members of the group, Morisot devoted her career to the creation of images that depict, with elegance and spontaneity, intimate scenes from daily life. Often using her family as models, Morisot's paintings permit the viewer to enter a closed domestic realm populated mainly by women and children.

Morisot's art is characterized by delicate brushwork and elegant colors, juxtaposed in subtle harmonies. These "feminine" qualities of her paintings were regularly noted by critics evaluating her works but are actually stylistic elements also found in the paintings of her male Impressionist colleagues. Both technically and thematically, Morisot belongs with the Impressionists. Her exhibition strategy was the same as that of Renoir, Monet, Degas, or Pissarro, because she also avoided the official Salon and submitted her works only to the private group shows held between 1874 and 1886.

There was little in her background to predispose her to the life of a dedicated avant-garde artist. Morisot was born in Bourges into an upper-middle-class family. When she was 7, the family moved to Paris. She and her sister, Edma, were given drawing lessons at an early age. Both sisters showed greater dedication to their art than was expected from or appropriate for women of their class. One of their teachers, Joseph Alexandre Guichard, warned Mme. Morisot:

> Considering the characters of your daughters, my teaching will not endow them with minor drawing room accomplishments; they will become painters. Do you realize what this means? In the upper class milieu to which you belong, this will be revolutionary. I might almost say catastrophic. Are you sure that you will not come to curse the day when art, having gained admission to your home, now so respectable and peaceful, will become the sole arbiter of the fate of two of your children?[17]

In 1861 the Morisot sisters were introduced to Camille Corot, who became their mentor for the next five years. Berthe Morisot's early paintings reveal Corot's influence in the rendition of effects of early morning light and in the closely toned color harmonies in her landscapes.

In one of her few surviving landscapes from the 1860s, *Thatched Cottage in Normandy* (1865), Morisot had moved far beyond Corot's technique to create what could be defined as the most sophisticated use of paint to indicate grass and foliage of any of her Impressionist colleagues. The work exhibits a remarkable versatility in handling paint as light and texture that will only be achieved by Monet, for example, later in the 1870s at Argenteuil.[18]

In 1868 Morisot met Edouard Manet and, through him, most of the members of the Impressionist group. Morisot encouraged Manet to take up painting outdoors. In 1874 she married his younger brother, Eugène Manet. Although Edma stopped painting after her marriage, Berthe pursued her career throughout her lifetime, with only a brief interruption for the birth of her daughter.

Lady at Her Toilette is one of a series of images by Morisot which are focused on an anonymous female in the privacy of her boudoir. Charles Stuckey relates this work to a painting by Manet of a similar subject.[19] It demonstrates Morisot's ambition to conquer all the subjects of contemporary life explored in the art of her male colleagues, despite the inherent difficulties of identifying with the female figure as an object of aesthetic or sexual attraction, a gendered response more appropriate to a male artist and/or viewer.

The canvas is filled with a flood of active brushstrokes of high valued, closely related tones revealing Morisot's superb, mature technique. Local color and specific object textures are subordinated to the energy of visible paint. Whether articulating the two-dimensional surfaces of mirror and wall or the three-dimensional figure, Morisot's paint dominates in a manner similar to the gestural force of the Abstract Expressionists of the post-World War II era.

As a full-fledged member of the Impressionist group, Berthe Morisot occupies a secure position in the history of art. United by common interests with the Impres-

Fig. 13–3. Berthe Morisot, *Lady at Her Toilet.* c. 1875. Oil on canvas, 60.3 x 80.4 cm. *(photograph © 1995, The Art Institute of Chicago. All Rights Reserved. Stickney Fund, 1924.127)*

sionists, Morisot developed a personal style of originality, fluidity, and delicacy. Along with her male colleagues and Cassatt, Morisot and the others in the Impressionist group valued the private women's world of home and family and created pleasantly delightful images of beauty and elegance.

- ### Mary Cassatt, *Woman with a Pearl Necklace in a Loge*

Like Berthe Morisot, Mary Cassatt (1844–1926) was an active and loyal member of the Impressionist group. Born in Pittsburgh into an upper-middle-class family similar in status to Morisot's, Cassatt also possessed the personal strength and force of her convictions to pursue a career as an avant-garde painter, eschewing official recognition and juried competitions. Stimulated by the exciting environment of Paris, Cassatt became, in the view of many scholars, the best American artist, male or female, of her generation.

Cassatt overrode her family's initial resistance to her decision to become an artist. In 1861 she entered the Pennsylvania Academy of Fine Arts, one of the first art academies in the world to open its doors to women. After four years of study there, she recognized the limitations that America imposed on artists. Like the women of the "White Marmorean Flock" and many male and female artists of her generation, she traveled to Europe in the late 1860s to study the old masters. After 1872 she settled permanently in Paris and pursued her artistic training. Her sister Lydia and her parents joined her in 1877. Although she became most famous for her paintings of mothers and children, Cassatt never married. She continued to paint until the age of 70 when her eyesight began to fail. Her achievement was recognized, relatively late in her life, by the award of the medal of the French Legion of Honor in 1904.

Cassatt possessed a brilliant instinct for determining what the history of art has deemed most important in the confusingly active world of late-nineteenth-century Paris. She told her biographer that by the late 1870s, when Degas invited her to participate in the Impressionist exhibitions, "I had already recognized who were my true masters. I admired Manet, Courbet and Degas. I hated conventional art. I began to live."[20] Cassatt learned from these artists without losing her individuality and personal style.

In the late 1870s and 1880s, Cassatt's works reflect the influence of Impressionism. *Woman with a Pearl Necklace in a Loge* (Fig. 13–4), a painting of the artist's sister, Lydia, was exhibited in the fourth Impressionist exhibition of 1879 and is characteristic of Impressionism in several ways. Degas and Renoir had previously painted women at the opera, so the subject is typical of the Impressionists' taste for scenes of the amusements of Parisian life. The relaxed asymmetrical pose of the sitter, with one arm cropped by the picture frame, is also a typical Impressionist device. Degas would often "cut" his figures to convey a sense of immediacy, almost like a snapshot photo. In this painting, Cassatt was extremely interested in the effects of artificial light on

Fig. 13–4. Mary Cassatt, *Woman with a Pearl Necklace in a Loge.* 1879. Oil on canvas, 31⅝ x 23 in. *(Philadelphia Museum of Art, Bequest of Charlotte Dorrance Wright)*

flesh tones. Like Degas's studies of ballerinas on the stage, also illuminated by artificial gas lights, Lydia's face and shoulders are unnaturally radiant. Despite these glowing effects of artificial light, the figure is firmly modeled and her contours are well defined. Brushstrokes are evident in Lydia's dress, fan, and the reflected background. The spontaneity of Cassatt's touch is another element that connects her style with Impressionism. This work is painted with a sophisticated and original color sensibility. The pink dress is beautifully contrasted with the ruby-red banquette. The colors shimmer and sparkle in the gaslight of the theater at intermission. An innovative aspect of this work is the use of a mirrored background. This device conveys a reflection of the space, in which the viewer must also sit, without creating an actual illusion or description of deep space. Thus, the picture includes an image of the environment of the opera without violating the flat two-dimensionality of the picture surface. Cassatt's use of a mirrored background anticipates Manet's similar use of a mirror in his famous work, *The Bar at the Folies-Bergères* (1881–82).

Pollock has mapped out the physical spaces of masculinity and femininity in late-nineteenth-century Paris to elucidate the relationship between the territory of modernism and the dominant position of male painter and spectator in that formulation. The theme of women at the opera fascinated Cassatt precisely because it is one of the few physical places in which the private spaces of femininity, such as balconies and interiors, and the public spaces of popular entertainment intersect. Cassatt was sensitive both as an upper-middle-class woman and as an artist to the boundaries of these spaces and the places where they can be bridged. Pollock defines this issue as the "problematic of women out in public being vulnerable to a compromising gaze." The act of being looked at was a factor of risk for the middle-class woman in this epoch. "To enter such spaces as the masked ball or the café-concert constituted a serious threat to a bourgeois woman's reputation and therefore her femininity. The guarded respectability of the lady could be soiled by mere visual contact for seeing was bound up with knowing."[21] This image exists, therefore, on a "frontier of the spaces of femininity," the place of demarcation between the public/private dichotomy so crucial to women of the bourgeoisie living in urban environments such as Paris in the nineteenth century.

- **Mary Cassatt, *The Coiffure***

Mary Cassatt also made an important contribution to the history of printmaking. In 1891, inspired by an exhibition of Japanese woodblock prints, she created a series of ten prints using an unprecedented technique. *The Coiffure* (Fig. 13–5) was created with a combination of etching and engraving techniques. Cassatt applied the beautiful and subtle earth-toned inks directly to the copper plate for each print. Each image is executed with the strictest economy of lines.

Both Griselda Pollock and Anne Higonnet address the complexities of the woman artist of the avant-garde confronting the female nude. Pollock is interested in the class relationship between nude model and female artist and notes that the nudity of these women defines them as working class, probably domestic servants.[22] Higonnet discusses the ways in which women artists were positioned differently in the act of painting the female nude:

Fig. 13–5. Mary Cassatt, *The Coiffure*. c. 1891. Drypoint and soft-ground etching in color, 17 x 12¼ in.   *(Chester Dale Collection, © 1995 Board of Trustees, National Gallery of Art, Washington)*

If she [the woman artist] painted a female nude she would be painting a kind of reflection of her own body. She would therefore have to transform desire into being desired and enjoy pleasure by giving pleasure. For a woman who wanted to do the looking—and no one, arguably, needs to look more actively than an artist—identifying with a masculine point of view meant being two contradictory things at once: the one who looks and the one who is looked at. To paint a successful nude demanded that a woman artist paint a version of her own body and offer it completely to masculine viewers.[23]

This is the only image of frontal nudity in Cassatt's oeuvre, and Higonnet argues that it is closely related to Morisot's *At the Psyche*. Both works use a mirrored image as the "crux" of the work. "The mirror warns that the nude offered for our sensual pleasure might only be an image. By reframing their nudes within the mirror Cassatt and Morisot remind us that we are looking at the picture, not a person."[24] Higonnet stresses the importance of Japanese prints for both artists. We know that Cassatt was very enthused and invited Morisot to attend with her the exhibition of Japanese prints at the *Ecole des Beaux-Arts* in the Summer of 1890.

Neither Cassatt nor Morisot attempted the male nude. This was a theme outside their world. To their generation "the nude" meant "the female nude." Women artists would have lacked any technical training to study male anatomy with live male models, as well as the logistics to paint them.[25] As the Stephens image shows (Fig. 11–6), even in Eakins's class at the Pennsylvania Academy, the most "advanced" art school, women were only permitted to study the female, not the male, nude.

Griselda Pollock has termed such highly compressed pictorial environments, so prevalent in the compositions of both Morisot and Cassatt, as "the spaces of femininity." She argues convincingly for an interpretation of such shallow picture spaces as a comment on the restricted sphere of movement permitted women of this class in nineteenth century France.[26]

Mary Cassatt possessed both superb technical skills and great talent. Her dedication and devotion to the highest standards for her art helped her overcome the "handicap" of being a woman. As an American in Paris, at a time when Paris was the center of the art world, she absorbed the best innovations in her contemporary world of painting. Cassatt developed an independent style based on precise draftsmanship, refined color sensibility, and a gift for creative compositions.

Suggestions for Further Reading

Bonheur

ASHTON, DORE, and DENISE BROWNE HARE, *Rosa Bonheur: A Life and Legend* (New York: Viking, 1981).

BOIME, ALBERT, "The Case of Rosa Bonheur: Why Should a Woman Want to Be More Like a Man?" *Art History*, 4 (December 1981).

STANTON, THEODORE, *Reminiscences of Rosa Bonheur* (London, 1910; reprinted by Hacker Art Books, 1976).

Bashkirtseff

The Journal of Marie Bashkirtseff, trans. Mathilde Blind, introduction by Roszika Parker and Griselda Pollock (London: Virago Press, 1985).

UFPS

GARB, TAMAR, *Sisters of the Brush: Women's Artistic Culture in Late Nineteenth-Century Paris* (New Haven, CT: Yale University Press, 1994).

Women Impressionists

GARB, TAMAR, *Women Impressionists* (New York: Rizzoli, 1986).

POLLOCK, GRISELDA, "Modernity and the Spaces of Femininity" in *Vision and Difference: Femininity, Feminism, and the History of Art* (London: Routledge, 1988).

Morisot

ADLER, KATHLEEN, and TAMAR GARB, *Berthe Morisot* (Ithaca, NY: Cornell University Press, 1987).

EDELSON, T.J. (ed.), *Perspectives on Morisot* (NY: Hudson Hills Press, 1990).

HIGONNET, ANNE, *Berthe Morisot* (New York: Harper and Row, 1990).

HIGONNET, ANNE, *Berthe Morisot's Images of Women* (Cambridge, MA: Harvard University Press, 1992).

ROUART, DENIS (ed.), *The Correspondence of Berthe Morisot* (London: Lund Humphries, 1957, republished 1986).

STUCKEY, CHARLES F., and WILLIAM P. SCOTT, *Berthe Morisot: Impressionist* (New York: Hudson Hills Press, Mount Holyoke College Art Museum in Association with the National Gallery of Art, 1987).

Cassatt

BREESKIN, ADYLYN, *Mary Cassatt: A Catalogue Raisonné of the Oils, Pastels, Watercolors and Drawings* (Washington, DC: Smithsonian Institution Press, 1970).

HALE, NANCY, *Mary Cassatt* (Garden City, NY: Doubleday, 1975).

MATHEWS, NANCY MOWLL, *Cassatt and Her Circle: Selected Letters* (New York: Abbeville Press, 1984).

MATHEWS, NANCY MOWLL, *Mary Cassatt* (New York: Abrams, in association with the National Museum of American Art, Smithsonian Institution, 1987).

MATHEWS, NANCY MOWLL, *Mary Cassatt: The Color Prints* (New York: Abrams, 1989).

Chapter 14

· · · · · · · · · · ·

The Early
Twentieth Century:
1900–1940

GERMAN EXPRESSIONISTS: 1900–1910

German women who aspired to become artists acquired their training under highly discriminatory conditions. As late as the 1890s, women were still not permitted to study at the state-sponsored art academies in Germany or Austria. Women wishing to pursue a career in the visual arts could attend applied- and decorative-arts schools in Germany. But the official government schools for "fine arts" were closed to them. In response, the Verein der Künstlerinnen, the official women's art organization, ran independent schools in Berlin, Munich, and Karlsruhe, organized around a traditional academic curriculum.

This reflected the broader educational climate of Germany, since all German schools were sexually segregated. This situation differed from that of the women's art organizations of England and France, which sought to integrate women students into the male educational establishments, the Royal Academy in England or the *Ecole des Beaux-Arts* in France.

The Berlin school was opened sometime before 1885, when Käthe Kollwitz was enrolled. According to Diane Radycki, this school cost six times the tuition of the Prussian Royal Academy and offered a shorter, less rigorous course of study.[1]

If the goal was to prepare women artists for the Prussian Academy of Art, the difficulties of achieving full status were virtually insurmountable. The Prussian Academy conveyed only "honorary"—not regular—membership to women artists, the same category of membership available to males who were not artists but helped promote the arts in some manner. It was only in 1919, after the collapse of the Wilhelmine government, that Kathë Kollwitz became the first woman member of the Prussian Academy of Fine Arts. She held the directorship of the Graphic Arts department from 1928 until her resignation under Nazi pressure in 1933.

Paula Modersohn-Becker, Käthe Kollwitz, and Gabriele Münter may all be characterized as Expressionists (as defined by Shulamith Behr) despite their diverse styles and themes. Behr rightly points out that any number of male Expressionist artists did not paint in a uniform group style.[2] The three women developed original and unique avant-garde styles independently.

- **Paula Modersohn-Becker,** *Self-Portrait with Amber Necklace*

Before her premature death at the age of 31, Paula Modersohn-Becker (1876–1907) was working in an innovative style based on a synthesis of French Post-Impressionism and native German art forms. Her mature paintings, which include some recognized masterpieces, reveal a talented and original artist whose works bear comparison with the best paintings of her European contemporaries in the Post-Impressionist era.

Paula Becker was born in Dresden, Germany, into a cultured, upper-middle-class family. She first became interested in becoming an artist when, at age 16, she was given art lessons as part of her finishing school education. Visiting wealthy relatives in London, she attended St. John's Wood School of Art, which prepared students for admission to the Royal Academy.

As Radycki notes, when Becker studied at the St. John's Wood School in London, a private drawing school but one with the best reputation of preparing students for the Royal Academy, she was in a serious, coeducational environment aimed at conferring professional status and expertise.[3] This situation contrasted markedly with the Berlin school of the Verein der Künstlerinnen. By the time Becker arrived there, in 1896, there were separate departments of drawing, painting, and graphics. Four of the six male teachers were affiliated with the Prussian Academy. A few women also taught there. Käthe Kollwitz joined the faculty and taught figure drawing and graphics from 1897 to 1902.

After two years of this traditional instruction, Becker moved to the artists' colony located in Worpswede, a small village in northern Germany. The Worpswede artists, such as Fritz Mackensen and Otto Modersohn, used the local peasants and the bleak landscape as subjects and painted with a dark earth-toned, naturalistic palette. Becker studied with Mackensen and at first adopted the realistic style of this painter.

On New Year's Eve, 1900, Becker left Worpswede for Paris. This was her first visit to the world's art capital. Over the next seven years, Becker spent long periods in Paris, where she acquired more art training and absorbed the latest developments in French avant-garde painting. Becker joined many other women artists who were studying art in Paris at the turn of the century. She worked at the Académie Colarossi where, for a small fee, an aspiring artist could paint or draw from the live model and receive some criticism from established masters. Becker also benefited from the recent opening of classes to women at the *Ecole des Beaux-Arts.*

Returning to Worpswede, Becker married the recently widowed Otto Modersohn in 1901. Even after marriage, Modersohn-Becker continued to make independent journeys to Paris. In 1903, 1905, and during a prolonged stay from February 1906 to April 1907, she abandoned the style of Worpswede naturalism for an avant-garde method that attained a greatly simplified monumentality.

Her *Self-Portrait with Amber Necklace* (Fig. 14–1) was created during this prolonged stay in Paris. It is a fascinating work, both formally and iconographically. The painting clearly reveals the impact of contemporary avant-garde French painting. The densely painted surface and saturated colors are indebted to Van Gogh, while the smoothly flowing synthetic contours and frontal nudity relate the work to Gauguin's Tahitian imagery, exhibited at the Salon d'Automne, 1906. The generalized form and

Fig. 14–1. Paula Modersohn-Becker, *Self-Portrait with Amber Necklace*. 1906. Oil on canvas, 24$^1/_2$ x 19 in. *(Offentliche Kunstsammlung, Basil)*

darkened contours also show her knowledge of Cézanne's late bather paintings, although Modersohn-Becker was back in Worpswede by the time of the major retrospective of Cézanne's works at the Salon d'Automne in 1907, mentioned in a letter to Clara Rilke-Westhoff. As in Artemisia Gentileschi's *Self-Portrait as the Allegory of Painting* (Fig. 8–10), the artist here compresses two traditions: the active male realm of artistic creation with the female world of the instinctual, the natural, the fertile and vegetal. She is both passive receptacle of nature's processes and active formulator of her own self-image. Remarkably, she is both present, in the features of her face and her treasured amber necklace, and distanced from her own image, in the simplified forms and generalized features of the abstracted nude body.

This was one of hundreds of works labeled as "degenerate" by the Nazis and confiscated in 1937. It was shipped to Switzerland and auctioned in 1939; it survived the war there and today hangs in the Basel Kunstmuseum.

- **Paula Modersohn-Becker,** *Kneeling Mother and Child*

In this painting Modersohn-Becker has created an image that is outside any historical framework, an impersonal archetype of fertility. As opposed to Cassatt's mothers and children, which are always portraits, or Kollwitz's mothers, who are forces for political change, Becker emphasizes the biology of creation. It is important to appreciate the different messages these images communicate. Women artists often approach the specifically female experience of maternity, as well as every other subject, in distinctive ways. Factors such as nationality, political views, and family background influence the outlook and philosophy of an artist at least as much as, and perhaps more than, the artist's sex. Becker's *Kneeling Mother and Child* is related more closely to Gauguin's paintings of Tahitians than to the works of Cassatt or Kollwitz.

As early as 1898 Modersohn-Becker was attracted to the theme of the nursing mother. She wrote in her journal:

> I sketched a young mother with her child at her breast, sitting in a smoky hut. If only I could someday paint what I felt then! A sweet woman, an image of charity. She was nursing her big, year-old bambino, when with defiant eyes her four-year-old daughter snatched for her breast until she was given it. And the woman gave her life and her youth and her power to the child in utter simplicity, unaware that she was a heroine.

Behr believes her interest in the motif was reinforced by her familiarity with the Swedish writer Ellen Key, whose book *Lines of Life* (1903) "considered the positive and cultural implications of motherhood within the general advance of women's rights."[4]

Fig. 14–2. Paula Modersohn-Becker, *Kneeling Mother and Child*. 1907. Oil on canvas, 113 x 74 cm. *(Staatliche Museen zu Berlin—Preussischer Kulturbesitz Nationalgalerie)*

Otto Modersohn followed his wife to Paris in 1906. She became pregnant and returned with him to Worpswede in 1907. It is possible that Becker was already pregnant when she painted *Kneeling Mother and Child*. She died three weeks after giving birth to a daughter, tragically ending a career that had just reached maturity. Nevertheless, she had lived long enough to create a group of paintings of great artistic power and originality. As the first German artist to forge an original style that incorporated the innovations of French painting from the 1890s, her importance within the European Post-Impressionist avant-garde is firmly established.

- ### Käthe Kollwitz, *Outbreak*

Käthe Kollwitz (1867–1945) shares a common nationality and generation with Paula Modersohn-Becker. However, aside from the fact that both women created works of great force and originality often focused on women's primordial role as mother, their styles are quite distinct.

From the beginning of her career, Kollwitz chose to concentrate on drawings and prints in black and white. Her self-imposed restriction to the graphic media stems from both personal inclination and political conviction. While still an art student, Kollwitz was fascinated by the demands of the printmaking process. She did not feel the need of color to express her powerful political messages. A print is less expensive than a painting because a number of original copies can be made from one source. Therefore, Kollwitz's graphics could be bought if not by the destitute workers, whom she depicted so sympathetically, then at least by the middle-class people who shared her political beliefs.

Käthe Schmidt was born into an unusual family in the small Baltic seaport of Königsberg (now Kaliningrad). Her father was an ardent believer in socialism and an activist in the Social Democratic Worker's Party. Käthe absorbed these political beliefs, and throughout her lifetime her works express her sympathies for the oppressed poor and her strongly anticapitalist convictions. Her family encouraged her artistic talents and gave her drawing lessons with a local artist. In 1885 she studied art in Berlin at the school for women established by the Verein der Kunstlerinnen. After a few years at home, in 1889 she entered the Verein's school in Munich where the cultural environment was more stimulating.

In 1884 she became engaged to Karl Kollwitz, who shared her family's political convictions. Fearful that marriage might interfere with her ambition to become an artist, she postponed the wedding until 1891, when Karl had completed his medical studies and was a practicing doctor in a working-class neighborhood in Berlin. During the 1890s she bore two sons and worked on her first major graphic series, *The Revolt of the Weavers*, completed in 1897. The work was inspired by a play that told the true story of the 1844 armed rebellion of a group of destitute linen weavers in the German province of Silesia. This subject contains many recurrent themes that Kollwitz was to illustrate throughout the rest of her life: the misery of the impoverished working classes, the omnipresence of death, and a sympathy with armed revolt to improve inhuman conditions. *The Revolt of the Weavers* was greeted with great critical praise when it was displayed in 1898. The six prints that constitute this work established Kollwitz as one of Germany's leading graphic artists. Although she was nominated for a gold medal, the Kaiser denied her the award because of the radically leftist political content of the series.

Kollwitz's next major print cycle. *The Peasant War* (1902–8), was inspired by an uprising of German peasants in the sixteenth century. Kollwitz believed that women could be a force for political change, and she was attracted to this particular event because the leader of the revolt was a woman, known as Black Anna. *Outbreak* (Fig. 14–3) depicts Black Anna inciting the men, who are armed with primitive weapons. In this extraordinarily powerful image, a peasant army races across the scene with a seemingly invincible force. Here Kollwitz retained enough descriptive details to characterize the individual features of the peasants, and there is an element of naturalism in the figure of Black Anna. The tension of the scene is intensified by presenting Black Anna with her back to the viewer. Kollwitz used her own body as a model for her great back. In this manner, emotion and energy are expressed through posture and gesture rather than mere facial expression. Technically, Kollwitz employed a mixture of etching techniques, aquatint, and soft ground to achieve the range of textures, shadings, and details of the finished work.

The experience of World War I was a great trauma for Kollwitz. In 1914 her son

Fig. 14–3. Käthe Kollwitz, *Outbreak*. 1903. Mixed technique, 20 x 23$\frac{1}{4}$ in. *(Courtesy of the Library of Congress)*

Peter was killed in Belgium. Kollwitz channeled her grief and fury into many prints and sculpture in which she made statements about the futility of war and the destruction of young sons.

Kollwitz's humanitarianism is so self-evident in the themes of her work that it is also important to remember that she resisted specific political affiliations. As Elizabeth Prelinger notes, her pre-World War I work did not generally carry revolutionary or even specifically political overtones. While her compassion was sincere and universal, she remained indecisive in her political beliefs.[5]

Kollwitz's later works continue to explore the themes that had fascinated her in her youth. Many images focus on the horrors of sudden death, the pains and joys of motherhood, and the injustice of the economic exploitation and political oppression of one class by another. Avoiding the abstraction and stylistic innovations of many avant-garde artists, Kollwitz maintained a somewhat naturalistic style throughout her career, although her works became more simplified and forms more generalized in the 1920s and 1930s. Her talents were widely recognized during her lifetime. In 1919 she became the first woman to be elected to the Prussian Academy of the Arts. In 1928 she became director of graphic arts at this school. It was not until the Nazis assumed power in Germany that, like so many other artists, she experienced discrimination and was forced to resign from the Academy in 1933.

Kollwitz's compassion extended not only to the oppressed but also to her fellow women artists who were not as famous as herself. She was elected president of the Frauenkunstverband (Women's Art Union) in 1914. The main goal of this group was "securing the right of women to teach and study in all public art schools."[6] In 1926 she helped found GEDOK (Society for Women Artists and Friends of Art), a feminist organization "dedicated to showing, sponsoring, and contributing to the work of women artists."[7]

Kollwitz continued working into her seventies. She witnessed the annihilation of yet another generation of German youth in World War II. Her grandson, Peter, named after the son who had perished in World War I, also died in battle. The works she left to posterity are loaded with the fullest possible range of human emotions. Her images express her convictions as a woman, a mother, and a political being. They are frequently painful and always emotionally stirring.

- ### Gabriele Münter, *Boating*

Gabriele Münter (1877–1962), like Kollwitz and Modersohn-Becker, studied at the school of the Verein der Kunstlerinnen. Dissatisfied with the level of instruction there, she enrolled in Wassily Kandinsky's class at the "alternative" Phalanx School in 1902. As Anne Mochon notes, Kandinsky "was the first teacher to offer her consistent and careful instruction which recognized and respected the intuitive nature of her ability."[8] From 1903 to 1914 Münter and Kandinsky lived, traveled, and worked together. In 1908 they settled in Murnau, a small village in the Bavarian Alps. *Boating* was painted during the summer of 1910 on the lake at Murnau, the Staffelsee.

In Murnau, Münter and Kandinsky were close friends with the Russian artist-

Fig. 14–4. Gabriele Münter, *Boating.* 1910. Oil on canvas, 49¹/₄ x 28⁷/₈ in. *(Milwaukee Art Museum, Gift of Mrs. Harry Lynde Bradley)*

couple Alexei Jawlensky and Marianne von Werefkin. Jawlensky had been in Matisse's studio in 1907 and was familiar with the Symbolist theories of Paul Sérusier. All four artists exhibited at the first show of the New Artists' Association in 1909.

Boating is one of three versions of the theme executed that summer. It is the largest one, and it may be the work exhibited at the Munich New Artists' Association show of 1910 and at the Salon des Independents of 1912 in Paris.

The painting is a record of the importance of Münter's relationships in this period. The little boy is Jawlensky and Werefkin's son, Andreas. The seated woman in the red hat is Werefkin, who was seventeen years older than Münter. Münter's admiration for her is documented in at least one portrait.[9]

Dominating the composition at the apex of the triangle is the standing figure of Kandinsky, silhouetted against the green field and blue mountains of the background. However, one cannot ignore the fact that it is Münter herself who steers the boat.

Positioned with her back to the viewer, she is looking at this scene, controlling both the viewpoint and the safety of her passengers. With the approaching storm, indicated by the dark grey sky, her role as oarsman is crucial and unique. The broad expanse of her back, painted in an unmodulated flesh tone, is centered in the composition and provides the zone of highest value attracting the viewer's eye to the lower half of the composition. This visually balances the shapes of the upper portion, i.e., the figure of Kandinsky, the mountains, and the threatening grey sky.

In 1911 Münter participated in the activities surrounding the new avant-garde group, the Blue Rider. But World War I proved to be a time of great disruption for Münter. She moved to Stockholm in 1915 when Kandinsky returned to Russia. When Kandinsky married another woman in 1917, Münter's painting production tapered off dramatically. She never again found an avant-garde community in which her artistic practice could truly flourish.

THE AVANT-GARDE IN EUROPE: 1914–1925

Simultanism

- **Sonia Terk-Delaunay, *Electric Prisms***

Just before World War I Sonia Delaunay (1885–1979) created a painting system that employed brilliantly colored discs to create an effect of rhythmic movement. Her style, known as "Simultanism," is an important and influential contribution to twentieth-century avant-garde painting. Sonia Delaunay possessed a finely developed sensitivity to colors and their interrelationships.

Born in the Ukraine in 1885, at the age of 5 Sonia was adopted by her maternal uncle, Henry Terk, and raised in the wealthy, cultured environment of his home in St. Petersburg. Sonia Terk's artistic talents were encouraged, and from 1903 to 1905 she studied art in Germany. Her artistic training began in earnest when she arrived in Paris in 1905. Like Modersohn-Becker, who was also in Paris during these years, Terk absorbed the latest developments of French Post-Impressionism and Fauvism.

In 1908 she had her first one-woman exhibition in the gallery of Wilhelm Uhde, but she did not exhibit her works in public again until 1953. The following year she married Uhde, but she divorced him in 1910 to marry the painter Robert Delaunay (1885–1941). Each of their talents complemented the other's, and their lives became a team effort that enhanced their individual gifts. Both Sonia and Robert Delaunay acknowledged the influence the other exerted on his or her art, especially between 1910 and 1914 when they both were formulating their definitive styles.

A major turning point in Sonia Delaunay's development was triggered by the creation of a quilt for her infant son in 1911. Unlike the American quilt makers discussed in Chapter 11, Delaunay was prepared to appreciate the possibilities of this abstract language for painting. The results of this breakthrough were soon visible in her work.

Electric Prisms (Fig. 14–5) is one of her most important pre-World War I paint-

Fig. 14–5. Sonia Delaunay, *Electric Prisms*. 1914. Oil on canvas, 98$\frac{1}{2}$ x 98$\frac{1}{2}$ in. *(Musée National d'Art Moderne)*

ings. This large canvas (about 8 feet square) was inspired by the electric lamps that had recently replaced gaslights on the Parisian boulevards. Using concentric circles divided into quadrants, the alternating and repeating colors create an optical effect of pulsating, brilliant light. These colored sections are arranged in a complex pattern of disks and are divided by straight lines and waving arclike sections.

The exploration and depiction of "colored rhythms" or "rhythms of color" (both frequent titles of her works) was to be Delaunay's lifelong obsession. Her paintings, gouaches, and other two-dimensional works show a ceaseless inventiveness in the arrangement of colors to express movement and syncopation. Musical analogies seem unavoidable in the description of her pictorial language because she uses colored units like notes in a musical scale. Delaunay employs only the most basic elements of painting to construct her works. She defined her aesthetic system in the following way:

> The pure colors becoming planes and opposing each other by simultaneous contrasts create, for the first time, new constructed forms, not through chiaroscuro but through the depth of color itself.[10]

The term "simultaneous contrasts" refers to Chevreul's law, which states that when two complementary colors, such as red and green, are juxtaposed, their contrast is intensified. Delaunay once explained her devotion to abstraction by stating: "Beauty refuses to submit to the constraint of meaning or description."[11]

Delaunay lost her personal income during the Russian Revolution, so after World War I she turned increasingly to commercial, income-producing activities. She became a successful and highly innovative fashion designer. In 1925, at the famous and influential International Exhibition of Decorative Arts, she displayed her fashions and fabrics at a "Boutique simultanée." Vivid colors and geometric patterns characterize her textile designs, which were shown as loose-fitting full skirts and tunics. Such styles, which liberated the wearer from the confines of the wasp-waisted, corsetted, pre-War silhouette, were very popular in the new culture of the 1920s. The Depression of 1929 put her out of business. Sonia Delaunay's activity in the decorative arts industry demonstrated her unorthodox, independent attitude toward the conventional hierarchies of fine versus applied art and male versus female realms.[12] She did not perceive her activities outside of easel painting as inherently less important or intellectually demanding.

The fact that Sonia Delaunay did not exhibit her paintings between 1908 and 1953 has affected the public's knowledge of her artistic achievement. However, since the 1950s her works are more widely known. Major retrospective exhibitions of her works were held in Paris in 1967 and in the United States in 1980. Sonia Delaunay has escaped the fate of many a woman artist married to another artist. Both Sonia and Robert Delaunay have received full recognition, individually and as a team, for their contributions to the history of art.

Berlin Dada, 1919–1920

- #### Hannah Höch, *Cut with the Kitchen Knife*

This extraordinary photomontage was exhibited quite prominently at the First International Dada-Messe (Dada-Fair) of 1920, held in Berlin. It was shown with works by other members of the Dada group such as George Grosz, John Heartfield, and Raoul Hausmann, with whom Höch had been living since 1915. Höch (1889–1978) occupied a marginal position in the group as the only woman and was connected to the others mainly via her relationship with Hausmann. However, she did participate in all the major Berlin Dada exhibitions.

Höch was born in 1889 into a bourgeois family with no artistic inclinations. Her high school education was interrupted when she was 15, and at age 22, she left home to pursue an artist's education. Between 1912 and 1916 she studied at several applied arts schools in Berlin. From 1916 to 1926 Höch worked for Ullstein Verlag as a pattern designer in the handicrafts department, which produced instructions for knitting, crocheting, and embroidery. Her relationship with Hausmann was quite volatile since he was married and had a daughter. The definitive break occurred in 1922.

Maud Lavin has provided a fascinating reading of this large-scale, highly complex, and satirical image which "functions as a Dadaist manifesto on the politics of Weimar society."[13]

The upper-right quadrant, labeled "anti-dadaistische Bewegung" or "anti-Dada movement," is dominated by the image of Kaiser Wilhelm II, recently deposed as ruler of Germany. Four army officers are in the extreme upper-right corner. Just below them is an image of people waiting on line at an employment office.

In the lower-right quadrant, labeled "Die grosse Welt dada/Dadaisten" (The Great Dada World/Dadaists), the small figure of Hausmann in a diver's suit looks out at the viewer. From his head is a mass of machinery symbolizing the world of tech-

Fig. 14–6. Hannah Höch, *Cut with the Kitchen Knife.* 1919. Collage, 114 x 90 cm. *(Staatliche Museen zu Berlin—Preussischer Kulturbesitz Nationalgalerie)*

nology. At the extreme lower-right corner is a map of Europe in which the countries where women could vote are indicated in lighter tones.

The upper-left quadrant is dominated by Albert Einstein, from whose head springs the word "DADA." Five large wheels are also included, another reference to technology. The modernism of the entire image is made explicit by the use of photos from a specific newspaper, the Berliner Illustrierte Zeitung, the newspaper of widest circulation in Weimar German and published by Ullstein Verlag, the company where Höch worked during this time.

In these images, men disseminate Dada through words. however, there are a number of images of women, who, as Lavin argues, "occupy the principal revolutionary roles."[14] Female dancers and athletes move with physical freedom and liberation across the surface of the work. The body of a dancer is placed at the pivotal center of the composition. Just above the dancer's body floats the head of Käthe Kollwitz, who had just been appointed as the first woman professor of the Berlin Art Academy. Although Kollwitz's art was quite different from the Dadaists, her presence may be interpreted as "an inter-generational tribute, a sign of both admiration and difference."[15]

This work is a celebration of modernity and the "New Woman," a stereotype promoted by the mass print media that defined a new social role for women. In sum, this image is optimistic and utopian, projecting a new freedom and empowerment for both women and artists of the era in the wake of the overthrow of the Kaiser's government.

WOMEN OF THE BAUHAUS

- **Gunta Stölzl, *5 Choirs***

Sigrid Weltge has supplied a much more complete understanding of the experiences and contributions of women to the avant-garde art school known as the Bauhaus. The pioneering spirit of the male leaders of this enterprise, such as Walter Gropius, did not prevent the implementation of the most conservative gender ideology for women who enrolled at this school. Stölzl (1897–1983), like almost all the women who presented themselves to the Bauhaus as students, had previous art training. They were all "passionately interested in painting. . . . What attracted them to the Bauhaus in the first place was the lure of the painters,"[16] especially Klee and Kandinsky. What they encountered was the exclusion of women from all workshops by 1922, with the exception of the Weaving Workshop. As Weltge reports, "Instead of being fully integrated into the Bauhaus, they were segregated and given their own workshop—The Weaving Workshop—regardless of talent or inclination."[17]

Weltge identifies three categories of students in the Weaving Workshop: those who left without committing to a professional career, those who pursued artistic careers outside of the textile world, and those who embraced weaving as a career. Of this latter group, Gunta Stölzl and Anni Albers are the best known.

Products of the Weaving Workshop received very positive critical attention when shown to the public in two Bauhaus exhibitions. In 1925, a report of a delegation of the Dessau Trade Union noted that "The Weaving Workshop seems to be better than others. Its products clearly demand recognition, which cannot be said of the Carpentry Workshop."[18]

Gunta Stölzl was "the dominant presence in the Weaving Workshop."[19] She had been one of the first group of students to enroll in 1919, arriving at the Bauhaus with several years of training at the School of Applied Arts in Munich. By 1920 she was already playing a leading role in the Weaving Workshop. She had a natural affinity for materials and helped organize the workshop so works could be shown in the first official Bauhaus Exhibition in 1923. Textile designs incorporated the most sophisticated design principles and vocabulary articulated by the avant-garde painting masters, Kandinsky, Klee, van Doesburg, and Itten.

By 1928, when Stölzl created this hanging, she was able to incorporate Paul Klee's compositional ideas into "the most sophisticated Jacquard weaving produced at the Bauhaus . . . this work . . . shows her supreme mastery of this demanding medium. Her complex color scheme use of abstract pattern and shape shows the complexity and beauty of which her finest works are capable."[20]

Despite Stölzl's brilliance, the number of students in the Weaving Workshop steadily decreased during the 1920s. Weltge believes this is due in part to the growing emphasis on industrial textile design and the inability of some women to perceive themselves as integrated into a world of industry. However, by 1930, Stölzl, Albers, and the other women of the Bauhaus Weaving Workshop accepted the responsibilities of designing textiles for practical industrial production, aimed at all classes of society. Like the Russian Constructivists, they participated in the utopian avant-garde

Fig. 14–7. Gunta Stölzl, *5 Choirs*.
(photograph by Herbert Jäger)

attitudes of the post-World War I period. The startling creativity and originality of the Weaving Workshop is impressive. As Weltge points out, "What has now become commonplace—geometrical designs in stacked units, light/dark juxtapositions and transposed elements in a multiplicity of variations—was explored for the first time by Bauhaus weavers in the twenties."[21]

With the closing of the school and the dispersal of the members of the Weaving Workshop, some of these women eventually exerted a direct impact on American textile design in the post-World War II era.

RUSSIAN CONSTRUCTIVISM

In Russia, as in other countries of Europe, aristocratic women were often enthusiastic amateur painters. In 1842 the St. Petersburg Drawing School was opened to women. Later on there was a group of successful, if conservative, women artists active in the 1870s and 1880s, among whom Marie Bashkirtseff was perhaps the most famous. Such precedents established a base that at least partially explains the number of women artists in the pre- and post-Revolutionary Russian avant-garde.[22]

As opposed to the Berlin Dada circle in which Höch only grudgingly gained admittance via her relationship with Hausmann, the situation in Russia presents a concentration of women creators. After the revolution, a group of artists emerged who were politically engaged and eager to redefine and expand the role of the artist in the creation of "The Great Utopia" (the title of a major show at the Guggenheim Museum in 1993).

As one historian of the movement, Christina Lodder, notes, "the term Constructivism arose in Russia during the winter of 1920–21 as a term specifically formulated to meet the needs of these new attitudes toward the culture of the future classless society."[23] The identification with the new political and social order was at the core of the Constructivist enterprise, as was the call for the artist to go into the factory to move beyond art object and easel painting to transform life. This radical political agenda was formulated with women, as Nochlin notes "participating in the art process as equals or near-equals as never before—or since—in such numbers and with such impact."[24] In the landmark exhibition "5 x 5 = 25," three of the five artists participating—Popova, Stepanova, and Exter—were women.

Furthermore, according to Lodder, it was Popova and Stepanova who, with their male colleague, Tatlin, were the only members of this group who actually implemented the move into the factories and put their theoretical concepts of the artist-constructor into practical effect. Only the two women "entered mass production and formulated a constructivist approach and methodology to work in the area that correlated two design processes," textile design and clothing design.[25]

- **Lyubov Popova, *Architectonic Painting***

Lodder identifies Lyubov Popova (1889–1924) as "the most important" artist working prior to 1920 in two dimensions. The artist traveled to Paris in 1912 to study Cubism, and in the next years she painted in an abstract Cubo-Futurist style. In 1916 Popova worked with Kasimir Malevich on the publication of the Suprematist journal *Supremus*. This encouraged her break from a Cubo-Futurist monochromatic palette and tonal modeling. Her theoretical writing clarifies her approach to the creation of a work to be involved with the invention of a whole new pictorial language that concentrated on unmodulated color and the intersection of planes.

A typical example of the Constructivist style is *Architectonic Painting* (Fig. 14–8). This work consists of intersecting multicolored planes without any reference to objects in nature. Despite a certain amount of overlapping, it is impossible to say that these forms exist in a three-dimensional space. The traditional technique of modeling is employed nontraditionally because one cannot perceive these planes as rounded objects. Colors are also selected arbitrarily. This work is constructed with the most basic elements of painting, manipulated in a totally new way, overturning the Western tradition of painting since the Renaissance.

Popova, Stepanova, and other women artists who painted in a Constructivist style became active in "production art," which included theater sets and costumes, as well as industrial, graphic, and textile designs. As early as 1918, despite the political upheavals in Russia, the Visual Arts Section of the People's Commissariat for Enlight-

Fig. 14–8. Lyubov Sergeievna Popova, *Architectonic Painting*. 1917. Oil on canvas, 31$\frac{1}{2}$ x 38$\frac{5}{8}$ in. *(The Museum of Modern Art, New York. Philip Johnson Fund. Photograph © 1995 The Museum of Modern Art, New York)*

enment opened a special Subsection for Art-Industry, organized and directed by Olga Rosanova (1886–1918). The purpose of this group was to restructure the industrial design of the country. Rosanova encouraged many existing schools to join this organization.[26] She also devised a plan to reorganize the museums of industrial art in Moscow, which was eventually implemented. Many of her ideas were incorporated into the manifestos of Constructivism in the 1920s.

- **Varvara Stepanova, *Sportodezhda* (Designs for Sports Clothing)**

Varvara Stepanova (1894–1958) was a key member of the Constructivist group. Since 1916 she had been living in Moscow with Alexander Rodchenko, another member of this avant-garde circle. As with Modersohn-Becker, Delaunay, Münter, Höch, and others, romantic liaisons with male members of avant-garde groups did not overwhelm the unique creativity of these women, but provided a liberating base in which that creativity could flourish.

In collaboration with Popova, Stepanova identified the area of textile and clothing design as essential for the Constructivist utopian vision. In an article titled "Present Day Dress—Production Clothing," Stepanova formulated the concept that clothing design had to be organized toward its uses. The freedom of movement and energy of these designs for sports clothing is a clear example of this philosophy. Stepanova wrote:

> Fashion which psychologically reflects a way of life, customs and esthetic taste, give[s] way to clothing organized for work in different fields as defined by social movements, clothing which can prove itself only in the process of working in it, not presenting itself as having an independent value outside real life, as a special type of "work of art."[27]

These designs for sports clothing, *sportodezhda*, are characterized by a minimum of clothing, ease of putting on and wearing, and the special significance of color effects to distinguish individual sports and teams.[28] Between 1924 and 1925, Stepanova designed over 150 fabrics at the First Textile Printing Factory.

Popova also designed highly innovative fabrics and clothing and worked on the overalls for the actors in Meierkhold's production of *The Magnanimous Cuckold* of 1922. The overalls were actually prototypes for workers' clothing, and designed to al-

Fig. 14–9. Varvara Stepanova, *Sportodezhda* (Designs for Sports Clothing). *(photo courtesy of Christina Lodder)*

РАБОТЫ СТЕПАНОВОЙ

Проэкты спорт-одежды

low complete freedom of movement. Like those of Stepanova, Popova's clothing designs were simple, uncomplicated, and revolutionary. Both Stepanova and Popova
"saw the replacement of traditional Russian plant and flower patterns by geometri-
cally based designs as an essential aspect of the design process of cloth production."[29]
Each design was composed of one or two geometric shapes with black, white, and a
maximum of two other colors.

Stepanova and Popova actively pursued the revolutionary program of liberating
avant-garde design from the aesthetic sphere of the art object to directly impact the
lives of the working classes.

WOMEN OF THE LEFT BANK: PARIS BETWEEN THE WARS

• Romaine Brooks, *Una, Lady Troubridge*

Romaine Brooks (1894–1970) was born in Rome and lived a highly unusual
existence in her early life, moving frequently between Europe and the United States.
She attended private schools in New Jersey, Italy, and Geneva, Switzerland prior to
her study of painting at the Scuola Nazionale in Rome. In 1898 Brooks was the only
female student at the Scuola. Sandra Langer tells us that "From the beginning, Romaine Brooks was in revolt against family obligations, society and, to a lesser extent,
her youthful indecision."[30]

The most productive period for Brooks's art was in the post-World War I environment of Paris and in the lesbian community which flourished there, described by
Shari Benstock in her study, *Women of the Left Bank*. Brooks became the lover of author Natalie Barney and a key member of the group of talented women drawn to
this writer and *Salonnière*. Lesbianism was a courageous and self-conscious rejection
of patriarchal gender constructions for this circle. Chadwick notes that medical models in this epoch "constructed lesbianism around notions of perversion, illness inver-
sion and paranoia."[31] "Brooks's choice of style was a symbol of personal emancipation
from the structures of feminine roles."[32]

In 1924 Brooks painted this portrait of Una Vincenzo, who became the second
wife of Admiral Sir Ernest Charles Thomas Troubridge in 1908, then left her husband
in 1915 to live with the author Radclyffe Hall until the latter's death in 1943. Hall
described their relationship and the life of this group of artists in a novel, *The Well of
Loneliness*. The dachshunds were a gift to the sitter from Hall.[33] Una usually dressed in
male clothes and sported a monocle. Langer identifies her costume as "a little Lord
Fauntleroy suit, the epitome of what a well-dressed lesbian of fashion might wear at
home or for intimate evenings among friends."[34] Langer argues for an interpretation
of this and other portraits of lesbians in the circle "as positive visions of emancipated
lesbians . . . Her work . . . is . . . a visual expression of deeply held social, political and
esthetic beliefs."[35] This reading is much more sensitive to the choices and life-style of
Brooks than Adelyn Breeskin's simple dismissal of the image as a "caricature."

The shallow space and monochromatic palette are typical of Brooks's works in
this decade and relate to her personal creation of a coloristic system derived from
Whistler's closely toned symbolist technique.

Fig. 14–10. Romaine Brooks,
Una, Lady Troubridge. 1924. Oil
on canvas, 51$\frac{1}{8}$ x 30$\frac{1}{8}$ in.
*(National Museum of American Art,
Washington DC / Art Resource, NY)*

WOMEN ARTISTS OF SURREALISM

There is an irony inherent in the Surrealist position on the nature of women, the "other" sex. André Breton, the leading theorist of the Surrealist movement, valued woman as a primal force that he viewed with respect and awe. He advanced definitions of woman as catalytic muse, visionary goddess, evil seductress, and most significantly, as *femme-enfant*, the woman-child whose naive and spontaneous innocence, uncorrupted by logic or reason, brings her into closer contact with the intuitive realm of the unconscious so crucial to Surrealism. Breton exalted an abstract ideal of feminine sensibility as the primary source of artistic creativity, saying, "The time will come when the ideas of woman will be asserted at the expense of those of man."[36] However, Breton expected men to translate this intuitive woman's realm, viewed as closer to natural forces, into the culture as art. As flattering as his adulation of woman might seem, his theories relegated the "other" sex to the status of male-defined object, leaving little place for real women or women artists to develop independent identities. Thus, the women of Surrealism, as

Gloria Orenstein has suggested in a landmark article, had to struggle against limitations placed on them by the very concepts of Surrealism itself.[37]

Yet Surrealism, as a movement that sought to explore altered states of consciousness, to penetrate the realm of dreams, and to make the imaginary real, includes a number of women who produced significant works. Meret Oppenheim and Dorothea Tanning are among the leading women artists whose works fit within the Surrealist movement.

• Meret Oppenheim, *Object*

Raised in Switzerland and southern Germany, Meret Oppenheim (1913–1985) went to Paris at the age of 18 to become an artist. She became the subject of some of Man Ray's most beautiful photographs, and in 1933 she was invited by Alberto Giacometti and Jean Arp to exhibit with the Surrealists. She continued to participate in their exhibitions until 1937 and again after World War II until 1960.

In the catalogue of Surrealist imagery, one piece stands out as the paradigm of the disturbing object: the fur-lined teacup of Meret Oppenheim. Although this work, alternately titled *Object* and *Fur Breakfast* (Fig. 14–11), is frequently reproduced in standard texts, there is "a truly stunning absence of critical curiosity about Meret Oppenheim herself."[38]

Her fur-lined teacup remains a most potent example of the Surrealist goal to

Fig. 14–11. Meret Oppenheim, *Object [Le Déjeuner en fourrure]*. 1936. Fur-covered cup, saucer, and spoon. Cup 4³/₈ in. diameter; saucer 9³/₈ in. diameter; spoon 8 in. long; overall height 2⁷/₈ in. (7.3 cm). *(The Museum of Modern Art, New York. Purchase. Photograph © 1995 The Museum of Modern Art, New York)*

transform the familiar into the strange. Here, a mundane household object is rendered useless, while evoking the viewer's response to the sensation of drinking from wet fur. In another clever Surrealist object, Oppenheim trussed up a pair of women's high-heeled shoes like a holiday bird served on a silver platter, complete with paper frills. She also transformed a mirror by silk-screening onto the surface a face in the process of metamorphosis. She maintained a commitment to the ideas that formed the basis of Surrealism throughout her life. She wrote:

> Artists, poets, keep the passage to the unconscious open. . . . The unconscious is the only place from which help and advice can come to us.[39]

- ### Dorothea Tanning, *Maternity*

For Dorothea Tanning (b. 1910), too, personal identity can be seen as a central source of imagery. In her paintings women often appear in isolating and potentially menacing situations. One painting depicts young girls dressed in rags who seem haunted as they rip wallpaper into shreds along lonely corridors. In another work a woman, barefoot and half-clothed in a robe of dead branches, stands transfixed before a maze of doorways. She is accompanied by a fantastic creature with wings, tail, claws, and snout, who is her chimera or incubus.

Tanning's images speak to the condition of woman. This is most powerfully seen in *Maternity* (Fig. 14–12). In this work a barefoot mother and child, dressed in identical sleeping cap and nightgown, stand between two open doorways in an otherwise barren landscape, tenderly hugging each other. Their only companion is a pet Pekinese dog whose face bears a strong resemblance to Tanning's own features as a child. Dark storm clouds fill the sky above a sulfurous yellow desert. In the background a menacing figure, half-organic, half-machine, looms through a distant doorway. The woman's gown is shredded over her abdomen as a distended belly and engorged breasts push through, suggesting the violent wrenching of birth and the strong biological link that inextricably binds mother to child. Maternity, that experience unique to women, is here expressed as tender but bitter, uniting but isolating, a door that opens to some experiences but closes off others.

Although born in the United States in 1910 and not associated with the Surrealists in France until the 1950s, Tanning felt that unknowingly she had already become a Surrealist by the age of 7 when, in the small town of Galesburg, Illinois, she composed messages to secret loves and sealed them in paper cubes. But it was only after seeing the "Fantastic Art, Dada and Surrealism" exhibition at New York's Museum of Modern Art in 1937 that she realized that her artistic personality could be understood as part of a larger movement. Upon meeting her future husband, the Surrealist artist Max Ernst, who had emigrated to the United States during World War II, the links between her art and Surrealism became more direct. Together they spent the 1940s in Sedona, Arizona, where Tanning produced many of her best known works. In the 1950s and 1960s while living in France, she combined her painting with scenery and costume design; during the 1970s she experimented with soft sculpture. She, too, remains true to Surrealist principles. "Me, I want to seduce by means of imperceptible passages from one reality to another."[40]

Fig. 14–12. Dorothea Tanning,
Maternity. 1946. Oil on canvas,
44 x 57 in. *(Private collection)*

Oppenheim and Tanning each developed an independent style to explore highly personal subject matter while remaining loyal to the basic tenets of Surrealism. Recent research has begun to recognize and evaluate the contributions of these artists. Surrealism, a movement that exalted Woman as a creative force, may also be understood and valued for the women creators within it.

- **Frida Kahlo, *The Two Fridas***

Of all the women artists active in the twentieth century prior to 1950, Frida Kahlo (1910–1954) is today one of the most famous. Her life and her art are more closely interlocked than any other artist in this book. Her recurrent, even obsessive, focus on self-portraiture as her main subject formed an oeuvre of great honesty, power, and originality.

Kahlo married the noted Mexican mural painter Diego Rivera in 1929. Their stormy and passionate relationship was an important component of Kahlo's life. This work was painted during the period, lasting over a year, in which they were divorced. In *The Two Fridas*, Kahlo explores the dualities of her Mexican heritage and identity. On the left she wears a European-styled white lace dress, while on the right she presents herself in a Tehuana dress. This is the traditional costume of Zapotec women from the Isthmus of Tehuantepec. Janice Helland states that Zapotec women "represent[ed] an ideal of freedom and economic independence."[41] Kahlo's commitment to Aztec imagery and native dress can be connected to the nationalistic political movement of her youth, "Mexicanidad."

The two figures are united by their clasped hands and an artery that stretches between their two hearts. The extracted heart was a device used by Kahlo to show pain in love.[42] The artery emerges from the miniature painting of Rivera as a boy held by the Frida on the right. It reappears on the white dress and is clamped with a hemostat, dripping red blood. Helland notes that "Aztecs often represent the 'heart,' which they perceived as the life center of a human being, as drops of (or spurting) blood."[43] A phrase from a love poem by Elias Nandino that Kahlo had copied in her journal states, "My blood is the miracle that travels in the veins of the air from my heart to yours."[44] Hayden Herrera refers to this work as a "dramatization of loneliness."[45] Kahlo has only herself, with all her complexity of identity, to accompany herself in the world.

Kahlo's position in Surrealism is highly tenuous. Her works came to the atten-

Fig. 14–13. Frida Kahlo, *The Two Fridas*. 1939. Oil on canvas, 67 x 67 in. *(Collection of the Museo de Arte Moderno, Mexico City; photo by Jorge Contreras Chacel)*

tion of Julian Levy, who ran a small gallery oriented towards Surrealist art in New York. Kahlo had met André Breton, the theoretician of the Surrealists, and had entertained him as her houseguest in Mexico City. In 1939 she went to Paris, since Breton had promised to organize a show of her works. Her frustration and anger towards Breton and the French artists in his circle are clear in her letters from Paris. In 1952 Kahlo made the following statement concerning her relationship to Surrealism:

> Some critics have tried to classify me as a Surrealist; but I do not consider myself to be a Surrealist. . . . Really I do not know whether my paintings are Surrealist or not, but I do know that they are the frankest expression of myself. . . . I detest Surrealism. To me it seems to be a decadent manifestation of bourgeois art. A deviation from the true art that the people hope for from the artist. . . . I wish to be worthy, with my painting, of the people to whom I belong and to the ideas that strengthen me. . . . I want my work to be a contribution to the struggle of the people for peace and liberty.

THE UNITED STATES

Painting

- #### Georgia O'Keeffe, *Black Iris*

Georgia O'Keeffe (1887–1986) is widely recognized as one of the foremost American painters of the twentieth century. A highly individual artist, she cannot be easily classified with any movement or school of painters. Although she sometimes has been related to Precisionists such as Charles Sheeler, her largely organic abstractions and her painterly style separate her from the machine aesthetic of that group. O'Keeffe was truly an "original"—an independent American who remained uninfluenced by the contemporary European abstract movements.

Born on a farm in Wisconsin, O'Keeffe acquired some academic training at the Art Institute of Chicago and then at the Art Students League in New York. In 1912 she was exposed to the teachings of Arthur Wesley Dow, one of the few art educators in America who rejected academic realism in favor of the simplifications and flat patterning of Oriental art.

Between 1912 and 1916, O'Keeffe spent winters teaching art in Amarillo, Texas. Inspired by the vast expanse of the plains and responsive to Dow's concepts, she began drawing abstract shapes that came from her internal visual imagination. In 1916 she sent a friend some of these drawings. Her friend took them to Alfred Stieglitz, the noted photographer, who ran a gallery in New York that showed avant-garde European and American works. The following year O'Keeffe had the first in a series of one-woman shows at Stieglitz's 291 Gallery. In 1924 she and Stieglitz were married, and they lived mostly in New York City until his death in 1946.

O'Keeffe's ability to distill abstract shapes from natural phenomena is never more apparent than in her famous paintings of flowers. In *Black Iris* (Fig. 14–14), the flower is presented in a strictly frontal position, revealing its form to the viewer. From the mysterious mauve darkness of its center, one's eye moves outward to the violet-gray

Fig. 14–14. Georgia O'Keeffe, *Black Iris*. 1926 Oil on canvas, 36 x 29⁷/₈ in. *The Metropolitan Museum of Art, Alfred Stieglitz Collection, 1949. All rights reserved, The Metropolitan Museum of Art, 69.278.1)*

veil-like shapes at the peak. The black-gray lower section forms a base upon which the upper half of the flower is supported.

The interpretation of O'Keeffe's flower paintings is a complex issue. As Barbara Buhler Lynes and others have noted, it was Stieglitz who first promoted the interpretation of her art, even prior to the series of flower paintings of the 1920s, as a correlative of female sexual experience.[46] This concept dominated the reviews of O'Keeffe's first major exhibition of 1923 and continued throughout the decade. However, O'Keeffe herself consistently sought to distinguish her work from the label of "woman artist" and to deny all associations of her flowers with female anatomy.

Lynes documents O'Keeffe's participation in the National Women's Party (NWP) campaign for the Equal Rights Amendment.[47] O'Keeffe believed in equality between the sexes. She began her large-format flower paintings in 1924, the year after her abstractions had received so much comment in the press and, as Lynes proposes, perhaps wished to make more specific imagery that would not be open to interpretations of sexuality. The paintings sold well, and she continued to make them. In her published statement of 1939, she explicitly repudiates connections between this imagery and female genitalia:

> Everyone has many associations with a flower. . . . Still—in a way—nobody sees a flower—really—it is so small—we haven't time—and to see takes time, like to have a friend takes time. If I could paint the flower exactly as I see it, no one would see what I see because I would paint it small like the flower is small.

So I said to myself—I'll paint what I see—what the flower is to me but I'll paint it big and they will be surprised into taking time to look at it—I will make even busy New Yorkers take time to see what I see of flowers.

Well I made you take time to look at what I saw and when you took time to really notice my flower you hung all your own associations with flowers on my flower and you write about my flower as if I think and see what you think and see of the flower—and I don't.[48]

The "associations" from which O'Keeffe separates herself refer to the connections often drawn between images such as *Black Iris* and women's sexual anatomy.

However, Anna Chave has characterized O'Keeffe's art in the following terms: "O'Keeffe portrayed abstractly, but unmistakably, her experience of her own body, not what it looked like to others. The parts of the body she engaged were mainly invisible (and unrepresented) due to interiority, but she offered viewers an ever-expanding catalogue of visual metaphors for those areas, and for the experience of space and penetrability generally."[49] Chave connects this awareness with the political campaign for reproductive freedom through access to contraception, and one might add the feminist euphoria in the aftermath of the successful battle for female suffrage in the 1920s.

It is a tribute to the power of O'Keeffe's works that they can evoke a broad range of associations that vary from viewer to viewer. The relationship of this image to the female body is but one layer of metaphorical meaning that may be taken from it. Another interpretation might view it as fantasy architecture, an elaborate construction, or as a metaphor for a shelter, enclosure, or protection of a special being or sacred object. As Lloyd Goodrich has written, "The flower became a world in itself, a microcosm. Magnification was another kind of abstraction, of separating the object from ordinary reality, and endowing it with a life of its own."[50] The sheer formal power and brilliance of O'Keeffe's flower paintings secure their place among the most important American paintings of the twentieth century.

Beginning in 1929, O'Keeffe spent summers in New Mexico, where she felt a strong attraction to the stark beauties of the desert landscape. In addition to the geography of the desert, O'Keeffe repeatedly painted the bleached animal bones she found in the parched wilderness.

In 1949, after settling Stieglitz's estate, she moved permanently to the remote town of Abiquiu, New Mexico. O'Keeffe's art—spare, clear, and powerful—forces us to see that portion of nature she explored in a new and more profound way.

Photography

Whether to consider photography an art and photographers artists, rather than technicians or craftspersons, has been the subject of debate since the invention of photography in the nineteenth century. Although most nineteenth-century authorities thought of photography more as a science or craft than as an art, the consensus today is that photography is indeed an art form. Photographs are collected, displayed in museums and galleries, and subjected to critical evaluation. Major photographers are the subjects of scholarly monographs. Photography has its own history, with recognized masters, which parallels the history of painting and sculpture. Therefore, contemporary opinion justifies the inclusion of a select group of outstanding women photographers in this study.

- **Imogen Cunningham, *Portrait of Martha Graham***

Along with Edward Weston and Ansel Adams, Imogen Cunningham (1883–1975) is known for her sharply focused images of natural phenomena. Reacting against the style of "pictorial photography" favored by Alfred Stieglitz and others, these San Francisco photographers formed a rather unstructured organization known as the Group f. 64. An f. 64 setting on a camera is a very small lens opening that gives a sharply focused, finely detailed image along with a greater depth of field. Through the 1930s, the Group f. 64 was the most influential photography society in the country. Among Cunningham's most famous photos are very close-up studies of flowers and plants with strong light-dark contrast. This type of subject, as we have seen, was also favored by O'Keeffe.

Cunningham met the dancer and choreographer Martha Graham (Fig. 14–15) during the summer of 1931, when both women were living in Santa Barbara, California. Graham was visiting her mother, and Cunningham isolated her against the dark interior of the barn to achieve the dramatic light-dark contrasts of this image.[51] The expressive positioning of the hands is made even more exaggerated by the close-up focus and severe cropping of the image. Cunningham seems to have been inspired by the beauty, power, and intensity of Graham's choreography to create a photographic portrait worthy of this giant of modern dance. Cunningham's original vision established her reputation as one of the foremost women photographers of the twentieth century.

Fig. 14–15. Imogen Cunningham, *Martha Graham, Dancer.* 1931.
(© 1970 The Imogen Cunningham Trust)

• Dorothea Lange, *Migrant Mother*

Born of German immigrants in Hoboken, New Jersey, Dorothea Lange (1895–1965) had decided to become a photographer by the time she was 17 years old. While attending courses to become an elementary school teacher, she worked in several photographers' studios in New York learning her craft. Leaving home with a girl friend, Lange settled in San Francisco in 1918, where she established herself as a professional portrait photographer.

Lange's contribution to the history of photography dates from the 1930s, when she was hired by the Farm Security Administration both to document the plight of the migrant workers and to arouse sympathy for federal relief programs to aid them. *Migrant Mother* (Fig. 14–16) is the most famous photograph from this program. The circumstances surrounding the encounter with the subject of *Migrant Mother* have an almost eerie quality of intuitive recognition. Lange said, "I drove into that wet and soggy camp and parked my car like a homing pigeon."[52] This woman was only 32 years old. She and her children had been surviving on frozen vegetables gleaned from the fields and birds caught by the children. There was no more work since the pea crop had frozen. They could not move on because the car tires had just been sold to buy food. We do not really need to know this background saga of desperation. The anguish on this woman's face, her children who hide their faces from the photographer—these are immediately recognizable symbols of extreme poverty and stoical endurance. In fact, the image conveys this information so directly and eloquently that it has become one of the most memorable pictures of the last fifty years.

Fig. 14–16. Dorothea Lange, *Migrant Mother, Nipomo, California*. 1936. Gelatin-silver print, $12\frac{1}{2}$ x $9\frac{7}{8}$ in. *(The Museum of Modern Art, New York. Purchase Copy Print © 1995 The Museum of Modern Art, New York)*

- **Margaret Bourke-White,** *At the Time of the Louisville Flood, 1937*

Like Dorothea Lange, Margaret Bourke-White (1904–1971) was a documentary photographer. She is remembered as one of the most famous and prolific American photojournalists. Born in New York, she was an active amateur photographer by her freshman year at the University of Michigan in 1921. Her professional career began in Cleveland in 1927, following the collapse of a two-year marriage. In 1929 she was hired as a staff photographer for a new magazine, *Fortune*, published by Henry Luce. When Luce founded the magazine *Life* in 1936, Bourke-White was hired as one of its four original staff photographers. She continued to work for the immensely popular *Life* until 1956, when the debilitating effects of Parkinson's disease forced her into retirement.

Bourke-White was an aggressive, fearless documentary photographer. She traveled the globe in pursuit of images to inform the American people of the major world events of the epoch. Her courage and determination to get the right photo are legendary. She understood her pictures to be historical documents and, in fact, her images shaped the consciousness of millions.

Bourke-White traveled through the dustbowl of America's Midwest in the 1930s, recording the daily lives and the effects of poverty on the people of small-town America. Like the works of Lange, Bourke-White's images forced the readers of *Life* magazine to empathize with the plight of the unfortunate and destitute people captured in her photographs. *At the Time of the Louisville Flood, 1937* (Fig. 14–17), one of her most famous photographs, depicts homeless refugees lining up for emergency

Fig. 14–17. Margaret Bourke-White, *At the Time of the Louisville Flood, 1937.* (Life Magazine © 1937 Time Inc.)

supplies. The juxtaposition of these impoverished blacks and the billboard behind them proclaiming the prosperity of the "typical" American family is ironic social commentary.

Bourke-White was a courageous war photojournalist. At the end of World War II she arrived with General Patton to record the liberation of Buchenwald, one of the Nazi concentration camps. Her photograph of the emaciated and expressionless survivors, *The Living Dead of Buchenwald, 1945*, became an unforgettable image of the Holocaust. Bourke-White recorded her reactions to this experience in her book, *Dear Fatherland, Rest Quietly*:

> I kept telling myself that I would believe the indescribably horrible sight in the courtyard before me only when I had a chance to look at my own photographs. Using the camera was almost a relief; it interposed a slight barrier between myself and the white horror in front of me ... it made me ashamed to be a member of the human race.[53]

Bourke-White also created a unique photographic record of the Indian leader, Gandhi. According to Beaumont Newhall, author of the definitive *History of Photography*, one personality trait that unites these women photographers is "drive"—a combination of determination, persistence, and energy. Despite stylistic differences, each photographer possessed great force of personality that accounts, in part, for her success in this medium.

Architecture

- ### Julia Morgan, *San Simeon*

During a forty-seven-year career as a practicing professional architect, Julia Morgan (1872–1957) designed over 700 buildings, mainly in California. Her professional practice was based in San Francisco. Morgan worked in a broad range of styles and building materials and suited her designs to the tastes and needs of her patrons. Sara Boutelle has noted that light and color were a consistent preoccupation in her work, whether she used a Beaux-Arts, Arts and Crafts, or Mediterranean architectural vocabulary.[54]

Morgan was raised in the San Francisco Bay area and in 1890 enrolled in the University of California, Berkeley. Since there was no architecture school then, she became the only woman in the engineering program. In October, 1897, Morgan took the entrance examination for the Ecole des Beaux-Arts in Paris. Although she placed forty-second out of 376 applicants, that score was not good enough to secure her admission. However, on her third try, in October 1898, she became the first woman in architecture to be accepted to this prestigious art academy. Morgan returned to San Francisco in 1902, passed the State examination, and was certified for architecture in 1904.

According to Boutelle, Morgan's career should be understood in the context of a women's network of philanthropy and public activities. She built a large number of structures designed for women's use, from buildings on the campus of Mills College to a sorority house at Berkeley. In addition, the Young Women's Christian Association (YWCA) was a very important client for Morgan. She designed several YWCA structures, for example, in Asilomar, Oakland, and Riverside (now the home of the

Riverside Art Museum). Phoebe Apperson Hearst was a major patron of the YWCA, and Morgan had been working on additions to Mrs. Hearst's ranch in Pleasanton, "The Hacienda," since 1903. When the concept for a YWCA conference center was developed, Mrs. Hearst recommended Morgan for the job. Asilomar, which means "refuge by the sea," is "perhaps the largest institutional complex ever built in the Arts and Crafts style."[55]

The project for which Morgan is most famous is the elaborate structure built for Phoebe Hearst's son, William Randolph Hearst, known as San Simeon. In April, 1919, Hearst met with Morgan for the first time to discuss the construction of a home at "The Ranch" at San Simeon, two hundred miles south of San Francisco on the Pacific coast. This project would occupy much of Morgan's efforts for the next eighteen years. She traveled to the site nearly every weekend from 1920 through 1938. Hearst and Morgan worked in a close and cooperative collaboration on the construction of three guest houses or "cottages" and the main building.

Construction of the main building began in 1922. The reinforced concrete structure was designed with earthquake-proof standards in mind. The white facade was built of reinforced concrete and faced with stone. Initially, inspiration for the towers came from the church at Ronda in southern Spain, one of Hearst's favorites. The assembly room was two stories tall and measured about 80 × 30 feet, extending across the entire front of the building. The equally enormous refectory, with a 28-foot stone mantel, provided the inspiration for *Citizen Kane*'s Xanadu sets. Morgan also designed a movie theater, two elaborate pools, the Neptune pool and the Roman

Fig. 14–18. Julia Morgan, *San Simeon*. 1922–1926. Front entrance, Main Building.

pool, and a zoo for San Simeon. Boutelle records that the correspondence between Morgan and Hearst indicates that securing adequate funds to keep the building construction going was a constant problem.

Morgan closed her office in 1951, six years before her death in 1957. Her career was eclipsed by the predominance of the International Style in architecture in the post–World War II period.

Suggestions for Further Reading

German Expressionist Women

BEHR, SHULAMITH, *Women Expressionists* (New York: Rizzoli, 1988).

Modersohn-Becker

BUSCH, GUNTER, and LISELOTTE VON REINKEN (eds.), *Paula Modersohn-Becker: The Letters and Journals*, trans. Arthur S. Wensinger and Carole Clew Hoey (New York: Taplinger Publishing, 1983).

Paula Modersohn-Becker: zum hundertsten Geburtsdag (Bremen Kunsthalle, 1976). (German)

PERRY, GILLIAN, *Paula Modersohn-Becker: Her Life and Work* (London: The Woman's Press, 1979).

RADYCKI, J. DIANE (trans. and ed.), *The Letters and Journals of Paula Modersohn-Becker* (Metuchen, NJ: Scarecrow Press, 1980).

Kollwitz

HINZ, RENATE (ed.), *Käthe Kollwitz, Graphics, Posters, Drawings*, trans. Rita and Robert Kimber (New York: Pantheon Books, 1981).

KEARNS, MARTHA, *Käthe Kollwitz: Woman and Artist* (Old Westbury, NY: Feminist Press, 1976).

PRELINGER, ELIZABETH, et al., *Käthe Kollwitz* (Washington, DC: National Gallery of Art, 1992).

ZIGROSSER, CARL, *Prints and Drawings of Käthe Kollwitz* (New York: Dover Press, 1951; rpt. 1969).

Delaunay

BUCKBERROUGH, SHERRY A., *Sonia Delaunay: A Retrospective* (Buffalo, NY: Albright-Knox Gallery, 1980).

COHEN, ARTHUR A., *Sonia Delaunay* (New York: Abrams, 1975).

DAMASE, J., *Sonia Delaunay, Rhythms and Colors* (Greenwich, CT: New York Graphic Society, 1972).

DELAUNAY, SONIA, *Sonia Delaunay: Art into Fashion* (New York: G. Braziller, 1986).

Höch

LAVIN, MAUD, *Cut with the Kitchen Knife: The Weimar Photomontages of Hannah Höch* (New Haven, CT: Yale University Press, 1993).

Bauhaus Women

WELTGE, SIGRID W., *Women's Work: Textile Art from the Bauhaus* (San Francisco: Chronicle Books, 1993).

Russian Constructivism

GRAY, CAMILLA, *The Russian Experiment in Art: 1863–1922* (New York: Abrams, 1972).

LODDER, CHRISTINA, *Russian Constructivism* (New Haven, CT: Yale University Press, 1983).

WOOD, PAUL, et al., *The Great Utopia: The Russian and Soviet Avant Garde: 1915–1932* (New York: The Guggenheim Museum, 1992).

Popova

SARABIANOV, DMITRI V., and NATALIA L. ADASKINA, *Popova*, trans. Marian Schwartz (New York: Abrams, 1990).

Stepanova

LAVRENTIEV, ALEXANDER, *Varvara Stepanova: The Complete Work*, John E. Bowlt (ed.) (Cambridge, MA: MIT Press, 1988).

Brooks

BREESKIN, ADELYN, *Romaine Brooks, "Thief of Souls"* (Washington, DC: National Collection of Fine Arts, Smithsonian Institution Press, 1971).

LANGER, CASSANDRA L., "Fashion, Character and Sexual Politics in Some Romaine Brooks' Lesbian Portraits," *Art Criticism*, 1 (1981).

Surrealism

CHADWICK, WHITNEY, *Women Artists and the Surrealist Movement* (Boston: Little, Brown, 1985).

Oppenheim

WITHERS, JOSEPHINE, "The Famous Fur-Lined Teacup and the Anonymous Meret Oppenheim," *ARTS Magazine*, 52 (November 1977).

Tanning

BOSQUET, A., *Le Peinture de Dorothea Tanning* (Paris: Jean-Jacques Pauvert, 1966). (French)

PLAZY, GILLES, *Dorothea Tanning* (Paris: E.P.I. Editions Filipacchi, 1976). (French)

Kahlo

HERRERA, HAYDEN, *Frida: A Biography of Frida Kahlo* (New York: Harper and Row, 1983).

HERRERA, HAYDEN, *Frida Kahlo: The Paintings* (New York: HarperCollins, 1991).

O'Keeffe

CHAVE, ANNA, "O'Keeffe and the Masculine Gaze," *Art in America*, 78 (January 1990).

COWART, JACK, and JUAN HAMILTON, *Georgia O'Keeffe, Art and Letters*. Letters selected and annotated by Sarah Greenough (Washington, DC: National Gallery of Art, and Boston: New York Graphic Society, 1987).

GOODRICH, LLOYD, and DORIS BRY, *Georgia O'Keeffe* (New York: Whitney Museum of American Art, 1970).

LISLE, LAURIE, *Portrait of an Artist: A Biography of Georgia O'Keeffe* (Albuquerque: University of New Mexico, 1986, New York: Pocketbooks, 1987).

LYNES, BARBARA BUHLER, *O'Keeffe, Stieglitz and the Critics, 1916–1927* (Ann Arbor, MI: UMI Research Press, 1989).

O'KEEFFE, GEORGIA, *Georgia O'Keeffe* (New York: Viking, 1976).

Photography

SULLIVAN, CONSTANCE (ed.), *Women Photographers* (New York: Abrams, 1990).

Cunningham

DATER, JUDY, *Imogen Cunningham: A Portrait* (Boston: New York Graphic Society, 1979).

Imogen Cunningham: Photographs (Seattle: University of Washington Press, 1970).

Lange

MELTZER, MILTON, *Dorothea Lange: A Photographer's Life* (New York: Farrar, Straus and Giroux, 1978).

OHRN, KARIN BECKER, *Dorothea Lange and the Documentary Tradition* (Baton Rouge: Louisiana State University Press, 1980).

Bourke-White

BOURKE-WHITE, MARGARET, *Dear Fatherland, Rest Quietly* (New York: Simon and Schuster, 1946).

CALLAHAN, SEAN (ed.), *The Photos of Margaret Bourke-White* (Greenwich, CT: New York Graphic Society, 1972).

Morgan

BOUTELLE, SARA, *Julia Morgan, Architect* (New York: Abbeville, 1988).

CHAPTER 15

• • • • • • • • • • • •

THE POST-WORLD WAR II ERA: 1945–1970

Women artists have been increasingly influential and active as equal participants in the full range of developments in painting and sculpture since World War II. A cursory overview of works by women artists during more recent times indicates that sex alone is not a strong enough factor to determine any particular predisposition toward a specific style of art. The large numbers of women artists, of whom only a handful of the most oustanding have been selected for discussion in this chapter, have worked in a wide variety of styles in the most diverse media imaginable. In the absence of institutional barriers and with the increased equality of women in all phases of the postwar culture, women artists have demonstrated that they are capable of originality and can achieve the highest levels of creativity in the visual arts.

As Ellen Laudau has noted, women as art teachers and art patrons were already prominent in the 1920s.[1] By the 1930s, women comprised a significant percentage of the population of artists. The 1930 census identifies 40 percent of all practicing American art professionals as women. Women were also prominent as administrators of federally funded arts projects during the Depression. These programs were notably free of sex bias; 40 percent of those receiving assistance were women.[2] These statistics indicate that women artists were no longer interesting oddities or exceptions in a male-dominated profession. From that time to the present, the percentage of art students and artists who are women has steadily grown.

During the 1930s, especially in New York, many of the administrators of the local WPA Fine Arts Projects were women.[3] However, in the postwar period, women artists struggled in isolation from one another for recognition and success. As was the case for women in avant-garde groups earlier in the century, Landau concludes that influential male support was crucial for "even a modicum of mainstream success . . . Romantic entanglements with prominent artists, dealers, and critics had a key impact on the careers of a majority of artists . . . the entrée into the art world offered by these men proved critical to the women's success."[4] Landau also discusses the difficulties women experienced in combining the bearing and raising of children and having a professional career. Some women chose not to have children. "Women artists often had to play double roles and to prove themselves in ways not demanded of men, who could more easily integrate their personal and professional lives."[5] Women artists were subject to ridicule and condescension from critics, especially in the popular press.

"Typically overshadowed in the history books by their husbands, lovers, and male colleagues, women artists have also had their works incorrectly labeled as derivative."[6]

Many of these women were uncertain about the role of their gender in the creation and formation of their art. Alice Neel stated: "When I was in my studio, I didn't give a damn what sex I was. . . . I thought art is art."[7]

Women artists are often reluctant to accept the label "woman artist," which they perceive as a ghettoization and diminution of their talents. They have lacked the experience of institutional structures for mutual support, "doomed to work in relative isolation and to have their work belittled or ignored."[8]

Despite such oppressive isolation, however, we can see that in all trends of the mainstream art world women artists have been active and original contributors. Their achievements are a crucial part of the historical account of avant-garde artistic practices between 1945 and 1970.

ABSTRACT EXPRESSIONISM

• **Lee Krasner,** *Noon*

Lee Krasner (1908–1984) is the only woman artist of note in the first generation of Abstract Expressionist artists. Until recently, her role in the movement has been overshadowed by her position as the widow of Jackson Pollack. A reevaluation of her contribution was undertaken only a year before her death with a major retrospective exhibition at the Museum of Modern Art in New York.[9]

Born into a Russian Jewish family with absolutely no predispositions to the arts, Krasner was determined to become a painter by her teens. After studying on scholarship at Cooper Union in New York, she received very traditional academic training at the National Academy of Design. However, it was her years in the classes of Hans Hoffman that opened her art experience to the European masters Matisse, Picasso, and, of crucial importance, Mondrian.

From this grounding in the formal options of European modernism, she, like the other Abstract Expressionists, eventually rejected the cool, intellectual distance of that art in favor of the immediacy and spontaneity urged by Surrealism. Between 1942 and 1945 she shared Pollock's studio. These years mark a time of doubt and lack of direction for Krasner.

Anne Wagner has discussed the complexities which Krasner experienced as "Mrs. Jackson Pollock." In that role, she stuffed envelopes with announcements for Pollock's shows and kept track of details like the titles of his paintings. Of a joint exhibition titled "Artists: Man and Wife" at the Sidney Janis Gallery in 1949, an *Art News* critic wrote, "There is also a tendency among some of these wives to 'tidy up' the husbands' styles. Lee Krasner (Mrs. Jackson Pollock) takes her husband's paints and enamels and changes his unrestrained, sweeping lines into neat little squares and triangles."[10]

Leonore Krasner was known by the more gender-neutral name "Lee." She often used the initials "L.K." to sign her work. Wagner refers to these practices as "strategems . . . a resistance to her art being identified and thus seen 'as that of a woman,' a reluctance that went hand in hand with her refusal in 1945 to take part . . . in a group show of artists who were women."[11]

After meeting Pollock, Krasner stopped painting for a year and then endured a frustrating three-year period of "grey slabs," her term for the thickly encrusted paint and lack of image in work of the early 1940s.

In the spring of 1945, after Krasner and Pollock married, the couple moved out of New York City to East Hampton, Long Island. The following year both artists became preoccupied with allover compositions. Between 1946 and 1949 Krasner created the "Little Image" paintings, which may be divided into three series. These works, created simultaneously with Pollock's drip paintings, are executed on a smaller scale and with a greater degree of precision and control.

Noon (Fig. 15–1) is an example of the "mosaic" or divisionist pattern of the earliest group of "Little Image" works. Barbara Rose maintains that the original source for the all-over image was Mondrian's ocean and pier (or plus or minus drawings) and that it was Krasner who first drew Pollock's attention to the possibilities of this composition.[12] Pollock, in turn, encouraged Krasner to abandon her tenuous Cubist ties to physical nature.

Fig. 15–1. Lee Krasner, *Noon.* 1947. Oil on linen, 24 x 30 in. *(Private collection. Robert Miller Gallery, New York. Photo by Malcolm Varon)*

Noon is composed of an even, all–over surface of thickly impastoed paint in brilliant colors. Yellow, turquoise, orange, pink, and blue tonalities are evenly distributed over the surface. The sparkle of these juxtaposed hues creates an energetic and intense visual experience, related to the dots of Neo-Impressionism. The brushwork maintains a uniform density and rhythmic regularity. This totally abstract work exists in a highly compressed space. It communicates joy, energy, and exuberance. The other works in the "Little Image" series are composed of dripped webs of paint, inspired by Pollock's famous technique, and tight grids of hieroglyphics.

In 1951 Krasner showed her paintings for the first time after the 1949 "Artists: Man and Wife" show. Although she subsequently destroyed most of these paintings, the surviving works indicate a strategy to distinguish her art from that of Pollock. The paintings somewhat resemble early Rothkos, composed of bands or rectangles of colors in delicate ranges of related tones. Krasner would not show again until 1955. "In this instance negating Pollock ended up as a kind of neutrality too easily equated with the condition and mental habits of womanhood."[13]

• Lee Krasner, *Gaea*

Krasner's works after 1955, such as *Gaea*, reveal a great energy and self-confidence. From the aggressive, Dionysiac frenzy of *Celebration* (1959–60) to the precision and linear majesty of the "Majuscule" series (1971), Krasner's painting never settled into a signature style. Exploring the range of coloristic possibilities or restricting her palette to earth tones, using forms from nature or rejecting any organic illusionism, Krasner's art springs from sincerity, dedication to craft, and the strength of purpose found in the survivors of personal tragedy.

A painting such as *Gaea* (Fig. 15–2) illustrates one pole of Krasner's art. Active,

Fig. 15–2. Lee Krasner, *Gaea*. 1966. Oil on canvas, 69 in. x 10 ft. 5$\frac{1}{2}$ in.   *(The Museum of Modern Art, New York. Kay Sage Tanguy Fund. Photograph © 1995 The Museum of Modern Art, New York)*

visible, and seemingly spontaneous brushwork define the moving, energetic forms. The palette is characteristically restricted, in this case to black, white, rose pink, and a fleshy-toned, higher-valued pink. *Gaea* is the Greek name for the Earth Mother of the primordial past, a reference which underscores the sense of a prehuman, prehistoric life force pulsing through undifferentiated nature. Almost 7 feet tall and over 12 feet across, the sheer scale of the work overwhelms the viewer with its power and energy.

Krasner's restoration into the pantheon of Abstract Expressionists began in 1978 with her inclusion in an exhibition curated by Gail Levin and Robert Hobbs for the Whitney Museum's *Abstract Expressionism: The Formative Years* (1978). Her reputation, so consistently overshadowed by her position as the wife of Jackson Pollock, began to emerge independently when the artist was over 70. Feminist revisionism has helped us reevaluate the art of this major creator.

- ## Helen Frankenthaler, *Mountains and Sea*

Helen Frankenthaler is one of the major figures in the second generation of Abstract Expressionists. Her prominent position in the history of modern painting is secure because she invented a highly influential method of paint application known as the "soak-stain" technique. While O'Keeffe painted identifiable objects to reveal their abstract qualities, Frankenthaler uses abstract shapes to evoke the forms of the natural world.

Frankenthaler was born in 1928 into a distinguished upper-middle-class family. Her father was a Justice of the New York State Supreme Court. Frankenthaler received an elite, private school education in New York City. According to her own recollection, by age 15 or 16 she had decided to become an artist. She attended Bennington College, where she painted in a Cubist style. Upon graduation in 1949, she returned to New York, where the influential critic Clement Greenberg introduced her to the leading male artists of Abstract Expressionism. Frankenthaler and Greenberg were romantically linked for several years.

Frankenthaler's most significant painting historically is *Mountains and Sea* (Fig. 15–3), created in 1952. The canvas stretches almost 10 feet across. Inspired by Pollock's murals, which he placed on the floor and worked from all four sides, Frankenthaler used the same method. Edges were defined after the canvas was painted. However, Pollock's drip technique retained the thick texture of the paint, whereas Frankenthaler found a new, more luminous quality in oil paint by thinning the paint with turpentine. The colors soaked into the white canvas ground, decreasing the saturation of the hues and achieving an effect similar to the brightness of watercolors.

Unlike the single all-over texture that Pollock's drip method yields, Frankenthaler retains specific hues and shapes that float in an undefined space across the picture surface. While the viewer cannot actually identify water and mountains, one can sense both the color and light of a landscape. These qualities, combined with the sheer scale of the piece, make the viewer feel immersed in a watery natural environment. Frankenthaler painted this work in New York after spending the summer in Nova Scotia. She recalled: "I came back and did *Mountains and Sea* and I know the landscapes were in my arms as I did it."[14]

Fig. 15–3. Helen Frankenthaler, *Mountains and Sea*. 1952. 7 ft. 2³/₈ in. x 9 ft. 9¹/₄ in.   *(Collection of the artist)*

The drips and splatters that occur all over the canvas indicate that the painting of the work was a highly spontaneous, almost uncontrolled act made visible in the finished work. However, there is a clear centering of the main mass, a controlled balance that belies the apparent spontaneity of the technique. The potentialities for the "soak-stain" technique were appreciated by two major artists, Morris Louis and Kenneth Noland, who proceeded to develop their own staining techniques in the late 1950s.

Frankenthaler's contribution to the history of contemporary painting has long been recognized. In 1969 she was given a major retrospective at the Whitney Museum in New York. Her works reveal a unique color sensibility, an innovative method of paint application, and a personal imagery that conveys the beauty and vastness of nature in an abstract and nondescriptive, yet evocative, style.

SCULPTURE

• Louise Nevelson, *Sky Cathedral*

Louise Nevelson (1889–1988) is generally recognized as one of the major innovators in the history of twentieth-century sculpture. By the late 1950s she was making large-scale works that were technically and formally without art historical precedents.

Louise Berliawsky was born in Russia to Jewish parents. When she was 6 years old, the family emigrated to the United States, settling in Rockland, Maine. Louise's affinity for wood dates from her childhood, spent in the proximity of her father's lumber yard. In 1920 she married Charles Nevelson, whose family owned a cargo-shipping business. Two years later her son Myron was born. During the 1920s Nevelson studied voice, drama, and dance, as well as the visual arts. In 1931 she separated from her husband and began to focus her energies on her painting classes at the Art Students League. She continued her painting studies through the 1940s, but it was only when she began to make sculpture from pieces of wood, nailed together and painted a uniform color, that Nevelson found her identity as an artist. Her reputation rests upon a series of environmental structures that she began building in the 1950s.

These large-scale works are constructed from fragments of wood, arranged in compositions within box-like enclosures. They are always painted a uniform color. During the 1950s, the color was black, but later the color changed to white, then gold. However, the black sculptures are the best known and most characteristic of her works.

Sky Cathedral (Fig. 15–4) is one wall of an environmental installation typical of her style. The work is over 8 feet tall and 11 feet wide. By its sheer scale, it dominates the viewer and commands attention. The title evokes a sense of the sculpture as mysterious, awe-inspiring architecture. It is not a unified, coherently designed work. In this sense, Nevelson's aesthetic is diametrically opposed to the sculptures of contemporary Minimalism. *Sky Cathedral* is divided into boxlike enclosures so that the work operates on two levels: an overall impression and the compositions of each individual box.

Nevelson began to enclose her sculpture in boxes in 1956 for emotional reasons:

> I wanted to be more secretive about the work and I began working in the enclosures. . . . There's someting more private about it for me and gives me a better sense of security.[15]

From the confined limits of the box, Nevelson found the freedom to develop the fullest range of expressive potential in the interior compositions. However, she wanted to maintain a monumental scale for her sculpture, so she began piling these boxes on top of one another to create larger-scaled works:

> I attribute the walls to this: I had loads of energy. I mean, energy and energy and loads of creative energy. . . . So I began to stack my sculptures into an environment. It was natural. It was a flowing energy. I think there is something in the consciousness of the creative person that adds up, and the multiple image that I give, say, in an enormous wall gives me so much satisfaction. There is great satisfaction in seeing a splendid, big, enormous work of art.[16]

Part of the distinction of Nevelson's sculpture is that it operates very effectively on the microcosmic scale of the individual enclosures and the macrocosmic scale of a mural or piece of architecture.

Sky Cathedral contains great variety and diversity within its overall unity. Each of the enclosures has a distinctive composition, balanced and complete within its own confines. For example, the third box from the left, on the floor, is a study in curving versus straight elements. Two sweeping arcs are counterbalanced by four horizontal

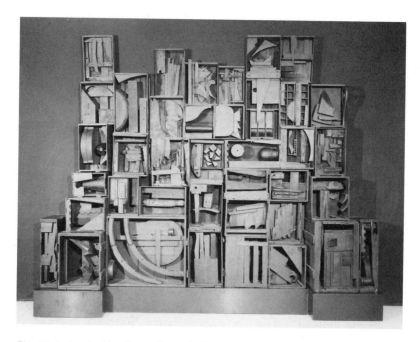

Fig. 15–4. Louise Nevelson, *Sky Cathedral.* 1958. Wood, 102½ x 133½ in. *(Albright–Knox Art Gallery, Buffalo, New York. George B. and Jenny R Mathews Fund, 1970)*

units. The circular shape is then repeated with a disk set on a third spatial level. It is very carefully arranged so that the abstract elements contain their own tensions. Unity is maintained by the overall black color and the consistency of the use of wood fragments.

Black is traditionally associated with death in our society. Yet Nevelson has said,

> . . . it's only an assumption of the western world that it means death; for me it may mean finish, completeness, maybe eternity.[17]

Nevelson's art, as has been noted, had variety and unity, complexity and a certain awesome simplicity. It is both very small and intimate in the box compositions and very large in overall impact. Nevelson believes that her work reflects her identity as a woman:

> I feel that my works are definitely feminine. . . . A man simply couldn't use the means of, say, fingerwork to produce my small pieces. They are like needlework. . . . My work is delicate; it may look strong, but it is delicate. . . . My whole life is in it, and my whole life is feminine. . . . Women through all ages could have had physical strength and mental creativity and still have been feminine. The fact that these things have been suppressed is the fault of society.[18]

It may be surprising at first to hear Nevelson relate her work—which uses nails, saws, and other tools, to needlework. But Nevelson has indeed taken bits and pieces of material, the debris of society, and transformed them, like a patchwork quilt, into a series of uniquely beautiful and impressive works of sculptural art.

Nevelson, who recognized her own isolation from the contemporary movement of Abstract Expressionism, made the following statement:

> Through personal choice and necessity, I never became involved with a group of artists. I don't belong to any movement. Of course, there is no mistake that the times I was living in had influence on me. We pool our energies with other creative people. I feel that, say, if some of our people weren't around where sparks fly, maybe I would not have come to this. That *must* be. My work is bound to be related to that of others. . . .
>
> But you know . . . I wouldn't feel in the right place if I was in the stream of Abstract Expressionism. Now I think they are marvelous. I love their art, and I love their energy. Nevertheless I had to go my own way. Yes, I believe artists reflect their time, but they have to stand on their own two feet . . . not on someone else's. I chose at quite an early age to be a soloist. Because I realized that the rhythms of people are different. Consequently, I wouldn't assume to impose that on somebody else. And by the same token, I had to make my decisions, I had to make my moves. Everything came back to *me*.[19]

• Claire Falkenstein, *U as a Set*

Over the course of a lengthy and prolific career, Claire Falkenstein (b. 1928) has created an enormously diverse oeuvre of highly innovative abstract sculpture. While her materials range from massive cedar logs of the *Forum, Memorial to A. Quincy Jones* to delicate welded wire, her works illustrate universal forces and processes as understood by twentieth-century science and philosophy.

Falkenstein was born in 1928 in a small rural community in Oregon, but her family moved to the San Francisco Bay area early in her life. She graduated from the University of California at Berkeley, where she studied anthropology and philosophy. These early intellectual interests would persist throughout her career and serve as sources for her aesthetic systems.

Alexander Archipenko was the first famous sculptor with whom Falkenstein studied. Archipenko's interest in the expressive possibilities of negative spaces, although still tied to the human form, was influential for Falkenstein, who would pursue her exploration of sculptural form freed from enclosing volumes throughout her career. In the late 1940s she taught sculpture at the California School of Fine Arts with such noted Abstract Expressionist painters as Clyfford Still.

A significant turning point occurred in her career when she moved to Paris in 1950. She lived and worked in Europe until 1962. Like the experiences a century earlier of sculptors such as Harriet Hosmer, Falkenstein matured as an artist during these years abroad, creating a significant body of works of great originality. Like Sam Francis, Joan Mitchell, and Ellsworth Kelly, Falkenstein found Paris inspirational. Like Barbara Hepworth, direct contact with European masters such as Brancusi, Arp, and Giacometti, coupled with access to works of the School of Paris and the freedom of movement far from the competitive environment of New York, made Paris a liberating and fruitful environment. In the welded wire sculptures known as the "Sun Series," Falkenstein created work that demonstrated her rejection of the closed, defined, and measurable world of Euclidean geometry in favor of an active curved space illustrative of her understanding of topology. The flowing and continuously expanding forms of topological space are related directly to Falkenstein's understanding of Einstein's theory of relativity:

> So when I'm talking about expanding space, I'm thinking in terms actually Einsteinian, the Einstein attitude of the expanding universe. I'm thinking about total space, that you do not make something to displace space but whatever you do is part of space. It's a through thing. It's not something that pushes space away from it, but space goes through it.[20]

Thus, one underlying principle of Falkenstein's art is never to create objects or images that imply that one can entrap or separate space from the unity of the natural world.

To illustrate this concept sculpturally, Falkenstein often employs "the sign of the U," a curved, open linear shape flattened at both ends. In the monumental *U as a Set* (Fig. 15–5) a mass of U signs made of copper tubing have been welded into a gigantic shape, which is also a "U" over twenty feet long. It is placed against a "wall" of fountain jets and isolated in its own reflecting pool on the campus of California State University in Long Beach. The interaction of active linear forms in the sculpture and the shooting sprays of water provide two parallel references to the motion of natural forces.

Falkenstein's works constantly surprise and confound programmed expectations of sculpture, painting, or architecture. Although she came to maturity in the era of second-generation Abstract Expressionism and her works can be seen in that histori-

Fig. 15–5. Claire Falkenstein, *U as a Set—A Fountain.* 1966. California State University, Long Beach, CA. Copper tubing, 14 x 20 x 10 ft. *(courtesy Claire Falkenstein)*

cal context, they do not fit easily or securely within a specific period, movement, or group. Emerging from a firm philosophical base, their quality resides in a high level of distinctive, individual expression.

MINIMALISM AND OP ART

- **Agnes Martin, *Untitled***

The mature works of Agnes Martin such as *Untitled* concentrate on the use of a grid drawn in pencil on a luminous ground. Her paintings are early and characteristic examples of Minimalism, a movement that affected a number of artists in the 1960s. Reacting against the painterly emotionalism of Abstract Expressionism, Martin's extremely delicate, humble paintings are conceptually crystalline, eliminating any elements of chance or spontaneity in their execution. Her works are holistic because the entire surface is created through the repetition of module units. Martin's works were seminal influences for the next generation of artists, including Eva Hesse, who frequently employed grids.

Martin was born in 1912 on a wheat farm in Saskatchewan, Canada. Her father died when she was still very young, and the family moved to Vancouver. In 1941 Martin began attending Columbia University's Teachers College. By 1954 she had earned a B.S. and an M.A. degree in fine arts and arts administration at Columbia and was determined to become a painter. She was living in New York during the most active and formative era of Abstract Expresionism, but after graduation she moved to New Mexico, settling in Taos in 1956.

Not surprisingly, Martin's paintings of the early 1950s reveal the influence of Abstract Expressionist painters, such as Arshile Gorky and William Baziotes, through her use of biomorphic, abstract forms, which convey a symbolic or narrative content. By 1955 she was using geometric shapes placed on pale, luminous backgrounds. In 1957, with the support of the gallery owner Betty Parsons, Martin returned to New York. From this time onward, her works developed in the direction of increasing simplicity of structure and uniformity of surface. Her paintings either employ the repetition of a single form or the depiction of one large form.

By 1961 Martin was using the format of the grid on a square canvas. Her horizontal and vertical units created the effect of a veil suspended within the canvas edges. Her grids eventually expanded to cover the entire surface of the canvas, creating a total unity between the picture surface and the module. Martin's grids are usually subdivided into rectangular units. She explained her use of the rectangle in the following way:

> My formats are square, but the grids never are absolutely square, they are rectangles, a little bit off the square, making a sort of contradiction, a dissonance, though I didn't set out to do it that way. When I cover the square surface with rectangles, it lightens the weight of the square, destroys its power.[21]

Martin's characteristic use of pencil creates "channels of nuance stretched on a rack of linear tensions."[22] As opposed to a brush, a pencil offers greater resistance to

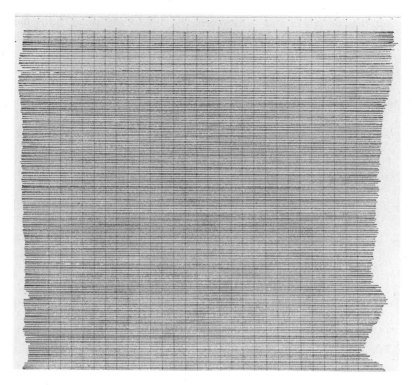

Fig. 15–6. Agnes Martin, *Untitled.* 1961. Ink and pencil on paper, 8 x 8¹/₄ in. *(courtesy Margo Leavin Gallery, Los Angeles)*

the artist's hand pressure. Therefore, the selection of pencil, as a medium, is a reaction against the gestural painters of Abstract Expressionism.

Although Martin has confined her art within a narrow set of limitations, there is great variety within the self-imposed confines of the grid. Her grids are never identical, but vary in proportions, size, and color. Furthermore, as Lawrence Alloway has noted, the selection of a conceptual order is just as personal as autographic tracks of the brush.[23]

The physical size of a work is irrelevant in Martin's systems. Whether on the small scale of Figure 15–6 or the much larger size of many of her canvases, Martin's images evoke the sense of the sublimely infinite in their accumulation of small, identical units. They seem as if they could be extended indefinitely to infinity. "A collection of similar bits, beyond easy counting, implies infinity; that is why the internal area of a Martin painting can seem highly expansive."[24] They are intended to evoke a mystical, meditative response in the viewer.

Martin's images, then, are deceptively simple. While one can grasp her system almost instantly, the implications of her images are complex. It is paradoxical but accurate to see in Martin's highly structured and impersonal surfaces a visual metaphor for the vastness of the universe and the multiplicity existing within nature.

- **Bridget Riley, *Fall***

Bridget Riley has received international recognition as one of the innovators in the Op Art movement. Her works concentrate on the dynamics of visual perception, the physiological core of the visual arts. Riley's paintings challenge the viewer to see in unaccustomed ways.

Born in London in 1931, Riley received her early training at Goldsmith's School of Art and at the Painting School of the Royal College of Art. She left school with no personal sense of direction and did very little painting until 1959. During that year she became interested in Georges Seurat, the theories of Pointillism, and the art of the Italian Futurists. By 1961 Riley had focused her energies on the creation of images in black and white in which basic units are altered to create a visual effect of motion. Unlike Martin, who maintains a uniformity in her grids, Riley's painting explores the effects of variations in regular patterning. In 1961 she saw works by Victor Vasarely for the first time. Encouraged by this artist's example, she pursued her interests in the optical "tricks" that can be achieved through the manipulation of geometric shapes.

Fig. 15–7. Bridget Riley, *Fall*. 1963. Emulsion on board, $55^1/_2$ x $55^1/_2$ in. *(The Tate Gallery, London. Reproduced by permission of the artist)*

Fall (Fig. 15–7) is a square canvas in which black and white lines of equal width undulate from top to bottom. Toward the bottom, the "visual frequency" (Riley's term) changes from the slow, even curves of the upper two-thirds of the canvas to shorter, more rapid undulations. The eye tries to mix the black and white lines unsuccessfully and perceives pulsations of gray. An almost painfully intense visual vibration results. As William Seitz observed: "The eyes seem to be bombarded with pure energy."[25] The image creates an illusion of movement. We feel as if these lines are actually moving through space. There is also a sense of sound waves, and the analogy to musical rhythms is unavoidable.

Riley's *Fall* and other Op Art paintings sacrifice narrative content and the entire Western tradition of optical illusion. There are few precedents for images that focus so exclusively on the way we see. Riley's creative input for this work resides in the selection of the unit sizes and in the changes in those units to alter the visual rhythm of the painting. As opposed to Frankenthaler's paintings, which reveal the technical skill and manual expertise of the artist, Riley's surfaces, like Martin's, are smooth and immaculate.

Riley participated in the seminal exhibition that defined and illustrated the artistic movement since named Op Art. "The Responsive Eye" opened at New York's Museum of Modern Art in 1965 with a reproduction of Riley's *Current* (1964) on the cover of the catalogue. Her paintings, then limited to back and white, elicited wide critical and popular success.

In the late 1960s Riley incorporated color into her systemic images. Retaining the use of repeating geometric units, her subtle color variations create beautiful and intriguing effects of movement. Her formative contribution to Op Art has long been recognized, and in 1971 she was given a major retrospective exhibition at the Hayward Gallery in London.

THE FEMALE BODY IN PAINTING AND SCULPTURE

Other artists in the 1960s eschewed the dominant mainstream forms of abstraction and instead opted to focus on works that direct attention to the female body.

• Alice Neel, *Pregnant Maria*

With total indifference to the trends in the art world since World War II, ignoring fluctuations of taste and the pervasive abstraction of the 1950s and 1960s, Alice Neel (1900–1984) created a body of works, almost all portraits, of supreme individuality and psychological intensity. After forty years of painting, it was only in 1974 with a major retrospective at the Whitney Museum in New York that her oeuvre became recognized outside of a small circle of cognoscenti. Neel's gifts spring from her unique ability to pierce the "protective strategies" which people assume, revealing the soul beneath the surface.[26] With deceptive modesty, Neel has said, "I usually know why people look the way they look."[27]

Born in a suburb of Philadelphia, Neel recalls always knowing she would become a painter. Avoiding the Impressionist-dominated Pennsylvania Academy of Fine Arts, she received her training in the more traditional academic curriculum of the Philadelphia School of Design for Women between 1921 and 1925. That year she married an artist from a wealthy Cuban family, Carlos Enriquez. The death of her first daughter, the disintegration of her marriage, and the impoverishment of the Depression led to a suicide attempt and total nervous breakdown in the early 1930s. From these painful experiences, Neel emerged to settle in New York City and eventually receive a small stipend from the WPA. Neel only began to receive some recognition in the art world when she won a prize for one of her portraits in 1962.

As Ann Sutherland Harris has observed, Neel has turned the conventions of portraiture inside out by operating outside of the confines of the commissioned work.[28] Without catering to the tastes or desires of her patrons, the artist selects her sitters, positioning them in her own studio rather than integrating them into their own environment. This absence of conventional portrait patronage has permitted Neel to paint some segments of humanity rarely, if ever, recorded in paint. Neel's sitters are drawn from the broadest range of social and economic classes. They include art world celebrities, such as Andy Warhol, members of the intelligensia, such as Linda Nochlin, and ordinary working-class minority persons, such as her Haitian housekeeper, Carmen, portrayed nursing her developmentally damaged child.

Between 1930 and 1978 Neel executed a series of nude portraits of pregnant women, sometimes reclining as in *Pregnant Maria*, at other times upright. Neel has justified her attention to pregnancy by noting its importance in life and its neglect by other artists.[29]

Fig. 15–8. Alice Neel, *Pregnant Maria*. 1964. Oil on canvas, 32 x 47 in.   *(courtesy Robert Miller Gallery, New York. © Estate of Alice Neel)*

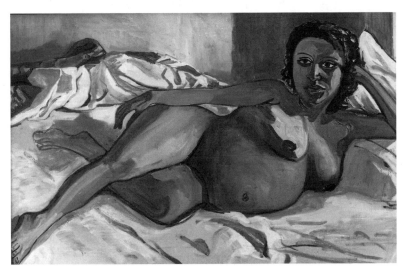

One of the most marked characteristics of Neel's images is their specificity. They never descend into stereotypes or generalizations. Even in the subcategory of nude pregnant portraiture, which Neel practiced sporadically throughout her career, the individual retains her own unique identity. This is clearly apparent in *Pregnant Maria*.

Like Manet's *Olympia*, *Pregnant Maria* presents an image of a whole person, unashamed of her nudity or obvious pregnancy, confronting the viewer with dignity and apparent lack of self-consciousness. No female fertility goddess or archetypal earth mother, this very real individual does not symbolize "Maternity," but embodies the physical human fact of childbearing.

Characteristically, Maria is positioned very close to the viewer in the extreme foreground, with little depth indicated. This forces a direct interaction between portrait subject and viewer. Also in a typical fashion, some portions of the canvas are treated with a great deal more detail and modeling than others. Maria's face, breasts, and distended belly are fully modeled, giving them a tangible presence, while the receding foot and background are undetailed and unmodeled. Clearly defined contour lines and visible brushwork also characterize the style of the painting.

Neel's talent lies in her unique ability to present the essence of her sitter, not merely his or her surface ornamentation. She calls this "telling the truth:"

> I do not know if the truth that I have told will benefit the world in any way. I managed to do it at great cost to myself and perhaps to others. It is hard to go against the tide of one's time, milieu, and position. But at least I tried to reflect innocently the twentieth century and my feelings and perceptions as a girl and a woman. Not that I felt they were all that different from men's.
>
> I did this at the expense of untold humiliations, but at least after my fashion I told the truth as I perceived it, and, considering the way one is bombarded by reality, did the best and most honest art of which I was capable.[30]

Linda Nochlin identifies this ability of telling the truth about an individual's personality as a characteristic most appropriate to the socialization processes of women:

> In the field of portraiture, women have been active among the subverters of the natural laws of modernism. This hardly seems accidental: women have, after all, been encouraged if not coerced, into making responsiveness to the moods, attentiveness to the character-traits . . . of others into a lifetime's occupation. What is more natural than that they should put their subtle talents as seismographic recorders of social position, as quivering reactors to the most minimal subsurface psychological tremors to good use in their art.[31]

Alice Neel, more than any other contemporary artist, has exploited this female trait of insight to generate a large body of extraordinarily powerful images.

• Niki de Saint-Phalle, *Hon (She)*

Born in 1930, Saint-Phalle spent her youth in New York, but her life as an artist began with her return to Europe in 1952. She had her first one person show in 1956 in Switzerland, and she was given a retrospective exhibition at the Pompidou Center, Paris, in 1980 and at the Nassau Museum, Long Island, in 1988.

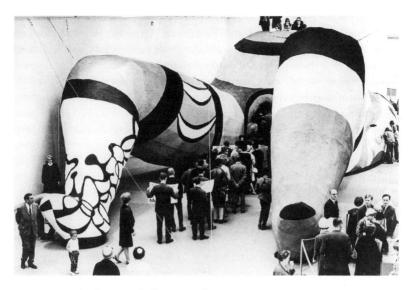

Fig. 15–9. Niki de Saint-Phalle, *Hon (She)*. 1966. *(The National Swedish Art Museums. © artist copyright de Saint-Phalle; © photo copyright Hans Hammarskiöld)*

Living with the artist Jean Tinguely, known for his late Dada-inspired performance art, Saint-Phalle's early work incorporated found objects. In works such as *Bride* and *Accouchment*, dolls and other small-scale toys are affixed to a figural image and then painted for uniformity. The immediate precedent for *Hon* was the series of giant *Nanas* she created beginning in 1965. Brightly painted, massive, and awesome, the *Nanas* took back the primordial power of the female body.

Created in 1966 as a temporary installation for Stockholm's Modern Museum, this work stretched 82 feet in length. Viewers entered the figure through a door in the vagina. A milk bar was installed in one breast and a film was projected in a different portion of the interior. Chadwick states that this work "reclaimed woman's body as a site of tactile pleasure rather than an object of voyeuristic viewing; the figure was both a playful and colorful homage to woman as nurturer and a potent demythologizer of male romantic notions of the female body as a 'dark continent' and unknowable reality."[32]

• Louise Bourgeois, *Femme Maison*

Bourgeois was born in 1911 into a French family in which her artistic talents were not only recognized but put to use. Her parents restored Aubusson tapestries, and her job as a child was to draw in the missing parts to guide the weavers. She received a classical education at the Sorbonne, where she studied philosophy and geometry. She also studied art history at the *Ecole du Louvre* and acquired academic training in the fine arts at the *Ecole des Beaux-Arts*, which she attended from 1936 to 1938. She moved to New York in 1938 and has lived there ever since.

Since the late 1940s Louise Bourgeois has created works of sculpture that express a highly personal symbolic system. Unaffected by the successive art movements that have dominated the art world since World War II, she has pursued personal goals, tenaciously seeking formal equivalents for the constants underlying the human condition. Working in a wide variety of media, ranging from traditional sculptural materials, such as marble, wood, and bronze, to impermanent latex, Bourgeois's works explore the relationship between man and woman and the concept of androgyny, as well as seeking equivalents for emotional states.

Femme Maison was first exhibited in 1947 and is clearly developed under the influence of Surrealism. Lucy Lippard selected this work to illustrate the cover of her book of collected essays on feminist art, *From the Center* (1976).[33] Since the mid-seventies, Bourgeois's work has been highly visible and well documented.

Charlotta Kotik identifies *Femme Maison* and the other works in the series on this subject as defining "a feminist vision [which] signaled the emotional intensity and narrative content that was to become the hallmark of Bourgeois's art. . . . The house becomes a major catalyst for memory, for it is in this certain and defined locale that the range of human relationships and feelings . . . take place."[34] The *femme maison* series would seem to be a particularly appropriate confirmation of Bourgeois's statement,

> My work is a very specific fight against specific fears, one at a time. It comes close to a defining, and understanding and accepting, of fear.[35]

Well into the 1980s the image of the house was used by Bourgeois in her sculp-

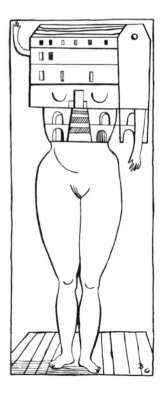

Fig. 15–10. Louise Bourgeois, *Femme Maison*. 1947. Ink on paper, 9$\frac{1}{16}$ x 3$\frac{9}{16}$ in. *(The Solomon R. Guggenheim Museum, New York. Photograph by David Heald © The Solomon R. Guggenheim Foundation, New York. FN 92.4008)*

ture. But in the more recent works the scale of the house is reduced to a diminutive box; it can no longer overwhelm the body as in the images from the 1940s.

- **Louise Bourgeois, *Cumul I***

In the late 1940s Bourgeois created simple wooden structures that convey a powerful and eerie presence. *The Blind Leading the Blind*, for example, consists of a double row of upright wooden posts that taper to pointed "feet." The posts are connected by an irregularly shaped lintel. The almost uniform uprights are easily interpreted as anonymous, unindividualized persons. The lintel binds them together, turning the separate posts into an architectural structure. Painted black, like Nevelson's later constructions, the work conveys a sense of monotonous menace. It is interesting and relevant that this work was created during the McCarthy Era, around the time when Bourgeois, Duchamp, and other artists were being investigated by the House Committee on Un-American Activities. It reflects the paranoia about communism that had temporarily seized the government machinery of the United States.

The use of a group of regular units is also seen in Bourgeois's "Cumul" series from the late 1960s (Fig. 15–11). In these works, most of which are carved in marble, rounded forms seem to be bursting through or growing out of undifferentiated matter. Like spores emerging from a sac, or a penis becoming erect, these rounded forms, which also could be interpreted as breast shapes, are symbols of a life force. They evoke a sense of eclosion and androgynous generation.

Bourgeois's works do not fit within a stylistic movement or a neatly defined category. She has worked in a wide variety of media and in a range of different styles, adjusting her formal means to fit her expressive intent. She deals with the most fascinating questions of the human spirit—the relationship between the sexes and the relationship between the individual and the society in which he or she lives.

Although Bourgeois often uses carved marble, that most traditional of all sculptural materials, her imagery is unique, and there is little point in trying to relate her works to other famous carvers such as Michelangelo or Rodin. Two major exhibi-

Fig. 15–11. Louise Bourgeois, *Cumul I*. 1969. Marble, 22³/₈ x 50 x 48 in. *(photo courtesy of the artist and the Musée Nationals d'art Moderne, Centre Georges Pompidou, Paris)*

tions, spaced about a decade apart in 1982 and 1993, indicate that Bourgeois's position in the history of contemporary art is finally secured.

PROCESS ART

- ### Eva Hesse, *Untitled*

Eva Hesse's (1936–1970) mature and significant career as an artist is concentrated within the brief span of five years, 1966 through 1970, the year she died from a brain tumor at the age of 34. During this time, she created a number of sculptures that differ in many ways from the prevailing contemporary aesthetic of Minimalism. As a post-Minimalist, Hesse's works were formally, technically, and conceptually innovative and influential for the direction of sculpture during the 1970s. Her oeuvre is well documented, and her contribution to the history of contemporary art is significant.

Born in Hamburg into a German Jewish family, she and her sister escaped extermination in the Holocaust by leaving Germany on a children's train bound for neutral Holland. Her parents rejoined them several months later, and the family settled in New York City in 1939. New traumas came when her parents were divorced and when, the following year, her mother committed suicide. By age 16, Hesse had decided to become an artist. She studied at several New York art schools: Pratt Institute, the Art Students League, and Cooper Union. From 1957 to 1959 Hesse attended Yale University's School of Art and Architecture. Returning to New York City, she integrated herself into the avant-garde art community. In 1961 she married the artist Tom Doyle, and in 1964 the couple spent a year in Germany. During this stay abroad, Hesse abandoned painting and started making three-dimensional, biomorphic reliefs, related in form and spirit to Surrealism.

In 1966 two emotionally traumatic events occurred in Hesse's life: Her marriage ended and her father died. She emerged from these crises a mature sculptor with a personal style and direction. That same year she participated, along with Louise Bourgeois, in a group show called "Eccentric Abstraction," curated by Lucy Lippard. This exhibition first defined the post-Minimal process-oriented attitude of a group of contemporary sculptors.

Hesse shared with Claes Oldenburg, Robert Smithson, Lucas Samaras, and Louise Bourgeois an aversion to the ponderous, architectural ambitions of Minimal sculpture. Hesse was one of the first artists to use a wide range of nontraditional materials to make her objects. Her earliest works were made from limp and pliable materials, such as cord, rubber tubing, or wire, emerging from boards mounted on a wall. Hesse's works often employed the repetition of similar units. She was very aware and deliberate about her intentions. In the last year of her life she told an interviewer:

> If something is meaningful, maybe it's more meaningful said ten times. It's not just an esthetic choice. If something is absurd, it's much more absurd if it's repeated . . . repetition does enlarge or increase or exaggerate an idea or purpose in a statement.[36]

In 1967 Hesse made *Repetition Nineteen*, in which nineteen nearly identical buckets are scattered about the floor. That same year she discovered latex rubber, a sensuous and flexible but impermanent material. The following year she also began working with fiberglass.

Anna Chave has analyzed Hesse's search for new and original ways "to articulate a feminine sexual subjectivity. . . . Rather than use her art to refuse the sociohistorically invisible position of being a woman, Hesse worked to attest to that very sense of vacancy or absence and the pain it entails."[37] Chave finds the body imagery in Hesse's work to be "a body in pain . . . mutilated, dismembered or flayed." Chave identifies the work illustrated (Fig. 15–12) as an example of what Hesse was trying to achieve in a series of negations. Hesse wrote in 1969,

> I wanted to get to non art, non connotive, non anthropomorphic, non geometric, non, nothing.[38]

Chave builds a case to understand Hesse as "more or less seriously ill throughout her life, and that she almost always viewed herself as sick."[39]

Hesse suffered from depression and anticipated her own death as a suicide, like that of her mother. She experienced severe pains in her legs in Germany, so severe that she could barely stand. Her materials, malleable, fragile, and soft, relate to spin-

Fig. 15–12. Eva Hesse, *Untitled (Rope Piece)*. 1969–1970. Latex over rope, string, and wire. Two strands: dimensions variable *(Collection of Whitney Museum of American Art. Purchase, with funds from Eli and Edythe L. Broad, the Mrs. Percy Uris Purchase Fund, and the Painting and Sculpture Committee. 88.17a–b. Copyright © 1995: Whitney Museum of American Art. Photo by Geoffrey Clements)*

ning, weaving, sewing, knitting, wrapping, and bandaging—all associated with women's work. "But in becoming a professional sculptor—one who courageously refused both academic and avant-garde orthodoxies—Hesse effectively declined such stultifying roles, while inverting the means and material of women's art into a mode of self empowerment."[40]

"The noisome scent of decay which seems to emanate from Hesse's sculpture helps explain its chilling effect on viewers, as it plays on our fears of contamination and dissolution, on our gnawing sense of our own mortality. . . . She made her art out of her illnesses, which substantially defined her identity as a woman and (to a lesser degree) as a Jew, as one of the disempowered and despised."[41]

The sculpture of Eva Hesse challenges many traditional attitudes concerning our expectations of the appearance of a piece of sculpture and the materials used in its construction. In a witty and understated way, Hesse's works are revolutionary, transforming the medium and the intellectual approach to the creation of a work of "art." Her sculptural oeuvre has been quite influential and her formative position within the history of contemporary art is widely acknowledged today.

Suggestions for Further Reading

General Reference Works

MUNRO, ELEANOR, *Originals: American Women Artists* (New York: Simon and Schuster, 1979).

NEMSER, CINDY, *Art Talk: Conversations with Twelve Women Artists* (New York: Scribner's, 1975).

SWENSON, LYNN F., and SALLY SWENSON, *Lives and Work: Talks with Women Artists* (Methuchen, NJ: Scarecrow Press, 1981).

Krasner

HOBBS, ROBERT, *Krasner* (New York: Abbeville Modern Masters, 1993).

ROSE, BARBARA, *Lee Krasner: A Retrospective* (New York: Museum of Modern Art, 1983).

Frankenthaler

CARMEAN, E. A., *Helen Frankenthaler: A Paintings Retrospective* (New York: Abrams and Modern Art Museum of Fort Worth, 1989).

ELDERFIELD, JOHN, *Frankenthaler* (New York: Abrams, 1989).

GOOSEN, E. C., *Helen Frankenthaler* (New York: Praeger, 1969).

ROSE, BARBARA, *Helen Frankenthaler* (New York: Abrams, 1971).

Nevelson

GLIMCHER, ARNOLD, *Louise Nevelson* (New York: Praeger, 1972).

NEVELSON, LOUISE, *Atmospheres and Environments* (New York: Clarkson N. Potter in association with the Whitney Museum of American Art, 1980).

NEVELSON, LOUISE, *Dawns and Dusks* (New York: Scribner's, 1976).

WILSON, LAURIE, "Bride of the Black Moon: An Iconographic Study of the Work of Louise Nevelson," *ARTS Magazine*, 54 (May 1980), pp. 140–48.

Martin

ALLOWAY, LAWRENCE, *Agnes Martin* (Philadelphia: Institute of Contemporary Art, University of Pennsylvania, 1973).

Riley

DE SAUSMAREZ, MAURICE, *Bridget Riley* (Greenwich, CT: New York Graphic Society, 1970).

RILEY, BRIDGET, *Paintings and Drawings, 1951–71* (Arts Council of Great Britain, 1971).

Neel

HARRIS, ANN SUTHERLAND, *Alice Neel: 1930–1980* (Los Angeles: Loyola Marymount University, 1983).

HILLS, PATRICIA, *Alice Neel* (New York: Abrams, 1983).

Bourgeois

KOTIK, CHARLOTTA et al., *Louise Bourgeois: The Locus of Memory, Works 1982–1993* (New York: The Brooklyn Museum and Abrams, 1994).

WYE, DEBORAH, *Louise Bourgeois* (New York: Museum of Modern Art, 1982).

Hesse

COOPER, HELEN et al., *Eva Hesse: A Retrospective* (New Haven, CT: Yale University Press, 1992).

LIPPARD, LUCY, *Eva Hesse* (New York: New York University Press, 1976).

CHAPTER 16

CONTEMPORARY ART: 1970–PRESENT

THE FEMINIST ART MOVEMENT OF THE 1970s

The energy and force of the women's liberation movement in America in the early 1970s generated new subjects, techniques, and inspiration for women artists. Largely bypassed by the coolly rational and ironic aesthetics of Pop Art and Minimalism, women artists began impacting very directly on the art world as a whole. In 1980, one critic looking back on the decade confidently proclaimed: "For the first time women are leading, not following."[1] That leadership role occurred in a number of different media and directions, exemplified by the artists included in this chapter.

Women artists first began incorporating subject matter derived from personal experience into the work of art. This inaugurated a shift from Minimalism to the era known as "Pluralism" or "Post-Modernism." Frequently subjects were autobiographical and focused on the specific experiences of being female. In an effort to integrate the private realm with the public activity of the art work, women artists adopted the feminist slogan, "The personal is the political." As one male artist succinctly observed: "Women have made subject matter legitimate again."[2]

Women artists employed a wide range of media for the expression of content. Whether it appeared in the traditional forms of painting or sculpture or in the rituals of performance art, the validity of using material summoned from the artist's life as a woman had immense consequences for the entire art world.

In *The Power of Feminist Art*, published in 1994, and edited by Norma Broude and Mary Garrard, the full extent and impact of women artists' creativity in the visual arts in this decade is given more complete discussion than is possible within the scope of this book. The following examples of works by a few artists active in the movement indicate the range and scale of this explosion of women's creativity in the 1970s. This period offers a marked contrast to the isolation often experienced by women artists in earlier times.[3] Women's political organizations and alternative exhibition systems were an important factor in building networks of support that encouraged this art to flourish.

The history of a contemporary feminist art movement is generally traced back to 1970, the year Judy Chicago founded the first feminist studio art course at Fresno State College in northern California.[4] It is also the year that Judy Gerowitz abandoned the patriarchal association of her father's name and selected the surname "Chicago" from the city of her birth and initial formal education at the Chicago Art Institute. That same year she showed the first images characterized by the centrality of vaginal imagery, which would dominate her art for the next decade. The following year, in 1971, she teamed up with Miriam Schapiro, who had been living in California since 1967. Together they developed a feminist art program at the California Institute of the Arts in Valencia.

The energy generated from these pedagogical experiments led to the communal art installation known as *Womanhouse*.[5] Working with a team of students from the University of California, Schapiro and Chicago supervised the renovation of a run-down building in Hollywood, designing installation works in each of the rooms. The walls and ceiling of the "Kitchen" (by Robin Weltsch) were covered in breast-shaped eggs. Schapiro, in collaboration with Sherry Brody, created a dollhouse whose forms and fabric elements would influence the course of her art for the next few years, while Chicago created the more aggressive "Menstruation Bathroom." Set into the sterile white environment of the typical American bathroom, a garbage can revealed the evidence of female menstruation cycles.

These artists' distinct contributions to *Womanhouse* are illustrative of the diverse directions their feminist art would take during the 1970s. *Womanhouse* was a catalytic force for Los Angeles's women artists' community and led directly to the founding in 1973 of the Los Angeles Woman's Building.

- ## Sylvia Sleigh, *The Turkish Bath*

The history of feminist art of the 1970s is intertwined with the establishment of alternative gallery spaces and exhibition strategies. In 1972 Womanspace in Los Angeles and A.I.R. (Artists in Residence) Gallery were founded. These were cooperative galleries in which a limited number of women paid dues and shared responsibilities for maintaining the gallery space. In its first years of operation A.I.R. achieved high visibility for its members in the New York art world. Sleigh was a founding member of another cooperative gallery, Soho 20, founded in 1973. Sleigh even painted a diptych group portrait of the members.[6] That same year, the Women's Building opened in Los Angeles, and for nearly two decades it would provide a center for feminist artists in southern California that included a full range of activities, not just an exhibition space.

Sleigh painted *The Turkish Bath* in that important year, 1973. She "appropriated" Ingres's famous image in the Louvre but substituted specific portrait likenesses of men for the anonymous women of Ingres's exotic Orientalist fantasy. In the foreground, most prominently displayed, is Lawrence Alloway, Sleigh's husband and a well-known art critic and educator in the New York art world. Alloway would become an early and enthusiastic supporter of the efforts of feminist artists in the 1970s. Immediately behind Alloway is John Perreault, also an art critic and an early defender of the pattern and decoration art movement. Paul Rosano, playing the guitar and depicted again on the far right, was one of Sleigh's favorite models of the time. The other two men, Scott Burton and Carter Ratcliff, were also critics.

Fig. 16–1. Sylvia Sleigh, *The Turkish Bath*. 1975. Oil on canvas. 76 x 102 in.
(courtesy Zaks Gallery, Chicago, and Stiebel Modern Gallery, New York)

Sleigh's image goes beyond simple sexual reversals to maintain the individual identities of these men who have both bodies and minds. She provides a model for escaping the "essentialism" so frequently characteristic of depictions of the female nude in the history of art.

• Audrey Flack, *Marilyn (Vanitas)*

Audrey Flack is one of the originators and most prominent artists in the 1970s movement known as Photo Realism. Like Don Eddy and Richard Estes, Flack uses photographic reproductions, i.e., color slides, projected onto the canvas to create her paintings. However, while Eddy and Estes merely select their subjects from the urban environment, Flack's paintings are wholly artificial still life arrangements. Her choice of objects and their juxtapositions and relative sizes are totally controlled by the artist. Her paintings always convey a precise message, sometimes with a biographical content, at other times with public or political significance.

Flack was born in New York and studied at the High School of Music and Art, where she was trained in Cubism. At Cooper Union, where the prevailing style was Abstract Expressionism, Flack absorbed the lessons of the gesture painters. She attended Yale University's Graduate School and continued her studies of the figure at the Art Students League. In the mid-1950s, Flack was one of the very few artists who displayed paintings of the human figure. Abstraction so dominated the art world at that time that her realistic art was little appreciated. Nevertheless, she persisted in retaining recognizable subjects in her art through the 1960s. The *Kennedy Motorcade* (1964) was the first painting in which she used a color photograph as a reference.[7] Thereafter, she continued to use photographs as sources for her paintings and in the early 1970s discovered the advantages of using a color slide projected directly on the canvas. In this way, she could increase the scale and achieve greater brilliance of color in her canvases.

In her characteristic paintings from the 1970s Flack uses an airbrush to create an immaculate surface that can imitate the textures of objects. She layers the three primary hues in transparent glazes so the colors are mixed optically. In this way, she eliminates line and brushstrokes but retains a precision useful for the description of a variety of reflective surfaces.

Joanna Frueh has characterized this work in the following description: "Audrey Flack's *Marilyn (Vanitas)* treats femininity as a willed choice. Powder puff, rouge, and eye shadow crown and halo Marilyn Monroe as a queen and saint of 'makeup,' the make-believe of feminine beauty. A levitating crimson lipstick and paintbrush dripping red pigment resonate as magical tools used by masters of illusion—visual artists who are painters and women who 'paint' themselves into the Eternal Feminine."[8]

This image recalls Gloria Steinem's frequently repeated phrase, "All women are female impersonators."

Fig. 16–2. Audrey Flack, *Marilyn (Vanitas)*. 1977. Oil over acrylic on canvas, 96 x 96 in. *(courtesy Louis K. Meisel Gallery, New York; photo by Bruce C. Jones)*

• Judy Chicago, *The Dinner Party*

Chicago's feminist activism culminated in the design and execution of the most monumental and well-publicized individual work to emerge out of the women's movement in southern California. *The Dinner Party* (Fig. 16–3) was conceived in 1974–75, exhibited at the San Francisco Museum in 1978, and traveled around the country, finally arriving at the Brooklyn Museum, New York, in 1980.

This major installation work is composed of a large triangular table, stretching 48 feet on each side. The triangle was selected as the earliest symbol of female power and the sign of the goddess. Each arm of the equilateral triangle supports thirteen place settings. The thirty-nine women selected for this homage range from early goddesses, through Eleanor of Aquitaine, Christine De Pisan, the noted feminist of the early fifteenth century, Artemisia Gentileschi, and Sojourner Truth, to the diverse achievements in the twentieth century of Margaret Sanger and Georgia O'Keeffe. Each of these place settings consists of a porcelain plate, 14 inches in diameter, designed by Chicago to reflect the specific achievements and experiences of these historic figures. The designs of all the plates are based on the central, vaginal imagery so critical to Chicago's aesthetic.

One of the most remarkable aspects of *The Dinner Party* was the complex and beautiful needlework runners that form a major part of the ensemble. These were executed by over one hundred skilled needleworkers. The use of china plate painting and needlework as the key components of this piece form a self-conscious reevaluation of "craft" media, most often practiced by women and barred from consideration as "fine art."

The monumental table is set on a raised platform, covered with 2,300 hand-cast tiles, on which are written the names of an additional 999 significant women in history.

Chicago's ambitious goal for this work was didactic and, in turn, political. By educating women about their unique contributions to history, she hoped to spark social change in today's world.

> So my *Dinner Party* would also be a people's history—the history of women in Western civilization. . . . I had been personally strengthened by discovering my rich heritage as a woman and the enormous amount of information that existed about women's contributions to society. This information, however, was totally outside the mainstream of historical thought and was certainly unknown to most people. And as long as women's achievements were excluded from our understanding of the past, we would continue to feel as if we had never done anything worthwhile. This absence of any sense of our tradition as women seemed to cripple us psychologically. I wanted to change that, and I wanted to do it through art.[9]

Whatever reservations one might have concerning the obsessive repetition of vaginal imagery and difficulties in viewing the needlework runners caused by the closed triangular form of the table, *The Dinner Party* fulfilled Chicago's expectations. Shown around the country, it impacted on a very large number of viewers, demonstrating the potential of a work of art, if it was large and clear and strong in its message, to touch the lives of many people in a very direct, immediate way.

Fig. 16–3. Judy Chicago, *The Dinner Party*. 1979. Multimedia installation, 48 x 48 x 48 ft. (© Judy Chicago, 1979; photo by Michael Alexander)

However, this work has had a deeply ambivalent reception within the art world. Even feminist art critics have distanced themselves from the imagery labeled in the 1980s as "essentialist." As Josephine Withers so accurately obsered, "It seems unrealistic to expect *The Dinner Party*—a late seventies embodiment of feminist dichotomized polemics—to also reflect the evolution of feminist critical thinking during the intervening years."[10]

The Dinner Party still lacks a permanent home. It was presented to the University of the District of Columbia in 1990, a black, urban land-grant institution. However, a heated debate in the House of Representatives, fueled by ultra-conservatives, resulted in the withdrawal of the gift. One can only hope that some permanent home for this historically significant work will be found in the future.

Since the late 1970s, Chicago has created two major ensembles, *The Birth Project* and *The Holocaust Project*, both dealing with themes of overwhelming human significance.

PATTERN AND DECORATION

• Miriam Schapiro, *Barcelona Fan*

Miriam Schapiro's contributions to the feminist art movement and the entire school of painting known as "pattern painting" or "decorative art" is well established. Her monumental compositions, which deal directly with the objects and life experiences of women, have received regular and consistently positive critical appraisals. Her ability to generate symbols based on historically grounded artifacts of women's life experiences provides a convincing case for the existence of a woman's culture that has survived and flourished through the centuries of patriarchy.

Born in 1923 and formally trained at Hunter College, Schapiro received her M.A. in fine arts from the University of Iowa in the early 1950s. Throughout that decade, she worked in an Abstract Expressionist style that contained veiled references to the human figure. Despite the execution in 1960 and 1961 of a large series of paintings that incorporated the personal symbol of the egg and the house as confining structure, by 1965 the artist had succeeded in erasing all personal metaphor and iconography from her abstractions.[11]

A turning point in her development occurred with the creation of the mural-scaled *Big OX #1* in 1968. The painting is dominated by an orange structure, hexagonal in shape, whose orifice is edged in a modeled pink. Four orange arms stretch to the corners of the composition, forming the "X" to the hexagon's "O" of the title. Despite the hard-edged style, the coloration and central imagery identify this transitional work as one loaded with female body imagery.

Her collaboration with Judy Chicago was a catalyst for Schapiro. After executing in 1972 (with Sherry Brody) the dollhouse, which was exhibited in *Womanhouse*, Schapiro began to explore and exploit the potential of patterned fabric to carry beauty and significance in a high-art context. By 1973–74 she had developed a style that combined fabric collage and painting, structured within an architectural framework. She named her new formal interest "Femmage": collages developed from materials and themes of concern to the lives of women. Bridging her return to New York in 1976, Schapiro worked on a series known as "Collaborations," which incorporated reproductions of works of art by women artists of the past.

Between 1976 and 1979 Schapiro exhibited a series of monumental works based on the form of the kimono, the fan, and the robe (the "Vestiture" series). These magnificent, impressive, and monumentally scaled works break down any meaningful distinction between the concerns of abstraction and the "merely" decorative use of patterning in craft objects or fabric design. Like the nineteenth-century American quilts, these works set new standards as complex abstract statements. Schapiro was now one of the leading figures in the postmodernist movement known as "pattern painting," defined by John Perrault in the following way:

> Pattern painting is non-Minimalist, non-sexist, historically conscious, sensuous, romantic, rational, decorative. Its methods, motifs, and referents cross cultural and class lines. Virtually everyone takes some delight in patterning, the modernist taboo against the decorative notwithstanding. As a new painting style, pattern painting, like patterning itself, is two dimensional, non hierarchical, all over, a-centric, and aniconic. It has its roots in modernist art, but contradicts some of the basic tenets of the faith, attempting to assimilate aspects of Western and non-Western culture not previously allowed into the realms of high art.[12]

Schapiro's role as a key generator of this new interest in pattern, which became widespread among a number of artists in the second half of the 1970s, cannot be overestimated.

An outstanding example of a fully developed "pattern painting" is the *Barcelona Fan* (Fig. 16–4). Stretching 12 feet across and 6 feet high, this enormous work is composed of alternating light and dark bands, which generate a continuous and rhythmic movement across the surface. The semicircular shape is divided into four major sections, each composed of alternating strips of fabric. Unity from the core to the outer

Fig. 16–4. Miriam Schapiro, *Barcelona Fan.* 1979. Fabric and acrylic on canvas, 6 x 12 ft. *(The Metropolitan Museum of Art, Gift of Steven M. Jacobson and Howard A. Kalka, 1993. All rights reserved, The Metropolitan Museum of Art, 1993.408)*

edges is maintained by the continuity of linear elements from the "handle" to the edge. *Barcelona Fan* is dazzling in its red and gold richness of flowered brocade. The form of the fan metaphorically reveals the unfolding of woman's consciousness. It was exhibited with the "Vestiture" series, which presents "ceremonial robes to cele- brate the new meaning of womanhood."[13] These works presented the artworld with a new use of fabric and a new definition of the "decorative" and its inescapable sig- nificance as "high art," as well as symbolic images suffused with feminist relevance.

In the 1980s Schapiro frequently employed the human figure in her art, often creating dancers. A dancing couple, *Anna and David* (1987), enlarged to 35 feet, was installed in a public space in Rosslyn, Virginia, a suburb of Washington, D.C.

In 1988 Schapiro created *Conservatory (Portrait of Frida Kahlo),* a monumentally scaled painting and fabric collage, stretching nearly 13 feet across. In this work, the figure of Frida Kahlo sits regally in the center, bearing a close resemblance to the fea- tures of Schapiro herself. It is hard to imagine an image which more directly testifies to the importance of the role models of women artists of the past, an image which addresses most directly the purpose of this book.

FEMINISM, POLITICS, AND AFRICAN-AMERICAN ARTISTS

Contemporary women of African descent have contributed significantly to the rich- ness of women's creative output in the past decades. However, it would be inaccurate to assume that African heritage alone is sufficient to unify these creative talents. As Leslie King-Hammond, in an introduction to a compilation of biographical entries on over 150 African-American women artists, describes: "There is not one voice. It is a collection of voices, which, through their combined synergy, vibrantly explore, challenge, invent, remember, reconfigure, innovate, improvise, act out, act up, cut up, piece, and perform their responses to the American experience in a complex 'exchange and re-exchange of ideas between groups'."[14]

Although sometimes marginalized, even from discussions of contemporary women artists' activities, the power, beauty, and variety of works created by African-American women is remarkable.

• Bettye Saar, *The Liberation of Aunt Jemima*

Bettye Saar is a noted African-American artist who developed a personal style to convey her distinctive vision outside the realm of the "fine arts" and the traditions of Western art. Born in Los Angeles in 1926, she studied art at Pasadena City College, graduating in 1949. During the 1950s she raised a family, but in the 1960s she began making constructions in boxes. Inspired by the works of Joseph Cornell, Saar gathered together objects, fabrics, and other bits and pieces with which she composed her imaginative tableaux. Using this assemblage technique, Saar discovered the formal means by which she could best express a personal content. In the mid–1960s and early 1970s Saar focused on the ready-made stereotypes of black people promoted by white society to make her political statements, using images such as "Uncle Tom" or

Fig. 16–5. Bettye Saar, *The Liberation of Aunt Jemima*. 1972. Mixed media, 11³/₄ x 8 x 2³/₄ in. *(University Art Museum, University of California at Berkeley. Purchased with the aid of funds from the National Endowment for the Arts; photo by Colin McRae)*

"Little Black Sambo." In *The Liberation of Aunt Jemima* (Fig. 16–5), Saar explodes the myth of the "good house nigger."[15] Aunt Jemima holds a broom in one hand and a rifle in the other. The anger and violence of the black revolution is here given a forceful symbol.

Bettye Saar's creative process is one of self-described ritual. She haunts junk shops and markets around the globe, searching for the materials which she will transform into her works of art. Her works then acquire layered, multiple meanings in the recontextualization from found object to "art." The pyramid, or tiered altar, moving from the lower, more tangible levels to the more metaphysical or esoteric symbolism at the top is a recurring element in her art, as are the symbols of the four elements: earth, air, fire, and water.[16]

Saar's daughter, Alison, is also an artist, one whose work is strongly influenced by African-American folk art and African sculpture.

• Faith Ringgold, *Die*

Faith Ringgold is an artist of impressive talents who also developed her personal style outside the Western Renaissance tradition. Born in Harlem in 1930, Ringgold studied art at the City College of New York. Like Saar, Ringgold's education was acquired through subsidized public schools for higher education. In the mid-1960s, inspired by the political upheavals of the civil rights movement, Ringgold painted a 12-foot-wide mural entitled *Die* (Fig. 16–6). Using flat, unmodulated colors, Ringgold achieves a decorative and original style for a vision of interracial violence. While black and white adults attack each other, two children huddle together in the center of the composition hoping to survive the massacre.

Ringgold recalls that she became a feminist in 1970 when she launched a protest

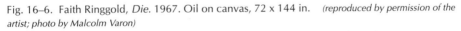

Fig. 16–6. Faith Ringgold, *Die*. 1967. Oil on canvas, 72 x 144 in. *(reproduced by permission of the artist; photo by Malcolm Varon)*

against an all-male exhibition at the School of Visual Arts in New York, in itself designed to protest war, racism, and sexism. Ringgold's feminism became incorporated into her art in 1973, when she abandoned oil painting and began making soft sculpture using sewing and other craft techniques. Her mother had been a fashion designer, and Ringgold recalls that when she was young her mother was always sewing. However, it was the feminist movement that sanctioned her use of these techniques for the creation of art.

> If I'd been left alone, I'd have done my own kind of thing earlier, based on sewing. As it was, it wasn't until the Women's Movement that I got the go-ahead to do that kind of work.[17]

During this time she had been teaching African crafts, such as beadwork, appliqué, and mask-making, at the Bank Street College in New York. Combining her interest in African crafts with her feminist consciousness of traditional women's art, she decided to make soft sculptures based on her memory images of black people. The results are the group of works known collectively as the "Family of Women." Using a variety of techniques, needlepoint, braided ribbon, beading, and sewn fabric, these images are imaginative presences with foam bodies. They are dressed in African-inspired clothing, and the sewn faces are derived from African masks.

Ringgold's works, formed with nontraditional materials, focus insistently on her identity as an African-American woman of the twentieth century.

> After I decided to be an artist, the first thing that I had to believe was that I, a black woman, could penetrate the art scene and that I could do so without sacrificing one iota of my blackness, or my femaleness, or my humanity.[18]

From this strong and focused sense of communal and individual identity, Ringgold has created a highly personal body of works of formal, technical, and iconographical originality. Her mature works are consistently outside of neatly defined categories of painting or sculpture, utilizing fabric, quilting techniques, and literary narrative in highly original ways.

• Faith Ringgold, *Tar Beach*

In the 1980s Ringgold produced a remarkable series of works that combine narrative stories with quilting techniques. *Tar Beach* is the best known in this series and reveals her imaginative and fantastic visions. Ringgold's works remain firmly rooted in her personal identity. Ringgold expressed her attitudes towards success and recognition in the art world with characteristic honesty:

> As far as the art world is concerned, I have not had to think about that, because I'm not a member of those groups that would profit from being on the cutting edge. I'm not a man and I'm not white. So I can do what I want to do and that has been my greatest gift. It's kind of a backhanded gift but it sets me free. I do what I want to do because I'm not lined up for those things anyway. I may get those things but I'm not in the lineup. I'm over here, you see, and that's fine. I believe that what you do in this world is figure out where you are and go ahead and do what you can do, and that's what I'm doing.[19]

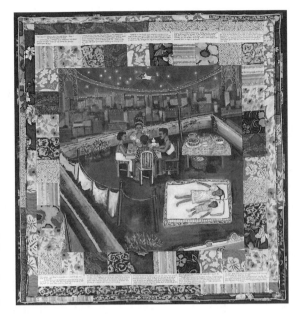

Fig. 16–7. Faith Ringgold, *Tar Beach (Woman on a Beach Series #1).* 1988. Acrylic paint on canvas bordered with printed and painted quilted and pieced cloth, $74^5/_8$ x $68^1/_2$ in. *(The Solomon R. Guggenheim Museum, New York. Gift of Mr. and Mrs. Gus and Judith Lieber, 1998. Photograph by David Heald © The Solomon R. Guggenheim Foundation, New York. FN 88.3620)*

By any standards of success in the art world, Faith Ringgold measures up to a level of creative excellence shared by only a small group of African-American women artists of her generation. In 1990, a major retrospective exhibition of her works began to tour the country, exhibited not only on both coasts but in selected sites throughout the Midwest and the South.

PERFORMANCE ART

During the 1970s, women artists interested in both exploring their gender-defined identities and in changing society's attitudes and behavior towards women turned to a totally new art form known as "performance art." As Moira Roth, a historian of this movement, defines it, performance art is "a hybrid form which combines visual art, theater, dance, music, poetry and ritual."[20] The presence of one or more performers, an audience, and the execution of the work in real time and space provides the performance artist with an immediacy and concrete reality appropriate for the communication of feelings, beliefs, and concepts that would receive much more highly abstracted representation in the traditional media of painting or sculpture.

Roth has identified three major trends in performance art of the 1970s. This "Amazing Decade" for women saw performance artists exploring autobiographical sources, the "personal clutter" of everyday lives as valid material for a work of art. The belief that the "personal is the political" lent a broadened significance to these performance pieces. A second trend focused on the developing interest in prehistoric matriarchies, goddess worship, and other forms of women's spirituality via the staging of rituals. The third trend involved highly structured events with a well-defined feminist political intent. Such events are intended in Lacy and Labowitz's term to serve as "models for feminist action."

By 1972 there were active centers of performance art on both the east and west coasts. Many performance events focused on the expression of personal feelings and experiences about the performers' lives as women. Such works have no equivalent in the aggressive "Body Art" of male artists such as Vito Acconci or Chris Burden. As precedents to concerns later explored by Cindy Sherman, "Women performers made attempts to study, expose, mock, and challenge stereotyped images of women."[21] Carolee Schneeman, a filmmaker, and Eleanor Antin have been among the leading performance artists in this trend. In 1975 Schneeman performed "Interior Scroll." Standing in the nude, she extracted a text from her vagina and defended and explained the need for the exposure of the personal in art. Eleanor Antin's art has involved the development of a series of alter-ego personae, including a nurse and Eleanora Antinova, a black ballerina in Diaghilev's Ballet Russes. Primarily through the medium of performance, Antin explores aspects of herself by playing out the lives of these fictional people.

• Mary Beth Edelson, *Gate of Horn/Fig of Triumph*

Mary Beth Edelson is one of the most important performance artists concerned with myths of female power in prepatriarchal, prehistorical cultures. The primary form in which she expresses these concerns is ritual. One of Edelson's most noted ritual pieces was staged in 1977 at the A.I.R. gallery (a woman's cooperative gallery) in New York. The artist created *Gate of Horn*, composed of photos of women's hands making the sign of the horn, the symbol of the Minoan great goddess, found at the Palace at Knosses (Fig. 4–1). Participants in this ritual passed through this *Gate of Horn* to an interior space defined by a flaming ladder to perform the ritual piece *Proposals for: Memorials to 9,000,000 Women Burned as Witches in the Christian Era*. Edelson connected the persecution of women as witches with the patriarchal, Christian need to eliminate goddess worship. On Halloween women reenacted the medieval meetings of witches and marched in procession, carrying long sticks holding candlelit pumpkins.

Other rituals were created to be performed in isolation, made public only through subsequent documentation. These private rituals often had more autobiographical significance to the performers and sought a transformation of personal circumstances into mythic dimensions.

In other images created that same year, 1977, Edelson used her own nude body in photographs in which she posed herself with uplifted arms in the gesture most closely associated with the cosmic energies of the Goddess.[22]

Edelson and other women artists, such as Buffie Johnson and Ana Mendieta, addressed the goddess as part of a feminist rejection of masculinist myths and patriarchal abuse of the environment. As Orenstein summarizes, the goddess ritual and imagery generated "a holistic vision of the interconnectedness of spirit and matter, heaven and earth, male and female, human and nonhuman life forms: . . . a contemporary movement that . . . sees art as the crossroads where feminist activism and feminist imagina-

Fig. 16–8. Mary Beth Edelson, *Gate of Horn/Fig of Triumph.* 1977. Installation from exhibition "Proposals for: Memorials to the 9,000,000 Women Burned as Witches in the Christian Era." *(© Mary Beth Edelson; photo by Eric Pollitzer)*

tion converge making for a revolutionary change in both consciousness and culture."[23]

Edelson insists on the nature of her art works as an expression of a "collective" identity. She says she wishes to reveal "Not who I am but who we are."[24] In one project, *22 Others*, she petitioned 22 individuals for suggestions about what sort of work she should make. One of the results was her clever poster, *Some Living American Women Artists/Last Supper*, of 1972, in which the heads of Jesus and the apostles of Leonardo's famous image are replaced with Georgia O'Keeffe as Jesus and a new contingent of women artists as the apostles. The same year she staged the memorial to the witches, she also staged another ritual, "Your 5,000 Years Are Up!," using humor to combat patriarchal domination. As Lippard notes, Edelson was "unwilling to separate social change from spiritual change, affirmative action from affirmative passion."[25]

- ### Leslie Labowitz and Suzanne Lacy, *In Mourning and In Rage*

Leslie Labowitz and Suzanne Lacy pioneered another trend in the type of performance art most closely associated with southern California. These performances are activist, interventionist, and political.

Labowitz spent five years in Germany during the 1970s, studying with Joseph Beuys and developing a consciousness and experience in the possibilities of carefully staged events to force political, media, and popular attention on issues of key concern to women. Lacy had been involved in Judy Chicago's feminist art program in Fresno in 1970 and also brought many years of involvement with feminist issues to their collaboration. Spurred by the crimes of the Hillside Strangler and the climate of fear being generated by the news media, Lacy and Labowitz staged *In Mourning and In Rage* on the steps of Los Angeles City Hall in 1977. A funeral procession first circled City Hall. Then, nine 7-foot-tall women, veiled in black, emerged from the hearse. Each of the nine black mourners read a statement that explicitly connected the murders of the Hillside Strangler with the entire range of crimes against women perpetrated by our society. As each mourner read her statement, a tenth figure, clothed in red, draped a red scarf around the black figures. The surrounding chorus chanted, "In memory of our sisters, we fight back!" The press was given a statement of the purpose of the event, and a list of demands for women's self-defense was presented to members of the City Council. In their explanation of the event, Labowitz and Lacy express their concern about the images as well as the condition of women in our culture.[26] They state three primary reasons for *In Mourning and In Rage*: first, to provide a public ritual for women to share their grief and rage over the recent tragedies; second, to provide a means for women's organizations and city government to share in a collective expression against this violence; and third, to create a media event controlled by the artists to permit a wider audience to learn of their concerns. The political artists here harnessed the power of television, radio, and written news media to communicate their viewpoint.

Fig. 16–9. Suzanne Lacy and Leslie Labowitz, *In Mourning and In Rage*. Los Angeles, California, 1977. *(courtesy Suzanne Lacy; photo by Susan Mogul)*

Breaking out of the confines and limitations of the traditional forms of the visual arts, performance artists invented a new genre of art, one which focused on the specific experience of women and spoke to those needs in a very direct form of communication.

OTHER TRENDS IN THE VISUAL ARTS

Many other women artists have produced original and exciting works which do not necessarily fall into the category of feminist art. It is important to recognize the diversity of techniques and interests in the works of women artists since the 1970s.

Painting: Extending the Boundaries of Abstraction

- **Jennifer Bartlett, *2 Priory Walk***

Jennifer Bartlett was born into an upper-middle-class family in Long Beach, California, in 1941. Her mother had been a fashion illustrator, and Bartlett was determined to become an artist from early childhood. She did her undergraduate work at Mills College, where Elizabeth Murray (see Fig. 16–11) was her best friend. She enrolled in Yale in the fall of 1963 with classmates Richard Serra, Chuck Close, Jonathan Borofsky, and Nancy Graves, receiving her M.F.A. in 1965.

In 1968 she decided to paint on 1-foot-square steel plates using them as the basic module unit of her work. This commercially manufactured material relates to the interests of "Minimalist" artists who were using industrial materials in the late 1960s. Bartlett emerged as an important artist with the 988-plate work, *Rhapsody*, installed in the Soho Gallery of Paula Cooper in May, 1976. *New York Times* art critic John Russell called it "the most ambitious single work of art that has come my way since I started to live in New York."[27] Marge Goldwater wrote that *Rhapsody* is characterized by qualities of "obsessiveness and ambition,"[28] qualities that are crucial aspects of all Bartlett's works.

Bartlett's paintings employ a self-limited set of motifs, which undergo transformations of scale, medium, or artistic style. Bartlett communicates her ideas through "re-presentation"[29] of repeating motifs. One very persistent and recurring motif for Bartlett is the house, an image that first appeared in Bartlett's work in 1969. In the series of paintings from 1977 of which *2 Priory Walk* is an example, the titles are actually addresses of houses carrying biographical or autobiographical references and personal significance. "For Bartlett . . . the house functions almost as an alter ego, a perfect metaphor for registering the shifts in mood and the different phases of her life."[30] Clearly the motif of the house, for Bartlett as for Louise Bourgeois and other women artists, carries powerful associations of both confinement and rootedness.

2 Priory Walk is typical of Bartlett's interest in juxtaposing "a range of styles and systems of depiction"[31] within a single work. Here, the flattened schematic house is visible in the lower-right quadrant. It is repeated in a dot-matrix image in the plate in the extreme lower-right corner as well as being embedded in the painterly, highly

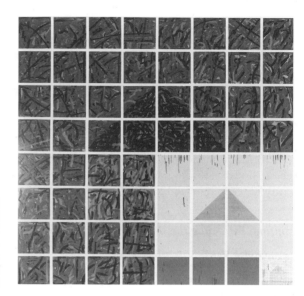

Fig. 16–10. Jennifer Bartlett, *2 Priory Walk*. 1977. Baked enamel, silkscreen, and enamel on steel, 8 ft. 7 in. x 8 ft. 7 in. *(Philadelphia Museum of Art. Purchased: Adele Haas Turner and Beatrice Pastorius Turner Fund)*

gestural technique used to cover the surface of the other plates. The compression of three distinct painting techniques calls into question the validity of a personal style.

In the winter of 1980, Bartlett occupied a dreary villa in the south of France, in Nice. She executed a series of drawings, *In the Garden*, from the view outside a window, using ten different media to generate nearly 200 images. This series was also greeted with critical success and led to a commission to decorate the dining room of influential art collectors Charles and Doris Saatchi's residence in London.

Bartlett's willingness to compress a broad range of styles and media into a single work without merging or blending these styles, and maintaining their distinctiveness, is characteristic of a Postmodernist distrust of the hierarchies and priorities of modernism. It is a testimony to her recurrent inventiveness and willingness to make visible the complexities of image making.

- **Elizabeth Murray, *Sail Baby***

Elizabeth Murray's witty, inventive paintings of the 1980s demonstrate the survival of abstraction as a viable mode in contemporary painting. However, Murray's style of abstraction is filled with organic forms, references to content, narrative, and synthetic Cubist still life objects and could not be further removed from the reductivist geometry of 1960s Minimalism or other formalist aesthetic systems.

Murray was born in Chicago in 1940 but received her masters in fine arts in 1964 from Mills College, in the San Francisco Bay area. Moving to New York in 1967, her development proceeded slowly through the 1970s. From an early interest in narrative and cartooning, Murray spent much of the 1970s experimenting with the formal possibilities of oil paint, enlarged scale, shaped canvases, and highly saturated color. Only in the early 1980s did Murray's painting acquire the self-assurance and control of formal means that make them fascinating and unique artistic statements. Murray's paintings generate multiple and ambiguous associations that avoid programmed or specific narrative content.

Sail Baby (Fig. 16–11) is characteristic of Murray's mature paintings on a number of levels. First, it is composed of three individual canvases. Murray's 1980s paintings most frequently employ multiple canvases, which echo or contradict the forms depicted on them. Often, as in this example, painted shapes are continued from one canvas to the other, generating an obvious tension between the physical facts of the painting, i.e., the separate canvases and the painted illusion that unifies those physically distinct canvases. Another characteristic of Murray's art is the presence of large areas of highly saturated colors. The frequently depicted coffee cup, here in a brilliantly saturated yellow with a sky-blue interior edge, is "supported" by a magenta saucer shape underneath.

Also, *Sail Baby* has a narrative meaning. Murray notes that this painting is "about my family. It's about myself and my brother and my sister, and I think, it's also about my own three children, even though Daisy wasn't born yet."[32] This painting expresses the tension between individual identity and the emotional bonding within families. In fact, every form in this painting helps to unify this image and work against the physical separation of the three canvases. The shape of the cup and saucer most obviously bridges the canvases. A serpentine emerald-green linear element weaves about in a continuous counterclockwise motion from the "hole" in the handle of the cup to its disappearance into the sky-blue interior of the cup. The whole form is set against a wine-red ground, which on its lower edges reveals a dripped paint surface of yellows and blue. Therefore, in terms of method of paint application, *Sail Baby* contains a range from gestural definition to hard edge, from evenly painted surfaces to dripping, residually Abstract Expressionist spontaneity.

The green serpentine is the most obvious element in *Sail Baby* that reveals Murray's obsession with movement. "Elizabeth Murray's art has always been in motion

Fig. 16–11. Elizabeth Murray, *Sail Baby*. 1983. Oil on canvas, 26 x 135 in. *(Walker Art Center, Minneapolis. Walker Special Purchase Fund, 1984)*

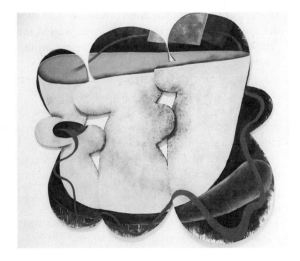

and about motion. . . . Everything is in flux, is undergoing a process of change and distortion that is visually strange and abstract, but also psychologically real. . . ."[33]

It is exciting to see an artist find ways of using the traditional medium of oil painting in a very innovative and also very personal way. Murray's paintings are full of formal surprises that remain engrossing because they resonate with human implications.

Both Murray and Bartlett demonstrate the ability of women artists to invent new formal means and content in the 1980s and each has been recognized for her achievements. The paintings of both artists can surprise, delight, and move jaded late-twentieth-century viewers through the traditional medium of painting.

Sculpture and Fiber Art

• **Magdalena Abakanowicz, *Embryology***

The work of Magdalena Abakanowicz is one of the most persuasive reasons to abandon any inherent devaluation of craft from the "fine art" of sculpture. The Polish artist is today widely recognized as the foremost artist working with fiber. She has built an international reputation since the 1960s, moving from her initial medium of weaving, to sculpture in fiber and wood, to other more permanent materials.

Born in 1930 into an aristocratic family of the Polish landed gentry, Abakanowicz's youth was spent in the upheavals of World War II and its aftermath in Poland. She studied from 1950 to 1954 at the Academy of Fine Arts of Warsaw without finding a clear direction as an artist. It was only in the early 1960s, on a borrowed loom, that her original vision found its means of expression. Exhibiting regularly in the Lausanne Biennial of Tapestry from 1962 through 1979, she began to receive international recognition for her extraordinary creations.

Her first major works were the huge woven structures known as *Abakans*. These enormous, freely hanging objects, full of slits and negative spaces, exist in three dimensions and transform the medium of tapestry into the realm of monumental sculpture. They signaled a new set of possibilities for the use of fiber. Beginning in 1973, Abakanowicz abandoned the loom and the weaving process while maintaining the use of nautral organic fibers, now pressed into molds. The "Seated Figures" and "Backs" series are evocative symbols of community and anonymity, individuality and similarity.

Mary Jane Jacob, curator of the major retrospective exhibition that traveled about the United States and Montreal from 1982 to 1984, identifies *Embryology*, created 1978 to 1980 (Fig. 16–12), as Abakanowicz's masterpiece.[34] Composed of hundreds of rounded forms of various sizes, the shapes are cut and stitched. Some are closed opaque shapes covered in rough burlap. Others are semitransparent, gauze-covered forms that reveal their interior stuffing. Composed of hand-made thread that the artist soaked, dyed, rinsed, and dried in a complex process, "the cycle is about the process of birth and growth in human beings and in nature and the changes that bodies or earth undergo when cut or altered."[35]

Abakanowicz has described associations connected with her chosen medium in the following statement:

Fig. 16–12. Magdalena Abakanowicz, *Embryology.* 1978–1980. *(courtesy Magdalena Abakanowicz; photo by Jan Nordahl, Sodertalje, Sweden)*

> I see fiber as the basic element constructing the
> organic world on our planet,
> as the greatest mystery of our environment.
> It is from fiber that all living organisms are built—
> the tissues of plants, and ourselves.
> Our nerves, our genetic code,
> the canals of our veins, our muscles.
> We are fibrous structures.
> Our heart is surrounded by the coronary plexus,
> the plexus of most vital threads.
> Handling fiber, we handle mystery.[36]

Although Abakanowicz has used the fibrous, natural material of wood in some sculptural pieces, her reputation and artistic identity is rooted in her sensitivity to the sculptural possibilities and expressive potential of fibers.

However, in the 1980s, Abakanowicz shifted from soft materials to the use of a full range of permanent materials for her sculpture, including aluminum and bronze casting. As documented in a monograph by Barbara Rose, it is clear that this artist no longer fits into the niche of "fiber art." Recent work reveals a shift from "environmental installation to contextually sited sculpture"[37] most vividly with the seven upright 12-ton disks of stone quarried in the Negev desert for *Negev*, commissioned for the sculpture garden of the Israel Museum in Jerusalem (1987).

- ### Nancy Graves, *Variability and Repetition of Similar Forms II*

Nancy Graves (1940–1995) made her first appearance in the art world with the exhibition of life-sized camels, frozen in midmotion, in 1968. While living in Florence, Italy, in 1965, Graves was inspired by the wax sculptures of an eighteenth-century anatomist, Clemente Susini. Sensing the sculptural possibilities of a recreation of the world of natural forms, she began her exploration of the camel, which would result by 1970 in the fabrication of twenty-five full-scale beasts.

Graves pursued an intensive study of the anatomy of these animals and constructed them on wooden armatures, using sheepskins and goatskins. Although the artist was quite conscious that these sculptures were not exact replicas, their scale, pose, and naturalistic components made them appear as effigies of the awesome beasts.[38] In the rarified atmosphere of the New York art world, then dominated by Minimalism, the camels brought sculpture back in touch with the vital world of organic nature in the most direct way possible.

Between 1969 and 1971 Graves made several works based on the forms of camel bones. Investigation of the camel skeleton led, in turn, to an interest in the fossilized prehistoric camel skeleton in the collection of the Natural History Museum in Los Angeles. After making two films in Morocco, both of which focused on the movements of camels, Graves created *Variability of Similar Forms*, a work that combined her interest in fossilized skeletons with the illusion of motion. Originally fabricated in wax over a steel armature and painted white, the piece was reworked several years later and then cast into bronze with a white patina developed by Ron Young of the Johnson atelier in Princeton, New Jersey. *Variability and Repetition of Similar Forms II* (Fig. 16–13) is the resulting work, which now can function as an outdoor sculpture. This piece is composed of thirty-six camel legs, which both retain her desire for a close connection with the natural world and become isolated linear forms of pure motion. The clear intent to create an illusion of motion was inspired, according to Graves, by the nineteenth-century time-lapse studies of animal and human locomotion of Edweard Muybridge.[39] Each leg is subdivided into thirds by two joints. While the bottom portion of each is identical, the upper sections are taken from both front and back legs of the prehistoric beast. The legs are positioned in a variety of different angles, so the effect of motion is inescapable.

Since 1979 Graves's desire to utilize objects and forms from the real world of living nature has found expression in over 200 sculptures cast directly from objects selected from the plant and animal world. Her extraordinarily vital sculptures employ plant leaves, vines, carob beans, sardines, and oyster shells among many other selected objects, which are then brightly colored.

The sculpture of Nancy Graves has been appreciated by a wide audience and has received positive critical evaluation. There was a major traveling exhibition of her works in 1987, with simultaneous publication of a catalogue raisonné. Her sculptures seem to satisfy a need for renewal with nature while exploring the full range of the formal possibilities of welding. Graves has developed an oeuvre that constantly surprises and seems endlessly inventive, yet springs from the multiplicity of forms in the natural world itself. These works translate the childlike awe and sense of wonder at

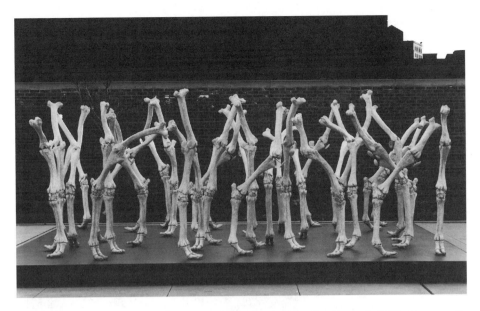

Fig. 16–13. Nancy Graves, *Variability and Repetition of Similar Forms II.* 1979. Bronze with white patina and Corten steel, 72 x 144 x 192 in.   *(Collection Akron Art Museum. Purchased with the aid of the Museum Acquisition Fund, the Mary S. and Louis S. Myers Fund, the Firestone Foundation, and the National Endowment for the Arts; photo by Rick Zaidan)*

the organic world into sophisticated sculptures of wide appeal, communicating a sense of a pulsating life force.

Earthworks, Site Sculpture, and Installations

Women artists have been important participants in the movement, which began in the late 1960s and early 1970s, to connect the work of art with a direct experience of the earth itself, outside of the gallery space. Rejecting the high-tech look and focus of Minimalism, earth sculptors introduced a new sense of geological and prehistoric time into their art. In the key works of both Nancy Holt and Alice Aycock, the direct participation of the viewer is absolutely essential for completion of the work of art.

- ### Alice Aycock, Fantasy Sculpture II

  The first large outdoor sculpture of Alice Aycock (born 1946) was *Maze* (1972), a twelve-sided wooden structure 32 feet in diameter and 6 feet high. This work was specifically intended to evoke the panic of entrapment in the viewer. The following year, Aycock designed the first structure in which the viewer had to crawl along the ground to experience the work. The viewer entered *Low Building Made with Dirt Roof*

Fig. 16–14. Alice Aycock,
Fantasy Sculpture II. 1990.
Installation: Abington Art
Center. Steel, wood, Plexiglas.
Height: 20 ft. Diameter: 15 ft.
(courtesy John Weber Gallery)

(for Mary) through a doorway only 30 inches high, which was the tallest point of the structure of which the other dimensions were 20 by 12 feet. Like *Maze*, the panic of claustrophobia was part of the intended result. Lucy Lippard has pointed out that Aycock's low buildings evoke both the fearful and hopeful aspects of the cave: fear in terms of claustrophobia, entrapment, and absorption and hopeful in the prehistoric sense in which caves were magical precincts located within the body of the Earth Mother. It is believed that in prehistoric times, caves were viewed as protective environments. They were the sites of fertility and childbirth rituals.[40]

By the late 1970s Aycock had abandoned the medium of wood and began building giant structures that resembled fantastic laboratory apparatus from horror movies of the 1930s. Jonathan Fineberg has characterized her works from this period as re-creating "the magic, the nostalgia, and the mysterious threatening forces of dreams."[41]

In the monumentally scaled construction, *Fantasy Sculpture II,* Aycock condenses visual ideas from sources as diverse as a Renaissance visualization of the cosmos, a roller coaster, the Christian image of a stairway or ladder to heaven, the tree of life, Native American totem poles, and a mini-amphitheater to create a compelling, evocative image. "Her work is inclusive and maximal instead of exclusive and minimal . . . it is about everything at once . . . undermining the fixed relations of a stable world view . . ."[42]

- ## Nancy Holt, *Sun Tunnels*

Nancy Holt's most famous and seminal site sculpture, *Sun Tunnels*, shares an isolated, barren desert setting with works by Smithson, Heizer, and de Maria. Its form is determined by a precise interaction with the environment to a much greater extent than most other works in this category. Like Aycock's site sculptures, *Sun Tunnels* and Holt's other works require a level of human interaction far beyond that of most other site sculptures.

Born in Massachusetts in 1938, Nancy Holt lived and worked on the East Coast until 1968, when, in the company of Robert Smithson and Michael Heizer, she traveled west to the Salt Lake deserts of Utah. According to her own recollection, "As soon as I got to the desert, I connected with the place."[43] Five years later she began a search for a site to install a set of four monumental concrete tubes, which would become the *Sun Tunnels*.

Sun Tunnels evolved naturally out of Holt's earlier invention of the concept of "locators." Not sculpture in the traditional sense of an object to be looked at, Holt's locators are meant to be looked *through*. The artist thus provides a means of controlling the viewer's perceptions of a given view or space. In 1972 she positioned eight locators at Missola Ranch in Montana and one at Narragansett Beach, Rhode Island.

Sun Tunnels consists of four huge concrete pipes, 18 feet long and slightly over 9 feet in diameter. Each pipe rests on a buried concrete foundation. The four pipes are arranged in an X configuration which, at its longest point, reaches 86 feet. The positioning of these pipes was determined with the help of an astrophysicist using the position of the sun at its most extreme points from the earth—the summer and winter solstices. Like a modern Stonehenge, giant shapes brought from a different place were erected to assist the primordial human need to comprehend the cycles of the universe.

The complexity of *Sun Tunnels* is increased when one becomes aware of the configuration of holes 7 to 10 inches in diameter drilled through concrete pipes that are 7 inches thick. The positions of these holes were determined by the location of stars forming four constellations. By day, the drilled holes permit sunlight to penetrate the tubes, casting elliptical forms on the inner surface. At night, when the moon is over a quarter, paler light forms may also be observed in the tubes. Like Monet's complex inversions of air and sky in the *Waterlilies* murals, Holt has "turned the world upside down" in an innovative way. She also transforms sunlit day into darkened night inside the protective shelter of the pipes.

Thus, *Sun Tunnels* is not a sculpture positioned in the desert but an observatory, which requires the participation of the viewer to function. According to the artist, one of the major goals of *Sun Tunnels* is the desire to bring "the vast landscape back to human proportion."[44] The larger openings at the ends of the pipes and the smaller drilled holes frame and limit the landscape vistas, defining a new relationship between the viewer and the vastness of the earth. Another way that Holt reconciles the imposition of these large, commercially fabricated objects into this uninhabited desert vastness is through the materials employed. She notes, "The color and substance of the tunnels is the same as the land that they are a part of."[45]

• **Jenny Holzer,** *Under a Rock*

Jenny Holzer (born 1950) is one of the most important artists to have generated highly original ways of communicating through words. Her verbal messages are exhibited in inventive ways not anticipated by any other artist. She has imprinted her words on a wide range of media such as printed signs, metal plaques, and stone benches, as well as on the Times Square Spectacolor Board in New York City and on electronic LED (light-emitting diode) boards of various sizes.

Born into a middle-class and unartistic family in Ohio in 1950, Holzer studied art formally at the University of Chicago, Ohio University, and the Rhode Island School of Design in Providence. She spent these years mostly painting abstract works.

In 1977, Holzer created her first mature series, *The Truisms*. In pithy one-liners, such as "Abuse of power comes as no surprise," she first committed herself to language as her primary medium. However, even in her first works Holzer was highly sensitive to the ways language communicates in a visual sense. The *Truisms* became posters, plastered in public on buildings in lower Manhattan, T-shirts, and billboards.

Beginning in 1982, she began using LED machines, which first displayed the Truisms. The LED boards are visible in *Under a Rock*, but are combined with another unprecedented medium, granite benches, arranged in a chapel-like formation on which are etched her provocative, even shocking text:

CRACK THE PELVIS SO SHE LIES RIGHT. THIS IS
A MISTAKE. WHEN SHE DIES YOU CANNOT REPEAT
THE ACT. THE BONES WILL NOT GROW TOGETHER
AGAIN AND THE PERSONALITY WILL NOT COME
BACK. SHE IS GOING TO SINK DEEP INTO THE
MOSS TO GET WHITE AND LIGHTER. SHE IS
UNRESPONSIVE TO BEGGING AND SELF-ABSORBED.

PEOPLE GO TO THE RIVER WHERE IT IS LUSH AND
MUDDY TO SHOOT CAPTIVES, TO FLOAT OR SINK
THEM. SHOTS KILL MEN WHO ALWAYS WANT.
SOMEONE IMAGINED OR SAW THEM LEAPING
TO SAVAGE THE GOVERNMENT. NOW BODIES DIVE
AND GLIDE IN THE WATER, SCARING FRIENDS
OR MAKING THEM FURIOUS.

LIGHT GOES THROUGH BRANCHES TO SHOW TWO
CHILDREN BORN AT ONCE WHO MIGHT LIVE.
THE MOTHER RAN FROM EVERY HAZARD
UNTIL THE BABIES EASED ONTO THE LEAVES.
WITH BOTH HANDS SHE BRINGS THEM TO HER
MOUTH, CALLING THEM TWICE THE USUAL
ANSWER TO MORTAL QUESTIONS. SHE IS
DELIGHTFUL AND MILKY SO THEY WILL WANT
TO GROW.

According to Diane Waldman, "Holzer's signs, benches and sarcophagi seem permanent and totemic no matter how swiftly her messages flash on and off the boards. The message is the medium and then some."[46]

Fig. 16–15. Jenny Holzer, *Under a Rock*. 1986. Installation, Barbara Gladstone Gallery, New York. L.E.D. electronic display signboard, 6 x 47 x 4 in. Nine Misty Black granite benches, each $17^{1}/_{4}$ x 48 x 21 in.   *(courtesy Barbara Gladstone Gallery, New York)*

A selection of these benches was installed at one of the entrances to Central Park in Manhattan. Holzer's media can move easily from gallery space to public setting because her format resides in the vernacular; it looks familiar while carrying a personal and culturally critical content. Holzer's art proceeds from a conceptual base. Her creative input is in the writing of the texts and control of their dissemination. Her interest in language is not unusual in the context of Postmodernism. As in the work of Mary Kelly and Barbara Kruger, words are simply too important, too powerful a means of communication to be banished from the work of art.

In 1989, Holzer took over the space of the Guggenheim Museum. By means of large LED boards her messages zapped around and across Frank Lloyd Wright's central void, finding yet another way in which the medium and the message could be reinvented.

- ## Maya Lin, *The Vietnam Veterans Memorial* (VVM)

By far, the most famous and important site-specific monument of our contemporary world is the extraordinary Vietnam Veterans Memorial (VVM). It is hard to conceive of a greater challenge to America's artists than the invention of a design for a memorial to those who died in Vietnam.[47] For a war in which winning and losing lost their significance, a war in which there were no heroes but only survivors, the task of finding a form that would honor and commemorate the dead without glorifying this inglorious war might seem an impossible task. The achievement of Maya Ying Lin, an undergraduate architecture student at Yale, in inventing the design of the memorial seems all the more remarkable.

The *Vietnam Veterans Memorial* owes its existence to the Vietnam Veterans Memorial Fund (VVMF) founded by Jan C. Scruggs in 1979. This group lobbied for a site in Washington and succeeded in this goal in 1980, when President Carter authorized the establishment of the monument on two acres of the Mall of the U.S. Capitol. With the securing of the site, an enormous open competition took place in which over 1400 final entries were submitted. Lin's winning design was announced on May 1, 1981. The Memorial was finished in 1983.

This powerfully simple work is neither sculpture nor architecture, but a hybrid form derived in its essential, utterly simple formal vocabulary from the tenets of Minimalism. The memorial consists of two triangular walls that form an arc, meeting at about 125°. The viewer moves along a 247-foot-long path on either end, constantly descending into the earth, to a depth of over 10 feet at the point of intersection. The visitor then makes his or her ascent. The walls create a structure without enclosing space. The descent into the earth is an extremely powerful aspect of the experience of the Memorial and one with an ancient history in funerary monuments. From the buried tombs of the Pharaohs to the tholos tombs of Mycenae, burial in the life-giving body of Mother Earth has provided solace for survivors and signified respect for the dead.

The cool simplicity of a Minimalist vocabulary seen in the identical triangular walls appears as a necessary form of intellectual control given the immense emotional power of the experience. As our national "wailing wall" with the ability to evoke such depths of mourning, the need for a spare language with an intellectually or rationally clear form seems appropriate.

The material for the walls, a very highly polished granite, was another important component of the overall design of the Memorial. A total of seventy granite slabs compose the two walls. Engraved into the slabs are the individual names of every person killed in Vietnam, listed chronologically by date of death. The years encompassing

Fig. 16–16. Maya Lin, *The Vietnam Veterans Memorial.*   (photo by Judy Scott Feldman)

the conflict, 1959 and 1975, are inscribed in the center angle. This most modern war memorial turns upside down the concept of the "tomb of the unknown soldier." One dead body does not abstractly symbolize all casualties. Every individual who died is evoked, one by one, by name. No trite generalizations are permitted to relieve the awareness of individual sacrifice.

The granite surface both contains the names of the dead and functions as a mirror reflecting the image of each visitor. Thus, no matter how aggressively one might wish to distance oneself from the consciousness of the human cost of Vietnam, every visitor is by definition a part of the memorial by the unremitting presence of one's own image reflected in the wall every step of the way. There is no way to remain "outside" the experience of the monument once one has initiated the descent. Lin has referred to the VVM as a "scar." She said "Take a knife and cut open the earth, and with time the grass would heal it."[48] Lin also intended the memorial to serve as "a cathartic healing process."[49] Charles Griswold believes that the "main purpose of the memorial is therapeutic, a point absolutely essential for an adequate understanding of the VVM."[50]

In the *New York Times*, on Veterans Day, November 11, 1994, journalist Gustav Neibuhr described the memorial as "something like a sacred shrine, where pilgrims come and devotions are paid."[51] The memorial regularly attracts more visitors than either the Washington Monument or the Lincoln Memorial. Over 30,000 items have been left at the site, and these, coupled with the reverence and the emotions visitors often display, encourage authorities on religion to relate the visitors' experience to that of pilgrims at religious sites such as Lourdes, Buddhist holy shrines, or the "Wailing Wall" in Jerusalem.

Despite the controversies at the beginning of the project and the addition of highly realistic statues, the power of this memorial seems to grow stronger through the years. The beauty, power, and immense originality of the VVM has penetrated into America's consciousness. This great work has redefined the form of a fitting monument to the dead and proven to be a magnet for an entire nation that lived and suffered through those terrible years. The VVM exists for everyone, not only the comrades and families of the slain.

FEMINIST ART SINCE THE 1980s

While critical consensus identifies the 1970s as an extremely active and fruitful epoch for women artists, this situation began to change in the early 1980s. Coinciding with the political rise of Reagan and the Moral Majority, coupled with the defeat of the ERA amendment, the cultural backlash against women artists was in full force by 1984, the year of the enormous inaugural exhibition of the newly refurbished Museum of Modern Art in New York City. In that international survey of trends in the arts, only 14 of 150 works were by women. The underrepresentation of women in that major show stimulated the formation of the "Guerrilla Girls," an anonymous activist group who appear in public wearing gorilla masks. They are the self-proclaimed "conscience of the art world." The Guerrilla Girls are another chapter in the struggle of women artists for recognition and equality in the most prestigious institutions of the art community. The abysmal record of the Whitney Museum in showcasing women artists has been a specific target of their attacks.

The declining fortunes of women artists in the 1980s could be measured economically. Funding by the National Endowment for the Arts for women artists' organizations such as cooperative galleries declined 35 percent between 1982 and 1985.[52] According to an NEA report, women artists made an average annual income of less than half that of men. While 38 percent of practicing artists were women, only a very tiny minority were able to maintain public careers as artists.

In the spring of 1987 the National Museum of Women in the Arts opened to the public in Washington, D.C., with a major historical exhibition of works by American women artists.[53] The establishment of this institution reopened the debate over the role of women artists and feminism in the art world.[54] Many people feel that the "ghettoization" of work by women in a separate museum is not a positive move. Others feel that the concept is valid only if the museum functions on a feminist agenda, working to improve the situation of living artists. The politically conservative founder, Mrs. Wilhelmina Cole Holladay, whose private collection forms the core of the museum's permanent collection, has publicly refused to use the museum as a feminist forum.

The 1990s have witnessed a renewed interest in "body art" by avant-garde creators. Women's bodily reproductive capacities have encouraged several avant-garde artists since 1990 to use the body as the means of expression for a broad range of political and emotional images. As Roberta Smith points out, the subjects of this art "are often highly flammable: domestic violence, racism, homophobia, bodily functions, rape, self-disgust . . . as well [as] the variety of feminist pleasure, desire and sexual power."[55] Among the most moving body images from the early 1990s are Hannah Wilke's courageous self-portraits documenting her ultimately unsuccessful battle with cancer.

Postmodern Feminism

Since the late 1970s, another group of women artists looked at the ways in which popular media contribute to gender identity construction. They began to formulate a critique of these genres in a highly conceptual way. Avoiding traditional painting media, Cindy Sherman and Barbara Kruger used photography in highly innovative ways to generate powerful images.

• Cindy Sherman, *Untitled Film Still #2*

Using the medium of photography paired with the life-sized or larger scale and color of painting, Cindy Sherman employs carefully staged pictures to expose the artifices of imagery and the power of that constructed imagery to manipulate the reality of women's lives. Since she began her career in 1977, her works have received consistent critical appreciation, culminating in a retrospective exhibition organized by the Akron Art Museum and shown at the Whitney Museum in New York in 1987. Part of the second generation of feminists, her true subject is a deconstruction of film, magazine, and all forms of popular imagery. As Lisa Phillips observed: "For Sherman the camera is a tool with which to explore the condition of representation and the myth that the photograph is an index of reality."[56] More recent works explore the appearances of a loss of sanity and the deterioration of the human into first animal then vegetable decay, rot, and defilement.

Born in New Jersey and raised on Long Island, Sherman emerged in the art world in the late 1970s with a series of "film stills." In these black and white, 8- by 10-inch photos, carefully staged, and using herself as actress, Sherman changes her own appearance to create a frozen moment out of a fictitious, but implied, continuous film narrative. Borrowing from the imagery of *film noir* movies of the late 1950s and early 1960s, these works aggressively appropriate content and imagery in a postmodernist stance. Her art is meant to engage the viewer, forcing him or her into an involvement with the self-consciously ambiguous scenario only hinted at in the single image.

Laura Mulvey, one of the leading voices in feminist film criticism, has characterized the complexities of the film stills in the following statement: "But just as she is artist and model, voyeur and looked-at, active and passive, subject and object, the photographs set up a comparable variety of positions and responses for the viewer. There is no stable subject position in her work, no resting point that does not quickly shift into something else."[57]

Thus, while male critics such as Arthur Danto perceive the persona in the film stills as "The Girl,"[58] an object of male desire, women critics such as Mulvey and Abigail Solomon-Godeau can read the images more as a critique of such stereotypes from *film noir*.[59]

In this particular film-still, Sherman explores the theme of the self-consciousness of the gaze mediated by the mirror, echoing the concerns of Cassatt in *The Coiffure* (Fig. 13–5). Krauss notes the pronounced graininess of the image, a signifier in photographic terms of distance, as if the image is captured via a telephoto lens.[60] The black bar on the left of the doorframe positions the viewer as "voyeur" peeping in on the scene from a distance, intruding on the self-conscious gazing of the figure draped in a towel and standing in a bathroom.

In 1980 Sherman began to use color, simultaneously enlarging the scale of the image. Her first fully mature series, the horizontal works of 1981, were inspired by pornographic centerfolds. Sparked by a request from *Artforum* to design a portfolio, these life-sized figures are "psychologically charged, unsettling, and disturbing."[61] For example, in *Untitled #92*, an adolescent girl in dated clothing crouches anxiously on the floor gazing up at an unidentified, looming presence. Spotlighting isolates Sherman, the actress, and the looming black shadows rob the viewer of any clear sense of context. This work is characteristic of Sherman's production in its implied narrative and self-conscious ambiguity. It is an exciting, yet supremely frustrating, task for the viewer, forcing a personal projection, like a Rorschach inkblot, onto the image.

Following the highly theatrical and idiosyncratically colored scenes of the 1983 "Costume Dramas," Sherman's work began a descent into a hellish world of madness

Fig. 16–17. Cindy Sherman, *Untitled*. 1977. Black and white photo, 10 x 8 in. *(courtesy Metro Pictures)*

and loss of rational control. Her images, still using herself as actress, are bizarre, distressing, and at times veering into the animal world. Her works from 1987 present a rotting landscape of death, decay, and waste, in which her presence has all but disappeared. If Ken Johnson is accurate, Sherman's work "therapeutically releases the contents of psychic disturbance through the clarifying sanity of a prolifically inventive and witty theatrical, photographical and artistic practice."[62]

Sherman would attack the entire history of art in her series based on famous and instantly recognizable "masterpieces." In using the icons of art history as raw material, Sherman includes the "high" art of painting with all the other media in a destabilizing project that questions the impact of imagery in gender construction of identity.

• Barbara Kruger, *Untitled (We don't need another hero)*

Like Cindy Sherman, Barbara Kruger deals in her work with the power, sexual politics, and hidden meanings of images inherited from the popular media of films, television, and magazines. Unlike Sherman, Kruger does not assume the role of actress in constructed scenarios, but manipulates "found" imagery. She combines these pictures with brief, pithy texts that she has written. This appropriation of images is an important trend in works by second-generation, postmodernist artists with well-developed feminist consciousness.

Born in Newark, New Jersey in 1945, Kruger studied with the photographer

Diane Arbus for a short time at the Parsons School of Design. Encouraged by Marvin Israels, another teacher at Parsons, she secured a job as a graphic designer at Condé Nast publications, working on *Mademoiselle* magazine, which she designed between 1968 and 1972. This crucial experience gave Kruger the familiarity with media layout formulas that she employs directly in her characteristic photomontages.

Inspired by a massive wall hanging by Magdalena Abakanowicz, Kruger began making works in the late 1960s that incorporated yarn and cloth. When she began combining her own photos with short written texts, she discovered a new, very personal direction in her art.

In 1981 she developed the form she uses today. An image appropriated from a source in popular culture is manipulated through enlargement or cropping and juxtaposed with a text, set in boldface type. Her large-scale works, often 4 feet tall and 6 feet wide, are fitted into bright red frames for exhibition. They announce their identity as art objects, commodities on the market.[63]

A characteristic example of Kruger's work is shown in Figure 16–18. Appropriating an antedated photograph of a movie marquee advertising a film from the 1950s, Kruger's superimposed text declares, "We don't need another hero." The text thus deconstructs the mythology of sexual stereotypes and female subservience promoted by such mass media instruments as "The Naked Spur." It is through the juxtaposition of text and image that a contemporary feminist message is communicated, clearly and unequivocally.

Kruger works with the specific intent of including women in her audience. She recognizes the distinct experiences women have in the culture. "I want to address difference that leads to gender distinctions. I'm not a separatist, I'm not a utopian."[64]

Fig 16–18. Barbara Kruger, *Untitled (We don't need another hero)*. 1987. Photographic silkscreen/vinyl, 108³/₄ x 157³/₄ in. *(courtesy Mary Boone Gallery; photo by Zindman/Fremont)*

Kruger's works have received wide recognition in the art world since their appearance in the early 1980s. Considered among the most important postmodernists, Kruger creates work that is "contentious, aggressive, and explosive."[65] Similarly, Kate Linker defines Kruger's work as "assertive, aggressive and argumentative."[66] In its power to communicate concepts directly and expose manipulative meanings of imagery, it points in the direction of a widened role for art to effect significant social change.

Kruger's artistic practice is rooted in the belief that gender is not essential and biologically determined but constructed in culture. Kruger is very intent on including women in her audience and developing an "active viewer" capable of deconstructing words and text.[67] Linker articulates the ways in which Kruger's work was impacted by a number of theoretical discourses. Like Foucault, Kruger views power as decentralized and anonymous, dispersed over a multitude of sites.[68] Her mission, then, is "to erode the impassivity engendered by the imposition of social norms." She wants her male and female viewers to critique cultural "stereotypes," perceived as prime instruments in the production of docile and submissive subjects.[69] Film is one important site for the dissemination of these stereotypes. Kruger is well aware of the ideas developed by feminist film theoreticians who have used the concepts of both Freud and Lacan concerning the construction of the self through visual stimuli. In this work, Kruger implicates the films of the 1950s as a component of the cultural construction of gender which institutionalized sexism.

- **Barbara Kruger, *Your body is a battleground***

This poster supports the issue of abortion rights and was created for the march on Washington in 1992 to encourage the Supreme Court to uphold the right to legalized abortions, symbolized by the landmark decision of *Roe* v. *Wade*. This was, in

Fig. 16–19. Barbara Kruger,
Untitled (Your body is a battle-ground). 1989. Photographic silkscreen/vinyl, 112 x 112 in.
(courtesy Mary Boone Gallery)

fact, the largest demonstration ever held in Washington, when over 750,000 people marched. In this image, Kruger demonstrates her political commitment to issues directly affecting women's health, and survival. The poster is direct and unequivocal, providing an unforgettable image designed to galvanize the often depoliticized groups in the post-Reagan era. At the same time, she addresses the issue of the corporeal body. The severely cropped face is divided vertically into a positive image and its photographic negative. "Your body is a battleground" was a political slogan from the 1960s and, in this context, alerts the viewer to the rootedness of gender politics in the actual bodies of real women. In addressing immediate political issues, Kruger's art is capable of direct engagement in issues of power. Here Kruger goes beyond much of Postmodernism's theoretical meditations on the nature of subjectivity, authorship, and gender formation to more direct action.

- ### Mary Kelly, *Post Partum Document*

Although she was born in Minneapolis, in 1941, Mary Kelly spent the formative years of her artistic career in London, from 1968 through the 1970s. Her *Post Partum Document*, first exhibited in 1979, is contemporary with Chicago's *Dinner Party*. A comparison between these two works reveals the very different nature of contemporary American and British feminism. Kelly was part of the consciousness-raising group that included psychoanalyst Juliet Mitchell and filmmaker-critic Laura Mulvey. In this environment, Kelly beame conversant with the post-Freudian psychoanalytic theories of Jacques Lacan and with Michel Foucault's theories on sexuality as embedded in the society's discourses and institutions. Begun in 1973, the *Post Partum Document* was exhibited at the Institute of Contemporary Art in London in 1979. It is a six-section, 135-part work that deals with the artist's relationship with her son from his birth until he entered school at the age of 6. Kelly focused on such developmental milestones as weaning from the breast, learning to speak, starting school, and writing. The whole is presented with pseudo-scientific objectivity "documented" with memorabilia such as soiled diapers, clothing, and the child's markings, which are exhibited as museum objects or in Kelly's word "fetishes." The records of these "events" are infused with awareness of Freud's and Lacan's psychoanalytical systems. What is resolutely and obviously avoided are visual images of the mother. As Kelly states:

> . . . I have tried to cut across the predominant representation of woman as the object of the look in order to question the notion of femininity as a pre-given entity and to foreground instead its social construction as a representation of sexual difference within specific discourses.[70]

In Kelly's view, imagery of women as object of the male gaze is suspect to essentialism and the oppression of women under patriarchy. In the form and the content of this original *opus*, Kelly moved to the core of the issues of Postmodern feminist analysis.

The *Post Partum Document* has been reproduced in book form (published in 1985). Sections of the original have been acquired by a number of museums, including the Tate Gallery in London.

BODY ART OF THE 1990s

• Hannah Wilke, *SOS Starification Object Series*

Hannah Wilke (1940–1993) occupies a significant position in the history of feminist body art and performance. In her latex works of the late 1960s and early 1970s she was among the first artists to use vaginal imagery, which would become the subject of works by many women artists in the 1970s. She made vulvas out of a wide range of nontraditional materials, such as kneaded erasers and chewing gum. The use of gum is visible in this series of photographs documenting her performance piece, *SOS Starification Object Series* of 1974. Wilke uses her nude body as a sort of "canvas" on which the gum "vulvas" are attached. Her work sought to "valorize female form and to criticize the cultural devaluation of the feminine."[71]

Wilke was awarded her B.F.A. degree from the Tyler School of Art in Philadelphia, but her professional life was based in New York. She taught sculpture at the School of Visual Arts in Manhattan for many years and was represented by the Ronald Feldman Gallery, beginning in 1972.

Wilke's persistent use of her own body should not be interpreted as self-absorption or hedonistic narcissism. Her sense of collective identity was highly developed. She told an interviewer that from the very beginning of her career, her art making carried a sense of communal identity and social responsibility:

> I felt it would interest me to create an iconography about a woman by a woman. I could be representative of every woman.[72]

Fig. 16–20. Hannah Wilke, *S.O.S. Starification Object Series.* 1974–1982. Mixed media, $40^{1}/_{2}$ x 58 in. framed.   *(courtesy Ronald Feldman Fine Arts, New York; photo by D. James Dee)*

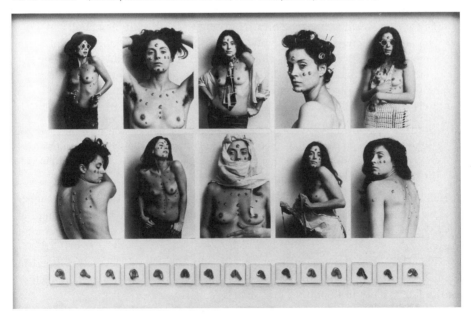

She connected this awareness directly to her identity as a Jew impacted by the Holocaust.

> I realized, the only universal is womanhood, which regenerates life. I was conscious of the destruction of so many people for all of man's ideals. I had to create something that was almost a new religion, that was a universal symbol for all humankind.[73]

As Joanna Frueh notes, "seeing the body through women's eyes was a crucial aspect of women's self-determination and self-actualization,"[74] since the 1970s.

- **Hannah Wilke, *February 19, 1992, #6 from Intra-Venus***

Wilke used photographs to document her mother's battle with cancer. Between 1978 and 1982 she took thousands of photos of her mother.

> I felt if I could get her [Wilke's mother] to have the same energy that I had when I made the art, possibly she would lose her cancer.[75]

The memorial exhibition, held in 1984, included a selection of life-sized photographs, sculpture, poems, and performances.

The enlarged photograph became Wilke's own medium a decade later in a series of thirteen over-life-sized prints which served as a powerful document of her own unsuccessful battle with lymphoma. Roberta Smith wrote that these self-portraits "seared the psyche."[76] The images that form the "Intra-Venus" series, such as Fig. 16–21, were selected from slides taken by her husband, Donald Goddard, during the last five years of her life. In this work, she is confronting the viewer through strands of hair, thinned by chemotherapy. In other images she is bald, and hooked to an IV (in-

Fig. 16–21. Hannah Wilke, *February 19, 1992, #6 from Intra-Venus.* 1992–1993. Chromagenic supergloss prints, 47$\frac{1}{2}$ x 71$\frac{1}{2}$ in. *(courtesy of Ronald Feldman Fine Arts, New York; photo by Dennis Cowley)*

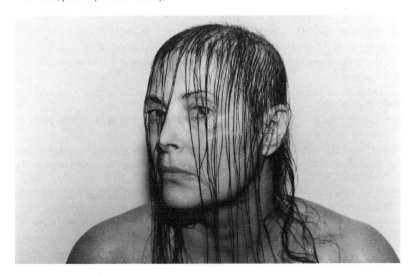

travenous) tube. The enlarged scale and direct, uncompromising gaze make these images powerful, indeed unforgettable, and somewhat "unbearable."[77]

Wilke's imagery forces the viewer to confront the artist, even as the creator is encased in a body ravaged by disease. In this project, Wilke's faith in the power of art as both witness and document ultimately affirms both her personal courage and integrity and the life force of every single human being.

CONCLUSION

The artists discussed in this chapter as in many previous epochs are not the only women creators to make important contributions to contemporary art. They have been selected for detailed discussion because each figure is an outstanding representative of a major avant-garde movement or trend in contemporary art history. The achievements of these few artists, however, do not represent the total contribution of women to the visual arts. There are many other productive women artists whose works are also worthy of attention and recognition.

I encourage the reader to use the list of suggested references at the end of this chapter to explore in greater depth than is possible in this text a fuller range of works of art created by women artists since 1970.

Without minimizing current concerns over the increasingly conservative nature of government funding or the political vulnerability of the National Endowment for the Arts, the future for women artists is filled with the possibilities of further achievements. The canon has been exploded, at least to the extent that the history of art can never again be retold without including the contributions of women in the story.

Suggestions for Further Reading

General Works on Contemporary Women Artists

BECKETT, WENDY, *Contemporary Women Artists* (New York: Universe Books, 1988).

BROUDE, NORMA, and MARY D. GARRARD (eds.), *The Power of Feminist Art: The American Movement of the 1970s, History and Impact* (New York: Abrams, 1994).

LIPPARD, LUCY R., *From the Center: Feminist Essays on Women's Art* (New York: E. P. Dutton, 1976).

LIPPARD, LUCY R., *Overlay: Contemporary Art and the Art of Prehistory* (New York: Pantheon Books, 1983).

POLLOCK, GRISELDA, *Framing Feminism: Art and the Women's Movement, 1970–1985* (Pandora, 1987).

RAVEN, ARLENE, CASSANDRA L. LANGER, and JOANNA FRUEH (eds.), *Feminist Art Criticism: An Anthology* (Ann Arbor: UMI Research Press, 1988), and *New Feminist Criticism: Art, Identity, Action* (New York: HarperCollins, 1994).

ROBINS, CORINNE, *The Pluralist Era: American Art, 1968–1981* (New York: Harper and Row, Icon Editions, 1984).

ROBINSON, HILARY (ed.), *Visibly Female: Feminism and Art Today* (New York: Universe Books, 1988).

ROSEN, RANDY et al., *Making Their Mark: Women Artists Move into the Mainstream, 1970–1985* (New York: Abbeville Press, 1989).

SMAGULA, HOWARD, *Currents: Contemporary Directions in the Visual Arts* (Englewood Cliffs, NJ: Prentice-Hall, 1983).

Flack

FLACK, AUDREY, *Audrey Flack* (New York: Abrams, 1981).

SIEGLE, JEANNE, "Audrey Flack's Object," *ARTS Magazine*, 50 (June 1976), pp. 103–5.

Chicago

CHICAGO, JUDY, *The Dinner Party: A Symbol of Our Heritage* (New York: Doubleday, and Garden City, NY: Anchor Books, 1979).

CHICAGO, JUDY, *Through the Flower: My Struggle as a Woman Artist* (New York: Doubleday, and Garden City, NY: Anchor Books, 1975).

Schapiro

GOUMA-PETERSON, THALIA, *Miriam Schapiro: A Retrospective: 1953–1980* (Wooster, OH: The College of Wooster, 1980).

African-American Artists

Gumbo Ya Ya: Anthology of Contemporary African-American Women Artists (New York: MidMarch 1995).

Performance

EDELSON, MARY BETH, *Seven Cycles: Public Rituals* (New York: A. I. R., 1980).

GOLDBERG, ROSELEE, *Performance Art: From Futurism to the Present* (New York: Abrams, 1988).

ROTH, MOIRA (ed.), *The Amazing Decade: Women and Performance Art in America: 1970–1980; A Source Book* (Los Angeles: Astro Artz, 1983).

Bartlett

BARTLETT, JENNIFER, *In the Garden* (New York: Abrams, 1982).

GOLDWATER, MARGE, *Jennifer Bartlett* (Minneapolis, MN: Walker Arts Center, 1985).

Murray

GRAZE, SUE, and KATHY HALBRIECH, *Elizabeth Murray: Paintings and Drawings* (New York: Abrams, in association with the Dallas Museum of Art and the MIT committee on the Visual Arts, 1987).

Abakanowicz

JACOBS, MARY JANE, *Magdalena Abakanowicz* (New York: Abbeville Press, 1982).

ROSE, BARBARA, *Magdalena Abakanowicz* (New York: Abrams, 1994).

Graves

GRAVES, NANCY, *The Sculpture of Nancy Graves: A Catalogue Raisonné* (New York: Hudson Hills Press, in association with the Fort Worth Art Museum, 1987).

Holt

HOLT, NANCY, "Sun Tunnels," *Artforum* 15 (April 1977), pp. 33–37.

Holzer

WALDMAN, DIANE, *Jenny Holzer* (New York: Guggenheim and Abrams, 1989).

Lin, Vietnam Veterans Memorial

BLUM, SHIRLEY NEILSEN, "The National Vietnam War Memorial," *ARTS Magazine*, 59 (December 1984), pp. 124–28.

MITCHELL, W.J.T. (ed.), *Art and the Public Sphere* (Chicago: University of Chicago Press, 1990).

Postmodernism and Feminism

LINKER, KATE, and JANE WEINSTOCK, *Difference: On Representation and Sexuality* (New York: New Museum of Contemporary Art, 1984).

Sherman

KRAUSS, ROSALIND, *Cindy Sherman* (New York: Rizzoli, 1993).

SHERMAN, CINDY, *Cindy Sherman* (New York: Whitney Museum of Art, 1987).

Cindy Sherman History Portraits, essay by Arthur C. Danto (New York: Rizzoli, 1991).

Kruger

LINKER, KATE, *Love for Sale: The Words and Pictures of Barbara Kruger* (New York: Abrams, 1990).

SQUIERS, CAROL, "Diversionary (Syn)tactics: Barbara Kruger Has Her Way with Words," *Art News*, 86 (February 1987), pp. 74–85.

Kelly

KELLY, MARY, *The Postpartum Document* (London: Routledge, 1985).

NOTES

Preface

1. Amy Richlin in Richlin (ed.), *Pornography and Representation in Greece and Rome* (New York: Oxford University Press, 1992) p. 179.

2. Michael Ann Holly, "Past Looking," *Critical Inquiry*, 16 (Winter 1990), p. 395.

Introduction

1. Griselda Pollock, "Feminist Interventions in the History of Art: An Introduction," in *Vision and Difference: Femininity, Feminism and the History of Art* (London: Routledge, 1988), pp. 1ff.

2. Griselda Pollock and Roszika Parker, *Old Mistresses: Women, Art and Ideology* (New York: Pantheon Books, 1981).

3. Deborah Cherry, *Painting Women: Victorian Women Artists* (London: Routledge, 1993), p. 52.

4. Mieke Bal and Normal Bryson, "Semiotics and Art History," *Art Bulletin*, 73 (1991), pp. 174–208.

5. Jonathan Culler, *On Deconstruction: Theory and Criticism after Structuralism* (Ithaca, NY: Cornell University Press, 1982), p. 131.

6. Ibid., p. 156.

7. Denise Riley, *"Am I That Name?": Feminism and the Category of "Women" in History* (Minneapolis: University of Minnesota Press, 1988), p. 2.

8. Bal and Bryson, op. cit., p. 180.

9. Pollock, op. cit., p. 11.

10. Ibid.

11. Bal and Bryson, op. cit., p. 177.

12. Mieke Bal, "Light in Painting: Dis-seminating Art History," in Peter Brunette and David Wills (eds.), *Deconstruction and the Visual Arts: Art, Media, Architecture* (Cambridge: Cambridge University Press, 1994), pp. 54–56.

13. Bal and Bryson, op. cit., p. 186.

Chapter 1

1. Margaret Ehrenberg, *Women in Prehistory* (Norman: University of Oklahoma Press, 1989). p. 66.

2. Ibid.

3. Stephanie Coontz and Peta Henderson (eds.), *Women's Work, Men's Property: The Origins of Gender and Class* (London: Verso, 1986).

4. Coontz and Henderson, "Introduction," p. 37.

5. Elizabeth Barber, *Prehistoric Textiles: The Development of Cloth in the Neolothic and Bronze Ages* (Princeton, NJ: Princeton University Press, 1991), p. 284.

6. Ibid., p. 290.

7. Paula Webster, "Matriarchy: A Vision of Power," in Rayna R. Reiter, *Toward an Anthropology of Women* (New York: Monthly Review Press, 1975), p. 143.

8. Ann Oakley, *Sex, Gender and Society* (New York: Harper and Row, 1972), p. 165.

Chapter 2

1. Julia Asher Grève, *Frauen in Altsumerscher Zeit*, Biblioteca Mesopotamica 18 (Malibu: Udena Publications), 1985.

2. For the following discussion I am indebted to the detailed, excellent study by Gerda Lerner, *The Creation of Patriarchy* (New York: Oxford University Press, 1986) and the briefer essay by Ilse Seibert, *Women in the Ancient Near East*, trans. Marianne Herzfeld (New York: Abner Schram, 1974).

3. Asher Grève, pp. 181ff.

4. Irene J. Winter, "Women in Public: *The Disk of Enheduanna*, the Beginning of the Office of En-Priestess and the Weight of Visual Evidence," in J. M. Durand, *La Femme dans le Proche-Orient Antique* (Paris: Editions Recherche sur les civilisations, 1987).

5. Asher Grève, p. 182.

6. The seal is reproduced in Seibert, *Women in the Ancient Near East*, p. 22.

7. Asher Grève, p. 182.

8. Winter, p. 200.

Chapter 3

1. Gay Robins, *Women in Ancient Egypt* (Cambridge, MA: Harvard University Press, 1993), p. 180.

2. Ibid.

3. Ibid., p. 55.

4. Ibid., p. 53.

5. Ibid., p. 189.

6. Ibid.

Chapter 4

1. Scully, *The Earth, the Temple, and the Gods*, pp. 11–24. Sections of this discussion are reprinted in Broude and Garrard (eds.), *Feminism and Art History: Questioning the Litany* (New York: Harper and Row, 1982), pp. 33–43.

2. Ehrenberg, *Women in Prehistory*, p. 116.

Chapter 5

1. Sarah B. Pomeroy, *Goddesses, Whores, Wives and Slaves: Women in Classical Antiquity* (New York: Schocken Books, 1975), p. 227.

2. Kate McK. Elderkin, "The Contribution of Women to Ornament in Antiquity," in *Classical Studies Presented to Edward Capps on His Seventieth Birthday* (Princeton, NJ: Princeton University Press, 1936), p. 125.

3. Barber, *Prehistoric Textiles*, pp. 365ff.

4. Jeffrey Henderson in David Halperin, John J. Winkler, and Froma Zeitlin (eds.), *Before Sexuality: The Construction of Erotic Experience in Ancient Greece* (Princeton, NJ: Princeton University Press, 1990), p. 3.

5. Michel Foucault, *The Use of Pleasure: The History of Sexuality*, vol. 2, trans. Robert Hurley (New York: Random House, 1985), pp. 217–25.

6. Ibid., p. 213.

7. Robert F. Sutton, Jr., "Pornography and Persuasion on Attic Pottery," in Amy Richlin (ed.), *Pornography and Representation in Greece and Rome* (New York: Oxford University Press, 1992), pp. 21–22.

8. Ibid., p. 24.

9. Dyfri Williams, "Women on Athenian Vases: Problems of Interpretation," in Averil Cameron and Amelie Kuhrt (eds.), *Images of Women in Antiquity* (London: Croom Helm, 1983), p. 94.

10. Sarah B. Pomeroy, "A Classical Scholar's Perspective on Matriarchy," in Berenice A. Carroll (ed.), *Liberating Women's History: Theoretical and Critical Essays* (Urbana: University of Illinois Press, 1976), pp. 220, 223.

11. Pomeroy, *Goddesses, Whores, Wives and Slaves*, pp. 64–78.

12. Eve Cantarella, *Pandora's Daughters: The Role and Status of Women in Greece and Roman Antiquity* (Baltimore, MD: Johns Hopkins University Press, 1987), p. 51.

13. Williams, in *Images of Women in Antiquity*, p. 97.

14. H. A. Shapiro, "Eros in Love: Pederasty and Pornography in Greece," in *Pornography and Representation in Greece and Rome*, p. 53.

15. See Fig. 1.7 in *Pornography and Representation in Greece and Rome*.

16. See Fig. 1.2 in *Pornography and Representation in Greece and Rome*.

17. Shapiro, in *Pornography and Representation in Greece and Rome*.

18. Elderkin, "The Contribution of Women to Ornament," pp. 125–26.

19. Giovanni Boccaccio, *Concerning Famous Women*, trans. with an introduction by Guido A. Guarino (New Brunswick, NJ: Rutgers University Press, 1963), p. 131.

20. Robert Rosenblum, "The Origin of Painting: A Problem in the Iconography of Romantic Classicism," *Art Bulletin*, 39 (1957), pp. 279–82.

21. These histories include: Ernest Guhl, *Die Frauen in der Kunstgeschichte* (Berlin, 1858); Elizabeth Fries Lummis Ellet, *Women Artists in All Ages and Countries* (New York, 1859); Octave Fidière, *Les Femmes artists à l'Académie royale de peinture et de sculpture* (Paris, 1885); Walter Sparrow, *Women Painters of the World* (London, 1905).

Chapter 6

1. Diana E. E. Kleiner, "The Great Friezes of the Ara Pacis Augustae. Greek Sources, Roman Derivatives, and Augustan Social Policy," in Eve D'Ambra (ed.), *Roman Art in Context: An Anthology* (Englewood Cliffs, NJ: Prentice Hall, 1993), pp. 27ff.

2. Herlihy notes that there were fewer girls reaching adulthood than boys, but he does not attribute this directly to female infanticide. David Herlihy, "Life Expectancies for Women in Medieval Society," in Rosemarie Thee Morewedge (ed.), *The Role of Women in the Middle Ages* (Albany: State University of New York Press, 1975), pp. 4–5.

3. Verena Zinserling, *Women in Greece and Rome*, trans. L. A. Jones (New York: Abner Schram, 1973), p. 64.

4. Natalie Boymel Kampen, "Between Public and Private: Women as Historical Subjects in Roman Art," in Sarah B. Pomeroy (ed.), *Women's History and Ancient History* (Chapel Hill: University of North Carolina Press, 1991), p. 243.

5. Ibid., p. 220.

6. Natalie Boymel Kampen, "Social Status and Gender in Roman Art: The Case of the Saleswoman," in *Roman Art in Context*.

7. Zinserling, *Women in Greece and Rome*, p. 58.

8. Pomeroy, *Goddesses, Whores, Wives and Slaves: Women in Classical Antiquity* (New York: Schoken Books, 1975), pp. 199–200.

9. Pliny, the Elder, *Naturalis Historia*, 147, trans. K. Jex-Black and E. Sellers, *The Elder Pliny's Chapters on the History of Art* (Chicago: Argonaut, 1968, photocopy of 1896 edition), p. 171.

10. Mary T. Boatwright, "The City Gate of Plancia Magna in Perge," in *Roman Art in Context*, p. 200.

11. JoAnn McNamara and Suzanne Wemple, "The Power of Women Through the Family in Medieval Europe: 500–1100," in Mary Hartman and Louise Banner (eds.), *Clio's Consciousness Raised* (New York: Harper Colophon Books, 1974), pp. 103–4.

12. Ramsay Macmullen, "Women in Public in the Roman Empire," *Historia*, XXIX/2 (1980), p. 212.

13. Elaine K. Gazda, "Introduction," in *Roman Art in the Private Sphere: New Perspectives on the Architecture and Decor of the Domus, Villa, and Insula* (Ann Arbor: University of Michigan Press, 1991), pp. 6–7.

14. Yvon Thébert, "Private and Public Spaces: The Components of the Domus," in *Roman Art in Context*, p. 229.

15. Molly Myerowitz, "The Domestication of Desire: Ovid's *Parva Tabella* and the Theater of Love," in Amy Richlin (ed.), *Pornography and Representation in Greece and Rome*, pp. 131ff.

16. Michel Foucault, "The Care of the Self," in *The History of Sexuality*, vol. 3, trans. Robert Hurley (New York: Random House, 1986), pp. 79–80.

17. Roy Bowen Ward, "Women in Roman Baths," *Harvard Theological Review*, 85:2 (1992), pp. 125ff.

18. Fikret Yegul, *Baths and Bathing in Classical Antiquity* (Cambridge, MA: MIT Press, 1992), p. 32.

19. Eve Cantarella, *Pandora's Daughters*, pp. 140–41.

20. Averil Cameron, *Procopius* (Berkeley: University of California Press, 1985), p. 67.

21. Ibid., pp. 53–54.

22. Ibid., chapters 4 and 5.

23. Ibid., p. 74.

24. Ibid., p. 68.

25. Ibid., p. 81.

Chapter 7

1. Dorothy Miner, *Anastaise and Her Sisters* (Baltimore, MD: Walters Art Gallery, 1974), pp. 10–11.

2. Ibid., p. 10.

3. Brenda M. Bolton, "Mulieres Sanctae," in Susan Mosher Stuard (ed.), *Women in Medieval Society* (Philadelphia: University of Pennsylvania Press, 1977), pp. 45–47.

4. Annemarie Weyl Carr, "Women Artists in the Middle Ages," *Feminist Art Journal*, V (1976), p. 6.

5. Caroline Bynum, *Holy Feast and Holy Fast: The Religious Significance of Food to Medieval Women* (Berkeley: University of California Press, 1987), pp. 264–65.

6. Quoted in Bynum, ibid., p. 260.

7. Ibid., p. 270.

8. Ibid., p. 274.

9. Margaret R. Miles, "The Virgin's One Bare Breast: Nudity, Gender and Religious Meaning in Tuscan Early Renaissance Culture," in Norma Broude and Mary D. Garrard (eds.), *The Expanding Discourse: Feminism and Art History* (New York: HarperCollins, 1992), p. 31.

10. Kathleen Casey, "The Cheshire Cat: Reconstructing the Experience of Medieval Women," in Berenice A. Carroll (ed.), *Liberating Women's History* (Urbana: University of Illinois Press, 1976), p. 247, note 7.

11. Susan Groag Bell, "Medieval Women Book Owners: Arbiters of Lay Piety and Ambassadors of Culture," in Mary Erler and Maryann Kowalski (eds.), *Women and Power in the Middle Ages* (Athens: University of Georgia Press, 1988).

12. Joan Kelly, "Early Feminist Theory and the *Querelle des Femmes*, 1400–1789," *Signs*, VIII (Autumn 1982), pp. 4–28.

13. Gerda Lerner, *The Creation of Feminist Consciousness: From the Middle Ages to Eighteen-Seventy* (New York: Oxford University Press, 1993), p. 139.

14. Millard Meiss, *French Painting in the Time of Jean de Berry* (London: Phaidon, 1967–1968), I, p. 3.

15. Dorothy Miner believes that Le Noir is identical with the artist identified by Meiss as the "Passion Master" (see *Anastaise and Her Sisters*, p. 19). While Meiss accepts the possibility that Le Noir might be the name of the artist whose works form a stylistic group, he uses the name "Passion Master" for this figure, stopping short of attributing these works to Jean Le Noir (*French Painting*, pp. 167–68).

16. Miner, *Anastaise and Her Sisters*, pp. 18–19.

17. Ann Sutherland Harris and Linda Nochlin, *Women Artists: 1550–1950* (New York: Knopf, and Los Angeles County Museum of Art, 1977), p. 26.

18. A. G. I. Christie, *English Medieval Embroidery* (Oxford: Clarendon Press, 1938), Appendix I.

19. See F. Stenton (ed.), *The Bayeux Tapestry* (London: Phaidon, 1957).

20. Roszika Parker, *The Subversive Stitch: Embroidery and the Making of the Feminine* (London: Women's Press, 1984), p. 27.

21. Ibid., p. 29.

22. Harris and Nochlin, *Women Artists: 1550–1950*, pp. 16–17.

23. For a detailed description of the Syon Cope, see Christie, *English Medieval Embroidery*, pp. 142–48.

24. Martha Howell, *Women, Production and Patriarchy in late Medieval Cities* (New Brunswick, NJ: Rutgers University Press, 1986), pp. 9ff.

25. Eileen Power, *Medieval Women*, ed. M. M. Postan (London: Cambridge University Press, 1975), p. 38.

26. Ibid., pp. 87–88.

27. Maryanne Kowalski and Judith M. Bennett, "Crafts, Guilds, and Women in the Middle Ages: Fifty Years after Marian K. Dale," *Signs*, 14 (1989), p. 480.

28. Ibid., p. 483.

29. Howell, op. cit., p. 179.

30. Merry E. Wiesner, *Working Women in Renaissance Germany* (New Brunswick, NJ: Rutgers University Press, 1986), pp. 157ff.

31. Ibid., pp. 163ff.

32. Ibid., p. 172.

33. Natalie Zemon Davis, "Women in the Crafts in Sixteenth-Century Lyon," in Barbara A. Hanawalt (ed.), *Women and Work in Preindustrial Europe* (Bloomington: Indiana University Press, 1986), p. 187.

34. Ibid., p. 189.

35. Sibylle Harksen, *Women in the Middle Ages*, trans. Marianne Herzfeld (New York: Abner Schram, 1975), p. 28.

Chapter 8

1. Judith Brown, "A Woman's Place Was in the Home: Women's Work in Renaissance Tuscany," in Margaret W. Ferguson et al. (eds.), *Rewriting the Renaissance: The Discourse of Difference in Early Modern Europe* (Chicago: University of Chicago Press, 1986), p. 209.

2. Ibid., p. 215.

3. Patricia Simons, "Women in Frames: The Gaze, the Eye, the Profile in Renaissance Portraiture," in Norma Broude and Mary D. Garrard (eds.), *The Expanding Discourse: Feminism and Art History* (New York: HarperCollins, 1992), pp. 39ff.

4. Joan Kelly-Gadol, "Did Women Have a Renaissance?" In Renate Bridenthal and Claudia Koonz (eds.), *Becoming Visible: Women in European History* (Boston: Houghton Mifflin, 1972), pp. 160–61.

5. J. O'Faolain and L. Martines, *Not in God's Image* (New York: Harper and Row, 1973), p. 145.

6. Hannelore Sachs, *The Renaissance Woman*, trans. Marianne Herzfeld (New York: McGraw-Hill, 1971), p. 9.

7. Ruth Kelso, *Doctrine for the Lady of the Renaissance* (Urbana: University of Illinois Press, 1956), pp. 59, 77.

8. Simons, op. cit., p. 41.

9. Ibid., p. 45.

10. Richard Goldthwaite, *The Building of Renaissance Florence: An Economic and Social History* (Baltimore, MD: Johns Hopkins University Press, 1980), pp. 77ff.

11. Ibid., p. 13–14.

12. Ibid., p. 108 (emphasis added).

13. Lilian Zirpolo, "Botticelli's *Primavera*: A Lesson for the Bride," in *The Expanding Discourse*, pp. 101ff.

14. Howell, *Women, Production and Patriarchy in Late Medieval Cities*, p. 16.

15. Harris and Nochlin, in *Women Artists: 1550–1950*, p. 106.

16. Margaret L. King, "Book Lined Cells: Women and Humanism in the Early Italian Renaissance," in Patricia Labalme (ed.), *Beyond Their Sex: Learned Women of the European Past* (New York: New York University Press, 1984).

17. Quoted in Harris and Nochlin, *Women Artists: 1550–1950*, p. 107.

18. Sondra Ilya Perlinghieri, *Sofonisba Anguissola: The First Great Woman Artist of the Renaissance* (New York: Rizzoli, 1992), p. 42.

19. Ibid., pp. 65ff.

20. Eleanor Tufts, *Our Hidden Heritage: Five Centuries of Women Artists* (New York: Paddington Press, 1974), p. 21.

21. Mario Praz, *Conversation Pieces: A Survey of the Informal Group Portrait in Europe and America* (University Park: Pennsylvania State University Press, 1971), p. 149.

22. Harris and Nochlin, *Women Artists: 1550–1950*, p. 111.

23. *The Age of Correggio and the Carracci: Emilian Painting of the 16th and 17th Centuries* (Washington, DC: National Gallery of Art, 1986), p. 132.

24. Tufts, op. cit., p. 32.

25. A complete transcript, translated into English, is published in Mary D. Garrard, *Artemisia Gentileschi: The Image of the Female Hero in Italian Baroque Art* (Princeton, NJ: Princeton University Press, 1989).

26. Ibid., p. 183ff.

27. Mieke Bal, *Reading "Rembrandt": Beyond the Word-Image Opposition* (Cambridge: Cambridge University Press, 1991), pp. 139ff.

28. Mieke Bal and Norman Bryson, "Semiotics and Art History," *Art Bulletin*, 73 (1991), pp. 205–6.

29. See Garrard, *Artemisia Gentileschi*, chapter 2, for a detailed discussion of the intellectual tradition of "Women Worthies" and *Querelle des Femmes* as background for the iconographic innovations of Gentileschi.

30. Ibid., p. 358.

31. All Artemisia Gentileschi's letters are reprinted in Garrard, *Artemisia Gentileschi*.

Chapter 9

1. E. de Jongh, *Still Life in the Age of Rembrandt* (Auckland, New Zealand: Auckland City Art Gallery, 1982), p. 65.

2. Ibid., p. 179.

3. James A. Welu and Pieter Biesboer, *Judith Leyster: A Dutch Master and Her World* (Worcester Art Museum, Yale University Press, 1993), p. 75.

4. Ibid., pp. 47–48.

5. Frima Fox Hofrichter, *Judith Leyster: A Woman Painter in Holland's Golden Age* (Doornspijk, The Netherlands: Davaco, 1989), p. 52.

6. Ibid., p. 47.

7. Welu and Biesboer, *Judith Leyster*, op. cit., p. 168.

8. Simon Schama, *The Embarrassment of Riches: An Interpretation of Dutch Culture in the Golden Age* (Berkeley: University of California Press, 1988), p, 407.

Chapter 10

1. Harris and Nochlin, *Women Artists: 1550–1950*, p. 161.

2. For a discussion of the Crozat Circle, see Thomas Crow, *Painters and Public Life in Eighteenth Century France* (New Haven, CT: Yale University Press, 1985).

3. Tufts, *Our Hidden Heritage*, p. 110.

4. For a translation of this text, see Wendy Slatkin, *The Voices of Women Artists* (Englewood Cliffs, NJ: Prentice Hall, 1993), pp. 18–19.

5. Patricia Labalme, "Women's Roles in Early Modern Venice: An Exceptional Case," in Labalme (ed.), *Beyond Their Sex: Learned Women of the European Past* (New York: New York. University Press, 1984).

6. Wendy Wassyng Roworth, *Angelica Kauffman: A Continental Artist in Georgian England* (Brighton: The Royal Pavilion Art Gallery and Museums, and London: Reaktion Books, 1992), pp. 15–17.

7. Ibid., p. 21.

8. Ibid., p. 91.

9. Ibid., pp. 92–93.

10. For a thorough discussion of this painting, see Joseph Baillio, "*Marie-Antoinette et ses enfants* par Mme. Vigée-Lebrun," *L'Oeil* (March–April 1981).

11. Lynn Hunt, "The Many Bodies of Marie Antoinette: Political Pornography and the Problem of the Feminine in the French Revolution," in Lynn Hunt (ed.), *Eroticism and the Body Politic* (Baltimore, MD: Johns Hopkins University Press, 1991), pp. 108ff.

12. For a discussion of the new issues of motherhood, see Carol Duncan, "Happy Mothers and Other New Ideas in Eighteenth-Century French Art," in Broude and Garrard (eds.), *Feminism and Art History*, pp. 201ff.

13. The discussion of Labille-Guiard is based on the detailed, authoritative study of the artist by Anne-Marie Passez, *Biographie et Catalogue raisonné des oeuvres de Mme. Labille-Guiard* (Paris: Arts et Metiers Graphiques, 1973).

14. Roseanne Runte, "Women as Muse," in Samia I. Spencer (ed.), *French Women and the Age of Enlightenment* (Bloomington: Indiana University Press, 1984), p. 144.

Chapter 11

1. Kathleen D. McCarthy, *Women's Culture: American Philanthropy and Art, 1830–1930* (Chicago: University of Chicago Press, 1991), p. 28.

2. Ibid., p. 8.

3. Ibid., p. 20.

4. Eleanor Tufts (ed.), *American Women Artists: 1830–1930* (Washington, DC: The National Museum of Women in the Arts, 1987), catalogue entry number 5.

5. Robin Bolton-Smith and William H. Truettner, *Lilly Martin Spencer: The Joys of Sentiment* (Washington, DC: Smithsonian Institution Press for the National Collection of Fine Arts, 1973), p. 11. The following discussion of Lilly Martin Spencer is indebted to this detailed, excellent catalogue.

6. Ibid., p. 69.

7. McCarthy, op. cit., p. 18.

8. Jane Mayo Roos, "Another Look at Henry James and the 'White Marmorean Flock'," *Woman's Art Journal*, 4 (Summer 1983), p. 32.

9. Susan Waller, "The Artist, the Writer, and the Queen: Hosmer, Jameson, and Zenobia," *Woman's Art Journal*, 4 (Summer 1983), pp. 21–28.

10. For a complete discussion of this work, see Tufts, *American Women Artists: 1830–1930*, catalogue entry number 107.

11. Ibid., p. 43.

12. Jo Ann Wein, "The Parisian Training of American Women Artists," *Woman's Art Journal*, 2 (Spring/Summer, 1981), pp. 41ff.

13. McCarthy, op. cit., p. 14.

14. Pat Ferrero, Elaine Hedges, and Julie Silber, *Hearts and Hands: The Influence of Women and Quilts on American Society* (San Francisco: Quilt Digest Press, 1987), p. 28.

15. Ibid., p. 11.

16. Wanda M. Corn, "Women Building History," in Tufts, *American Women Artists: 1830–1930*, pp. 26–29.

17. McCarthy, op. cit., p. 37.

18. Ibid., p. 84.

19. Corn, op. cit., p. 31.

20. For a complete discussion, see Jeanne Madeline Weimann, *The Fair Women: The Story of the Women's Building, World's Columbian Exposition, Chicago, 1893* (Chicago: Academy Chicago, 1981).

Chapter 12

1. Cherry, *Painting Women: Victorian Women Artists*, p. 78.

2. Nochlin, in *Women Artists 1550–1950*, p. 55.

3. Cherry, op. cit., p. 50.

4. Pamela Gerish Nunn and Jan Marsh, *Women Artists of the Pre-Raphaelite Movement* (London: Virago, 1989).

5. Reprinted in Pollock, *Vision and Difference*, pp. 91ff.

6. Ibid., p. 105.

7. Ibid., p. 97.

8. Gerish Nunn and Marsh, p. 70.

9. Ibid., p. 72.

10. Ibid., p. 73.

11. Roger Fry, quoted in *The Cameron Collection/Julia Margaret Cameron*, introduction by Colin Ford (New York: Van Nostrand and Reinhold, 1975), p. 136.

12. For a thorough discussion of *The Roll Call*, see Paul Usherwood and Jenny Spencer-Smith, *Lady Butler (1846–1933): Battle Artist* (London: National Army Museum, 1987), pp. 31ff, catalogue number 18. For the influence of French military painting, see pp. 163ff.

13. Matthew Lalumia, "Lady Elizabeth Thompson Butler in the 1870s," *Woman's Art Journal*, 4 (Spring/Summer, 1983), pp. 9ff.

14. Paul Usherwood, "A Case of Tokenism," *Woman's Art Journal*, 11 (Fall 1990/Winter 1991), pp. 14ff.

15. Paul Usherwood, "Elizabeth Thompson Butler: The Consequences of Marriage," in *Woman's Art Journal* (Spring/Summer, 1988), pp. 30ff.

Chapter 13

1. Marilyn J. Boxer and Jean H. Quataert (eds.), *Connecting Spheres: Women in the Western World, 1500 to the Present* (New York: Oxford University Press, 1987), pp. 102–9.

2. Harris and Nochlin, *Women Artists: 1550–1950*, p. 46.

3. Theodore Stanton (ed.), *Reminiscences of Rosa Bonheur* (London, 1910; reprint ed. New York: Hacker Art Books, 1976), p. 72.

4. Anna Elizabeth Klumpke, *Rosa Bonheur, sa vie, son oeuvre* (Paris: Flammarion, 1908), pp. 311–12 (author's translation).

5. For the discussion of Bonheur, I am strongly indebted to the excellent essay by Albert Boime, "The Case of Rosa Bonheur: Why Should a Woman Want to Be More Like a Man?" *Art History*, 4 (December 1981), p. 384.

6. James M. Salsow, "Disagreeably Hidden: Construction and Constriction of the Lesbian Body in Rosa Bonheur's *Horse Fair*," in *The Expanding Discourse*, p. 190.

7. Ibid., Fig. 8.

8. Whitney Chadwick, *Women, Art, and Society* (London: Thames and Hudson, 1991), p. 185.

9. Coral Landsbury, *The Old Brown Dog: Women, Workers and Vivisection* (Madison: University of Wisconsin Press, 1985).

10. Chadwick, op. cit., pp. 180ff.

11. Harris and Nochlin, *Women Artists 1550–1950*, p. 257.

12. Roszika Parker and Griselda Pollock, Introduction to *The Journal of Marie Bashkirtseff*, translated by Mathilde Blind (London: Virago Press, 1985), first published in English in 1890.

13. Quoted in ibid., vi.

14. Tamar Garb, *Sisters of the Brush: Women's Artistic Culture in Late Nineteenth-Century Paris* (New Haven, CT: Yale University Press, 1994), p. 111.

15. Ibid., p. 129.

16. Ibid., p. 165.

17. Denis Rouart, *The Correspondence of Berthe Morisot* (London: Lund Humphries, 1957), p. 14.

18. Charles F. Stuckey and William P. Scott, *Berthe Morisot: Impressionist* (New York: Hudson Hills Press, Mount Holyoke College Art Museum in Association with the National Gallery of Art, 1987). See colorplate 2 in the volume.

19. Ibid., pp. 88ff.

20. Adylyn Breeskin, *Mary Cassatt: A Catalogue Raisonné of the Oils, Pastels, Watercolors and Drawings* (Washington, DC: Smithsonian Institution Press, 1970), p. 9.

21. Griselda Pollock, "Modernity and the Spaces of Femininity," in *Vision and Difference*, p. 78.

22. Ibid., p. 88.

23. Anne Higonnet, *Berthe Morisot's Images of Women* (Cambridge, MA: Harvard University Press, 1992), p. 173.

24. Ibid., p. 187.

25. Ibid., p. 173.

26. Griselda Pollock, *Vision and Difference*, p. 63.

Chapter 14

1. J. Diane Radycki, "The Life of Lady Art Students: Changing Art Education at the Turn of the Century," *Art Journal*, 42 (Spring 1982), pp. 9–13.

2. Shulamith Behr, *Women Expressionists* (New York: Rizzoli, 1988).

3. Radycki, op. cit.

4. Behr, op. cit., p. 24.

5. Elizabeth Prelinger et al., *Käthe Kollwitz* (Washington, DC: National Gallery of Art, 1992), pp. 75ff.

6. Radycki, op. cit., p. 11.

7. Martha Kearns, *Käthe Kollwitz: Woman and Artist* (Old Westbury, NY: The Feminist Press, 1976), p. 192.

8. Anne Mochon, *Gabriele Munter: Between Munich and Murnau* (Cambridge, MA: Busch-Reisinger Museum, Harvard University, 1980), p. 16.

9. This work is in the Stadtische Galerie im Lenbachhaus (see catalogue entry no. 34 in Mochon).

10. Arthur A. Cohen, *Sonia Delaunay* (New York: Abrams, 1975), p. 61.

11. Ibid., p. 83.

12. For a discussion of this issue, see Clare Rendell, "Sonia Delaunay and the Expanding Definition of Art," *Woman's Art Journal*, 4 (Summer 1983), pp. 35–38.

13. Maud Lavid, *Cut with the Kitchen Knife: The Weimar Photomontages of Hannah Höch* (New Haven, CT: Yale University Press, 1993), p. 19.

14. Ibid., p. 23.

15. Ibid., p. 31.

16. Sigrid W. Weltge, *Women's Work: Textile Art from the Bauhaus* (San Francisco: Chronicle Books, 1993), p. 47.

17. Ibid., pp. 9–10.

18. Ibid., p. 89.

19. Ibid., p. 46.

20. Ibid., p. 104.

21. Ibid., p. 187.

22. Nochlin, in *Women Artists 1550–1950*, p. 62.

23. Christina Lodder, *Russian Constructivism* (New Haven, CT: Yale University Press, 1983), p. 3.

24. Linda Nochlin, "Matisse and Its Other," *Art in America* (May 1993), p. 94.

25. Lodder, op. cit., p. 146.

26. Camilla Gray, *The Russian Experiment in Art: 1863–1922* (New York: Abrams, 1972), p. 224.

27. Quoted in Lodder, op. cit., p. 148.

28. Ibid., p. 151.

29. Ibid.

30. Cassandra L. Langer, "Fashion, Character and Sexual Politics in Some Romain Brooks' Lesbian Portraits," *Art Criticism*, 1 (1981), p. 29.

31. Chadwick, *Women, Art, and Society*, p. 261.

32. Langer, op. cit., p. 30.

33. Adylyn Breeskin, *Romaine Brooks, "Thief of Souls"* (Washington, DC: National Collection of Fine Arts, Smithsonian Institution Press, 1971), p. 35.

34. Langer, op. cit., p. 34.

35. Ibid., p. 36.

36. Andre Breton, *Arcane 17*, quoted in Whitney Chadwick, "Eros or Thanatos—The Surrealist Cult of Love Reexamined," *Artforum*, 14 (November 1975), p. 50.

37. Gloria F. Orenstein, "Art History and the Case for the Women of Surrealism," *The Journal of General Education*, XXVII (Spring 1975); reprinted in *Feminist Collage: Educating Women in the Visual Arts*, Judy Loeb (ed.) (New York: Teacher's College Press, Columbia University, 1979), pp. 35–59. This situation receives expanded treatment in Whitney Chadwick, *Women Artists and the Surrealist Movement* (Boston: Little, Brown, 1985).

38. Josephine Withers, "The Famous Fur-Lined Teacup and the Anonymous Meret Oppenheim," *ARTS Magazine*, 52 (November 1977), p. 88.

39. From *Chronicle* (1958), quoted in Ibid., p. 93.

40. Dorothea Tanning, in *XX* Siècle* (September 1976), reprinted in the exhibition catalogue, *Dorothea Tanning: 10 Recent Paintings and a Biography* (New York: Gimpel-Weitzenhoffer Gallery, 1979).

41. Janice Helland, "Culture, Politics and Identity in the Paintings of Frida Kahlo," in *The Expanding Discourse*, pp. 399–400.

42. Hayden Herrera, *Frida Kahlo: The Paintings* (New York: HarperCollins, 1991), p. 135.

43. Helland, p. 401.

44. Herrera, op. cit., p. 135.

45. Ibid., p. 139.

46. Barbara Buhler Lynes, "Georgia O'Keeffe and Feminism: A Problem of Position," in *The Expanding Discourse*, p. 439.

47. Ibid., p. 442.

48. Georgia O'Keeffe exhibition catalogue, *An American Place, 1939*, reprinted in *Georgia O'Keeffe* (New York: Viking Press, 1976).

49. Anna C. Chave, "O'Keeffe and the Masculine Gaze," in *Art in America*, 78 (January, 1990), p. 119.

50. Lloyd Goodrich and Doris Bry, *Georgia O'Keeffe* (New York: Whitney Museum of American Art, 1970), p. 18.

51. *Imogen Cunningham: Photographs*, with an introduction by Margery Mann (Seattle: University of Washington Press, 1970).

52. Karin Becker Ohrn, *Dorothea Lange and the Documentary Tradition* (Baton Rouge: Louisiana State University Press, 1980), p. 79.

53. Margaret Bourke-White, *Dear Fatherland, Rest Quietly* (New York: Simon and Schuster, 1946), p. 73.

54. Sara Boutelle, *Julia Morgan, Architect* (New York: Abbeville Press, 1988), pp. 16–17.

55. Ibid., p. 95.

Chapter 15

1. Ellen Landau, "Tough Choices: Becoming a Woman Artist, 1900–1970," in Randy Rosen et al. (eds.), *Making Their Mark: Women Artists Move into the Mainstream, 1970–85* (New York: Abbeville Press, 1989), p. 29.

2. "Introduction" in *Seven American Women: The Depression Decade* (Vassar College Art Gallery, 1976), p. 7.

3. Landau, op. cit., p. 29.

4. Ibid., p. 39.

5. Ibid.

6. Ibid., p. 40.

7. Ibid., p. 39.

8. Ibid., p. 40.

9. Barbara Rose, *Lee Krasner: A Retrospective* (New York: Museum of Modern Art, 1983). My discussion is indebted to Rose's excellent, detailed essay.

10. Anne M. Wagner, "Lee Krasner as L. K.," in *The Expanding Discourse*, pp. 426–427.

11. Ibid., p. 429.

12. Rose, op. cit., p. 54.

13. Wagner, op. cit., p. 434.

14. Barbara Rose, *Helen Frankenthaler* (New York: Abrams, 1971), p. 54.

15. Quoted in Laurie Wilson, "Bride of the Black Moon: An Iconographic Study of the Work of Louise Nevelson," *ARTS Magazine*, 54 (May 1980), p. 144.

16. Louise Nevelson, *Louise Nevelson: Atmospheres and Environments* (New York: C. N. Potter in association with the Whitney Museum of American Art, 1980), p. 77.

17. Wilson, op. cit., p. 145.

18. Arnold B. Glimcher, *Louise Nevelson* (New York: Praeger, 1972), pp. 22–23.

19. Louise Nevelson, *Dawns and Dusks* (New York: Scribner's, 1976), quoted in Slatkin, *The Voices of Women Artists*, p. 254.

20. Claire Falkenstein, transcript from recorded conversation in *Los Angeles Art Community Group Portrait* (University of California, Los Angeles Oral History Program, 1982), p. 189.

21. Lucy Lippard, "Homage to the Square," *Art in America* (July—August 1987), p. 55; quoted in *Agnes Martin* exhibition catalogue (Institute of Contemporary Art, University of Pennsylvania, 1973), p. 9.

22. Lucy Lippard, *From the Center: Feminist Essays of Women's Art* (New York: E. P. Dutton, 1976), p. 65.

23. Lawrence Alloway, "Systemic Painting," in Gregory Battcock (ed.), *Minimal Art: A Critical Anthology* (New York: E. P. Dutton, 1968), p. 55.

24. Lawrence Alloway, *Agnes Martin* exhibition catalogue (Philadelphia: Institute of Contemporary Art, 1973), p. 10.

25. William C. Seitz, *The Responsive Eye* (New York: Museum of Modern Art, 1965), p. 31.

26. Linda Nochlin, "Some Women Realists: Painters of the Figure," *ARTS Magazine*, 48 (May 1974), p. 30.

27. Ann Sutherland Harris, *Alice Neel: 1930–1980* exhibition catalogue (Los Angeles: Loyola Marymount University, 1983), p. 3.

28. Ibid., p. 6.

29. Patricia Hills, *Alice Neel* (New York: Abrams, 1983), p. 162.

30. Ibid., p. 185.

31. Nochlin, "Some Women Realists," p. 29.

32. Chadwick, *Women, Art, and Society*, p. 312.

33. Landau, op. cit., p. 33.

34. Charlotta Kotik, "The Locus of Memory: An Introduction to the Work of Louise Bourgeois," in Kotik et al., *Louise Bourgeois: The Locus of Memory, Works 1982–1993* (New York: The Brooklyn Museum and Abrams, 1994), pp. 19–20.

35. Ibid., p. 29.

36. Cindy Nemser, "An Interview with Eva Hesse," *Artforum* (May 1970), p. 62.

37. Anna Chave, "Eva Hesse: A Girl Being a Sculpture," in Helen Cooper et al. (eds.), *Eva Hesse: A Retrospective* (New Haven, CT: Yale University Press, 1992), pp. 100–101.

38. Quoted in Ibid., p. 102.

39. Ibid., p. 103.

40. Ibid., p. 108.

41. Ibid., p. 112.

Chapter 16

1. Kay Larson, "For the First Time Women Are Leading, Not Following," *Art News*, 79 (October 1980), pp. 64–72.

2. Ibid., p. 68.

3. Mary D. Garrard, "Feminist Politics: Networks and Organizations," in Norma Broude and Mary D. Garrard (eds.), *The Power of Feminist Art: The American Movement of the 1970s, History and Impact* (New York: Abrams, 1994), pp. 88ff.

4. Faith Wilding, "The Feminist Art Programs at Fresno and CalArts, 1970–75," in *The Power of Feminist Art*, pp. 32ff.

5. Arlene Raven, "Womanhouse," in *The Power of Feminist Art*, pp. 48ff.

6. *The Power of Feminist Art*, pp. 110–111.

7. Cindy Nemser, "Conversation with Audrey Flack," *ARTS Magazine*, 48 (February 1974), p. 34.

8. *The Power of Feminist Art*, p. 194.

9. Judy Chicago, *The Dinner Party: A Symbol of Our Heritage* (Garden City, NY: Anchor Books, 1979), p. 12.

10. Josephine Withers, "Judy Chicago's Dinner Party: A Personal Vision of Women's History," in *The Expanding Discourse*, p. 462.

11. The most detailed discussion of Schapiro's work before 1980 is Thalia Gouma-Peterson, *Miriam Schapiro: A Retrospective: 1953–1980* exhibition catalogue (Wooster, OH: The College of Wooster, 1980). This catalogue was prepared for a major traveling exhibition of Schapiro's works.

12. John Perrault, "Issues in Pattern Painting," *Artforum* (December 1977), reprinted in Richard Hertz, *Theories of Contemporary Art* (Englewood Cliffs, NJ: Prentice-Hall, 1985).

13. Paula Bradley, "Placing Women in History: Miriam Schapiro's Fan and Vestiture Series," *ARTS Magazine*, 56 (February 1979), p. 148.

14. *Gumbo Ya Ya: Anthology of Contemporary African-American Women Artists* (New York: Mid March, 1995), p. vii.

15. Elaine Hedges and Ingrid Wendt, *In Her Own Image: Women Working in the Arts* (Old Westbury, NY: The Feminist Press, 1980), p. 289.

16. Lucy Lippard, entry for Alison and Bettye Saar, in *Gumbo Ya Ya*, op. cit., pp. 239ff.

17. Eleanor Munro, *The Originals: American Women Artists* (New York: Simon and Schuster, 1979), p. 410.

18. Thalia Gouma-Peterson, "Modern Dilemma Tales: Faith Ringgold's Story Quilts," in Eleanor Flomenhaft (ed.), *Faith Ringgold: A 25 Year Survey* (Hempstead, NY: The Fine Arts Museum of Long Island, 1990), p. 23.

19. Quoted in Ibid., pp. 14–15.

20. Moira Roth (ed.), *The Amazing Decade: Women and Performance Art in America: 1970–1980* (Los Angeles: Astro Artz, 1983), p. 8. For the following discussion of performance art, I am indebted to Roth's excellent essay.

21. Ibid., p. 20.

22. Gloria Feman Orenstein, "Recovering Her Story: Feminist Artists Reclaim the Great Goddess," in *The Power of Feminist Art*, p. 180.

23. Ibid., p. 187.

24. Mary Beth Edelson, *Seven Cycles: Public Rituals* (New York: A.I.R., 1980), p. 17.

25. Lippard, "Introduction," in Ibid., p. 9.

26. Leslie Labowitz-Starus and Suzanne Lacy, "In Mourning and In Rage . . ." *Frontiers: A Journal of Women's Studies*, 1 (Spring 1978), pp. 52–55.

27. Quoted in Marge Goldwater et al., *Jennifer Bartlett* (Minneapolis, MN: Walker Art Center, 1985), p. 29.

28. Ibid., p. 39.

29. Ibid., p. 83.

30. Ibid., p. 50.

31. Ibid., p. 120.

32. *Elizabeth Murray: Paintings and Drawings*, exhibition catalogue organized by Sue Graze and Kathy Halbreich, essay by Roberta Smith (New York: Abrams, in association with the Dallas Museum of Art and the MIT Committee on the Visual Arts, 1987), p. 64.

33. Ibid., p. 8.

34. *Magdalena Abakanowicz*, intro. by Mary Jane Jacobs (New York: Abbeville Press, 1982), catalogue organized by the Museum of Contemporary Art, Chicago, for traveling exhibition, p. 14.

35. Ibid., p. 15.

36. Ibid., p. 94.

37. Barbara Rose, *Magdalena Abakanowicz* (New York: Abrams, 1994), p. 124.

38. *Nancy Graves: A Survey 1969/1980*, essay by Linda L. Cathcart (Buffalo, NY: Albright-Knox Art Gallery, 1980), p. 13.

39. *The Sculpture of Nancy Graves: A Catalogue Raisonné* (New York: Hudson Hills Press, in association with the Fort Worth Art Museum, 1987), catalogue entry no. 23.

40. Lucy R. Lippard, *Overlay: Contemporary Art and the Art of Prehistory* (New York: Pantheon Books, 1983), p. 198.

41. Jonathan Fineberg, *Art Since 1940: Strategies of Being* (Englewood Cliffs, NJ: Prentice Hall, 1995), p. 391.

42. Ibid., p. 395.

43. Nancy Holt, "Sun Tunnels," *Artforum*, 15 (April 1977), p. 34.

44. Ibid.

45. Ibid., p. 35.

46. Diane Waldman, *Jenny Holzer* (New York: Guggenheim Museum and Abrams, 1989), p. 13.

47. For this discussion of the Vietnam War Memorial, I am indebted to Shirley Neilsen Blum, "The National Vietnam War Memorial," *ARTS Magazine*, 59 (December 1984), pp. 124–28.

48. Charles L. Griswold, "The Vietnam Veteran's Memorial and the Washington Mall: Philosophical Thoughts on Political Iconography," in W. J. T. Mitchell (ed.), *Art and the Public Sphere* (Chicago: University of Chicago Press, 1990), p. 106.

49. Ibid., p. 101.

50. Charles Griswold, Ibid., p. 109.

51. Gustave Neibuhr, "More Than a Monument: The Spiritual Dimension of These Hallowed Walls," *The New York Times*, Nov. 11, 1994, p. A12.

52. Eleanor Heartney, "How Wide Is the Gender Gap?" *Art News*, 86 (Summer 1987), p. 141.

53. The exhibition catalogue was written by Eleanor Tufts, *American Women Artists: 1830–1930*, with essays by Gail Levin, Alessandra Comini, and Wanda M. Corn (Washington, DC: The National Museum of Women in the Arts, 1987).

54. John Loughery, "Mrs. Holladay and the Guerrilla Girls," *ARTS Magazine*, 62 (October 1987), pp. 61–65.

55. Roberta Smith, "Body of Evidence," *Vogue* (August 1994).

56. *Cindy Sherman*, essays by Peter Schjeldahl and Lisa Phillips (New York: Whitney Museum of Art, 1987), p. 13.

57. Laura Mulvey, "A Phantasmagoria of the Female Body: The Work of Cindy Sherman," *New Left Review*, 188 (July/August 1991), p. 142.

58. Arthur C. Danto in Cindy Sherman, *Untitled Film Stills* (New York: Rizzoli, 1990), p. 10.

59. Abigail Solomon-Godeau, "Suitable for Framing: The Critical Recasting of Cindy Sherman," *Parkett*, 29 (1991), pp. 112ff.

60. Rosalind Krauss, *Cindy Sherman* (New York: Rizzoli, 1993), p. 56.

61. Phillips, op. cit., p. 15.

62. Ken Johnson, "Cindy Sherman and the Anti-Self: An Interpretation of Her Imagery," *ARTS Magazine*, 62 (November 1987), p. 53.

63. Carol Squiers, "Diversionary (Syn)tactics: Barbara Kruger Has Her Way with Words," *Art News*, 86 (February 1987), p. 84.

64. Ibid., p. 80.

65. Ibid., p. 75.

66. Kate Linker, *Love for Sale: The Words and Pictures of Barbara Kruger* (New York: Abrams, 1990), p. 12.

67. Ibid., p. 62.

68. Ibid., p. 27.

69. Ibid., p. 28.

70. Mary Kelly, *The Postpartum Document* (London: Routledge, 1985), pp. xvii–xviii.

71. Arlene Raven, "Hannah Wilke, 1940–1993," *The Village Voice* (Feb. 23, 1993), p. 81.

72. Garry Noland, "Art's Impact Depends on Feminist Content," *Forum*, 14 (Nov./Dec. 1989), p. 9.

73. Ibid., p. 10.

74. Joanna Frueh, "The Body through Women's Eyes," in *The Power of Feminist Art*, p. 192.

75. Cassandra Langer, "The Art of Healing," *Ms.* (Jan./Feb. 1989), p. 132.

76. Roberta Smith, "The Year in the Arts," *The New York Times* (Arts and Leisure Section), Dec. 25, 1994, p. 41.

77. Roberta Smith, "An Artist's Chronicle of a Death Foretold," *The New York Times* (Section 2), Jan. 30, 1994, p. 37.

ANNOTATED
Bibliography

General Works on the History of Women Artists

BACHMANN, D., and S. PILAND (eds.), *Women Artists: An Historical, Contemporary and Feminist Bibliography*. (Metuchen, NJ: Scarecrow Press, 1978). A thorough early listing of references on this subject, up to date of publication.

BROUDE, NORMA, and MARY D. GARRARD (eds.), *Feminism and Art History: Questioning the Litany* (New York: Harper and Row, 1982). A collection of scholarly articles that employs various methodological approaches, including analyses of works by women artists, to correct male-biased views of mainstream art history.

BROUDE, NORMA, and MARY D. GARRARD (eds.), *The Expanding Discourse: Feminism and Art History* (New York: HarperCollins, 1992). A recent volume which reprints twenty-nine key scholarly essays in feminist interpretations and re-evaluations of art, ranging from the late Middle Ages to the present.

CHADWICK, WHITNEY, *Women, Art, and Society* (New York: Thames and Hudson, 1990). Authoritative, concise overview of the history of women artists since the Middle Ages, which is integrated into a reframing of the discipline.

CLEMENT, CLARA ERSKINE, *Women in Fine Arts from the Seventh Century B.C. to the Twentieth Century* (Boston: Houghton Mifflin, 1904; reissued by Hacker Art Books, 1974). Provides interesting historical perspective.

ELLET, ELIZABETH FRIES LUMMIS, *Women Artists in All Ages and Countries* (New York: Harper and Co., 1859). An important early treatment of the subject.

FINE, ELSA HONIG, *Women and Art: A History of Women Painters and Sculptors from the Renaissance to the 20th Century* (Montclair, NJ: Abner Schram, 1978). Includes brief, interesting discussions of many artists. Each chapter is introduced with a concise, useful summary of women's social history. Useful bibliography.

GREER, GERMAINE, *The Obstacle Race: The Fortunes of Women Painters and Their Work* (New York: Farrar, Straus, Giroux, 1979). Contains useful information mixed with some distorted conclusions about a vast number of women artists. More important, Greer arranges the factors that prevented more women from achieving greater success in the visual arts into a series of obstacles and supports them with specific examples.

HARRIS, ANN SUTHERLAND, and LINDA NOCHLIN, *Women Artists 1550–1950* (New York: Alfred A. Knopf, 1976). Still a fundamental reference work. Written as a catalogue for a traveling exhibition, the introductory essays provide informative overviews, and the catalogue entries contain pertinent data on individual creators. Useful bibliography.

HELLER, NANCY G., *Women Artists: An Illustrated History* (New York: Abbeville Press, 1987). An adequate nonpolemic survey text loaded with quality illustrations and details.

LOEB, JUDY (ed.), *Feminist Collage: Educating Women in the Visual Arts* (New York: Columbia University Press, 1982). Collection of essays on both specific women artists and broader feminist topics.

MUNSTERBERG, HUGO, *The History of Women Artists* (New York: Clarkson N. Potter, 1975). Includes discussions of women artists in prehistoric, antique, and primitive civilizations, as well as chapters on graphic artists and photographers.

NOCHLIN, LINDA, *Women, Art, and Power and Other Essays* (New York: Harper and Row, 1988). A collection of seven key essays, including the author's seminal discussion of the issue "Why Have There Been No Great Women Artists?"

PARKER, ROSZIKA, and GRISELDA POLLACK, *Old Mistresses: Women, Art and Ideology* (New York: Pantheon Books, 1981). A thorough discussion of the stereotyping of women's art, ideological preconceptions of the discipline of art history, and women's relation to artistic and social structures. Avoiding biographical discussions, these English feminists present the first serious analysis of the relationship between the historical evaluation of women's art and the underlying criteria of the academic discipline of art history.

PETERSEN, KAREN, and J. J. WILSON, *Women Artists: Recognition and Reappraisal From the Early Middle Ages to the Twentieth Century* (New York: Harper Colophon Books, 1976). Contains a chapter on Chinese artists and many black and white reproductions. The text, however, tends to be superficial and is not consistently reliable. Useful bibliography.

POLLOCK, GRISELDA, *Vision and Difference: Femininity, Feminism and the Histories of Art* (London: Routledge, 1988). A collection of seven essays, including the major theoretical discussion on "Feminist Interventions in the Histories of Art: An Introduction."

SLATKIN, WENDY (ed.), *The Voices of Women Artists* (Englewood Cliffs, NJ: Prentice Hall, 1993). Sourcebook of edited autobiographical texts by women artists from Gentileschi to the present. Primary sources are introduced with contextual information on the artists and the institutional structures in which they worked.

SPARROW, WALTER, *Women Painters of the World* (London: Hodder and Stoughton, 1905). Contemporary with Clement's volume, Sparrow's work is equally extensive.

TUFTS, ELEANOR, *Our Hidden Heritage: Five Centuries of Women Artists* (New York: Paddington Press, 1974). Lively biographical essays of twenty-two major women artists.

WALLER, SUSAN, *Women Artists in the Modern Era: A Documentary History* (Metuchen, NJ: Scarecrow Press, 1991). Sourcebook which includes the writings of women artists, critical reviews of women's work in exhibitions, discussion of women's abilities as artists, and institutional records concerning women artists societies and schools. Texts date from the 1760s to the 1950s.

WITZLING, MARA (ed.), *Voicing Our Visions: Writings by Women* (New York: Universe, 1991). Edited collection of the writings of twenty nineteenth- and twentieth-century women artists, introduced with brief biographical sketches.

General Works on Women's History

The literature in this discourse has expanded dramatically in recent years. The following selected volumes should prove useful to the student reader as an introduction to the field.

BOXER, MARILYN J., and JEAN H. QUATAERT (eds.), *Connecting Spheres: Women in the Western World, 1500 to the Present* (New York: Oxford University Press, 1987). The editors' introductory remarks to the more specific essays provide a useful overview of women's history since the Renaissance.

BRIDENTHAL, RENATE, and CLAUDIA KOONZ (eds.), *Becoming Visible: Women in European History* (Boston: Houghton Mifflin, 1977). An interesting collection of early essays.

BRIDENTHAL, RENATE, CLAUDIA KOONZ, and SUSAN M. STUARD, *Becoming Visible: Women in European History*, 2nd ed. (Boston: Houghton Mifflin, 1987). Published a decade later than the first volume, this book adopts a more integrated, textbook approach. Individual chapters on selected topics from prehistory to the twentieth century are written by leading scholars in each field.

CARROLL, BERENICE A., *Liberating Women's History* (Urbana: University of Illinois Press, 1976). An informative and reliable collection of essays on a range of topics in women's history.

HARTMAN, MARY, and LOUISE BANNER (eds.), *Clio's Consciousness Raised* (New York: Harper, 1974). Authoritative collection of essays.

HELLY, DOROTHY O., and SUSAN M. REVERBY (eds.), *Gendered Domains: Rethinking Public and Private in Women's History* (Ithaca, NY: Cornell University Press, 1992). These essays originated in a session held at the Seventh Berkshire Conference on the History of Women. Useful revision of former dichotomies in "Introduction." Groups of interesting case studies.

OFFEN, KAREN, RUTH ROACH PEIRSON, and JANE RENDALL (eds.), *Writing Women's History: International Perspectives* (Bloomington: Indiana University Press, 1991). Essay by scholars in twenty-two countries documenting the "state of the art" of women's history in a wide range of historiographical contexts.

RILEY, DENISE, *"Am I That Name?": Feminism and the Category of "Women" in History* (Minneapolis: University of Minnesota Press, 1988). Well-written, brief discussion of the entire category "woman" as historical construct.

SCOTT, JOAN W., *Gender and the Politics of History* (New York, 1988). Key theoretical essays by one of the leading figures in women's history, including "Gender: A Useful Category of Historical Analysis."

SMITH, BONNIE G., *Changing Lives: Women in European History Since 1700* (Lexington, MA: D. C. Heath, 1989). Well-written textbook on the topic with useful bibliography.

Index

Page numbers with illustrations are in bold print.